Keely Laycock

Cambridge IGCSE® and O Level
Global Perspectives

Coursebook

CAMBRIDGE
UNIVERSITY PRESS

CAMBRIDGE
UNIVERSITY PRESS

University Printing House, Cambridge CB2 8BS, United Kingdom

Cambridge University Press is part of the University of Cambridge.

It furthers the University's mission by disseminating knowledge in the pursuit of education, learning and research at the highest international levels of excellence.

Information on this title: education.cambridge.org

© Cambridge University Press 2016

First published 2016

Printed in the United Kingdom by Latimer Trend

A catalogue record for this publication is available from the British Library

ISBN 978-1-316-61110-4 Paperback

Additional resources for this publication at education.cambridge.org

Cambridge University Press has no responsibility for the persistence or accuracy of URLs for external or third-party internet websites referred to in this publication, and does not guarantee that any content on such websites is, or will remain, accurate or appropriate. Information regarding prices, travel timetables, and other factual information given in this work is correct at the time of first printing but Cambridge University Press does not guarantee the accuracy of such information thereafter.

IGCSE® is the registered trademark of Cambridge International Examinations.

....

....

All summary questions and examination-style questions that appear in this book were written by the author.
In examination, the way marks would be awarded to answers like these may be different.

Contents

Acknowledgements

The authors and publishers acknowledge the following sources of copyright material and are grateful for the permissions granted. While every effort has been made, it has not always been possible to identify the sources of all the material used, or to trace all copyright holders. If any omissions are brought to our notice, we will be happy to include the appropriate acknowledgements on reprinting.

p. 7–8 from 'Why fresh water shortages will cause the next great global crisis' by Robin McKie in *The Guardian*, 8 March 2015, Copyright Guardian News & Media Ltd 2015; pp. 104–05 from 'Fur trade booming after swing from fashion faux pas to catwalk favourite' by Hannah Ellis-Petersen in *The Guardian*, 25 March 2015, Copyright Guardian News & Media Ltd 2015; p. 134 from 'Easing of China's one-child policy has not produced a baby boom' by Simon Denyer in *The Washington post*, 6 February 2015, © 2015 The Washington Post. All rights reserved. Used by permission and protected by the Copyright Laws of the United States. The printing, copying, redistribution, or retransmission of this Content without express written permission is prohibited;; p. 141 from ' New evidence that fast food is bad for kids' learning' by Kabir Chibber in *Quartz,* 21 December 2014, reproduced with permission; p. 147 adapted from 'World has zero chance of hitting education targets, warns UN' by Sam Jones in *The Guardian*, 26 June 2014, Copyright Guardian News & Media Ltd 2015; p. 175 excerpt from 'Minneapolis man handed out 520,000 sandwiches to homeless in one year' by Kimberly Yam in *Huffington Post*, 10 October 2014, © 2014 AOL Inc. All rights reserved. Used by permission and protected by the Copyright Laws of the United States. The printing, copying, redistribution, or retransmission of this Content without express written permission is prohibited; p. 198 from 'Globalisation: good or bad?' by Lewis Williamson in *The Guardian*, 31 October 2002, Copyright Guardian News & Media Ltd 2015; pp. 198–99 from 'Migration crisis: "Who can refuse these human beings? Who?" asks a UN official' by Sam Jones in *The Guardian*, Copyright Guardian News & Media Ltd 2015; p. 199 excerpt from 'Does migration change life for the better for people from poor countries?' by Claire Provost in *The Guardian*, 13 September 2013, Copyright Guardian News & Media Ltd 2015; p. 213 excerpt from 'Climate pledges by 140 countries will limit global warming – but not enough' by Reuters in *The Guardian*, 1 October 2015, from Reuters © 2015 reuters.com. All rights reserved. Used by permission and protected by the Copyright Laws of the United States. The printing, copying, redistribution, or retransmission of this Content without express written permission is prohibited.

The publishers are grateful to the following for permission to reproduce copyright photographs and material:

Cover Zoonar GmbH/Alamy; p.1 Africa Studio/Shutterstock; p.2 Elisabeth Burrell/Alamy; p.3 413x4sh/Shutterstock; p.40*tl* ppl/Shutterstock; p,40*tr* KAMONRAT/Shutterstock; p.53 Brian A Jackson/Shutterstock; pp.55/56 ifong/Shutterstock; p.75*tl* Syda Productions; p.75*tr* 06photo/Shutterstock; p.93 atm2003/Shutterstock; p.101*tl* Zuma Press Inc/Alamy; p.101*tr* Bill Cheyrou/Alamy; p.104 Cartoonstock; p.112 Robert Fried/Alamy; p.114 wavebreakmedia/Shutterstock; p.116 Krill PerchenkoEyeEM/Getty Images; p.121 Pixellover RMG/Alamy; p.123 Julian Rovagnati/Shutterstock; p.124 Peter Scholey/Alamy; p.125 Kevin Schafer/Alamy; p.145 AfriPics.com/Alamy; p.154*cl* Blend Images/Alamy p.154*cr* Joerg BoethingAlamy; p.158 Cultura Creative (RF)/Alamy; p.159 patrimonia designs lrd/Shutterstock; p.166 Design Pics Inc/Alamy; p.168 Friedrich Stark/Alamy; p.180 pruciatti/Shutterstock; p.181 Alexi Novikov/Shutterstock; p.182 Nadeza Grapes/Shutterstock; p.195 Zoonar GmbH/Alamy; p.214 xinhua/Alamy; p.216 Hemis/Alamy; p.217 incamerastock/Alamy; p.227*cl* Frank Metois/Alamy; p.227*cr* Artur Ish/Shutterstock; p.231 Vaclav Volrab/Shutterstock.

t=top, *b*=bottom, *c*=centre, *r*=right, *l*=left

Introduction

This book is for all students studying Cambridge IGCSE and O Level Global Perspectives, their teachers, and anyone else who wants to develop their information skills, critical thinking, independent learning, collaboration and communication skills, using global topics and issues to practise these skills.

Overview of IGCSE and O Level Global Perspectives

Cambridge IGCSE and O Level Global Perspectives provides opportunities for students to enquire into, and reflect on, global topics and issues from different perspectives: global, national/local and personal. It is intended that the activities within this book will give students plenty of practice to enable them to meet the aims of the Cambridge IGCSE and O Level Global Perspectives syllabus.

Overview of the Cambridge IGCSE and O level Assessment Components

On completion of their Global Perspectives course of study, students will be assessed by way of three components as follows:

Component 1

Component 1 is a written examination lasting 1 hour and 15 minutes, which includes reading time for the accompanying source material.

Students answer four questions based on the accompanying source material. Source material will present a global issue from a range of perspectives, and will be drawn from the list of eight topics identified for this component.

Component 2

Component 2 is the Individual Report. This is done as coursework in class. Students research one global topic (from a choice of eight given in the syllabus) and set a question. They use the research they do and the skills developed and practised in class to answer their question to produce their Individual Report.

Component 3

Component 3 is the Team Project. This is done as coursework in class. Students devise and work on a collaborative project into an aspect of one of the global topics (from a choice of eight). This choice of team project must allow for the exploration of different cultural perspectives.

The Team Project comprises two elements.

Team Element
As a team students produce one Outcome and one Explanation. The Outcome can be multimedia.

Personal Element
Each student writes a Reflective Paper on their research, contribution and personal learning.

How to use this book

The focus of this book is skill development using some of the global topics and issues from the syllabus as the vehicle for developing and practising skills. As such, not all the syllabus's global topics and issues are covered in this book. The intention is that any topic or issue can be used to acquire and develop the skills, but that those chosen will inspire students and teachers alike.

This book is divided into five chapters:

Chapter 1: Information skills
Chapter 2: Critical thinking skills
Chapter 3: Independent learning skills
Chapter 4: Collaboration skills
Chapter 5: Communication skills

Each chapter focuses on a skill set that students need to develop not only for their Global Perspectives course but for further study and future employment.

Within each chapter are sections that allow students to acquire and develop different skills within the chapter heading. These can be seen in the contents section of this book.

Learning objectives

Learning objectives

By the end of this chapter, you should be able to:

- understand the importance of developing information skills
- identify perspectives and viewpoints from written and spoken sources and use them in your own work
- undertake research to find a variety of relevant information
- analyse and synthesise information found
- plan well, creating SMART plans
- ask and answer a variety of questions.

Each chapter begins with a short list of the areas of focus and concepts that are explained within it.

Activities

ACTIVITY 1.03

Imagine you are in the 'Wilderness'. Close your eyes for a couple of minutes – see the wilderness, feel it around you, smell it, and hear it.
Open your eyes and write down all the words and phrase that express what you saw, felt, smelt and heard.

Activities are designed so that students can work independently, in pairs and in small groups/teams. There may also be occasions when the teacher wants to use one or more of the activities with students at the same time or the teacher can set activities for independent, collaborative or home learning.

Differentiated practice

Practising critical thinking skills

Each chapter also has fully differentiated practice sections at developing, establishing and enhancing levels. These allow students to practise the skills they have acquired and developed throughout the chapter. It is a good idea for students to complete the rest of the chapter before starting to work their way through these differentiated practice sections. Students can either work through these sections in order, from developing to establishing to enhancing, or they can choose the level (with guidance from their teacher) which they would like to focus on. If using the book in class, students practising at the same level can pair up for many of the activities. The topics covered for each of these sections are indicated in the contents page.

Discussion points

Discussion point
Share your perspective with a partner who is from a different country to your own.

You probably have different words and phrases from your partner, as you have envisaged the 'Wilderness' differently depending on your experiences (what you have already seen, heard and done in your life).

The purpose of the discussion points is to enable students to discuss their own thoughts and ideas with someone else, so that they not only get different opinions but can also clarify their own thinking by saying things out loud.

Reflection points

Reflection: Why do you think your partner had a different perspective to you?

Reflection points are included throughout the book so that students have the chance to think about how their skills are developing and the information they have explored and discovered.

Tip

TIP
Put the search terms '**ethics** in research' into a search engine to find out more about how to conduct primary research.

Tips are included throughout the book and include quick suggestions to remind students about key facts and highlight important points.

Global topics

Digital World is the topic. The <u>issue</u> is stated in the title – the digital divide is a cause of inequality. The first paragraph also states that 'the digital divide still exists' and gives <u>evidence</u>

Global topics are highlighted throughout the text, to allow students and teachers to quickly identify them, as they go through the book.

Key terms

KEY TERM

Assumption: something that is accepted as true or as certain to happen, without proof.

Key terms are included throughout the text and provide clear and straightforward explanations of the most important terms in each chapter.

Skills links

SKILLS LINKS

- Chapter 1: Information skills, 1.02 Research
- Chapter 1: Information skills, 1.05 Planning
- Chapter 5: Communication skills, 5.02 Writing

Skills links are at the beginning of each section and introduce relevant links to other essential skills in the book.

Summary

Summary

- Empathy is different from sympathy.
- Empathy helps us to build and maintain close friendships and develop strong communities.
- It's important to show empathy if doing any primary research for your Team Project.
- Empathy can be developed like any other skill.
- Imagine 'walking in another person's shoes' to develop your empathy.

There is a summary at the end of each section to review what the student has learned.

Summary questions

3.02 Note-taking

3 Explain why note-taking is a useful skill to develop.

4 Explain the benefits of a KWL chart for making notes.

Summary questions come before the Practice skills sections to help the student test their knowledge and understanding of each chapter.

Opportunities are also provided for students to gain feedback on the work they are doing, both from their peers and from their teacher. This is very important as feedback will enable students to develop their skills, thoughts and ideas further.

Suggested approaches for using this book

It will depend very much on the teacher how this book is used. It is recommended that students do not start work on their Individual Report or their Team Project until they have completed the activities in this book, as these activities will ensure that they are well prepared for all the assessment components.

Approach 1

One suggested approach is for the teacher to guide students through each of the chapters using the suggested activities as they stand to allow students to acquire and develop the skills. Students can then work through the differentiated practice sections to complete the whole chapter and each chapter in turn before they embark on their Individual Report or their Team Project.

Approach 2

Another way is for the teacher to supplement the activities within the book with their own activities and resources. Students might work through the first sections of each chapter, acquiring new skills, and then leave the practice sections until a later date, again before completing their Individual Report or their Team Project.

The teacher might also like to focus on the chapters that deal with the specific assessment components before embarking on a practice Written Examination, Individual Report or Team Project.

Although there is something of relevance to all components in all the chapters in this book, the following indicates the main focus for each chapter to help teachers with their planning.

Chapter 1: Information skills – particularly relevant for the Individual Report

Chapter 2: Critical thinking skills – focuses predominantly on skills for the written examination

Chapter 3: Independent learning skills – useful for study skills and the personal element of the Team Project

Chapter 4: Collaboration skills – useful for the Team Project

Chapter 5: Communication skills – encompasses all the assessment components and guides students in how to be more effective in their reading, writing, listening and speaking skills.

A final note

However you decide to use this book, we hope you find it a valuable resource for developing the skills needed to enjoy and be successful in Cambridge IGCSE and O Level Global Perspectives and any future studies.

Table of contents – IGCSE and O Level Global Perspectives

Chapter 1: Information skills	Topics introduced	Skills links (other relevant chapters)	Assessment links (component)
1.01 Perspectives	Globalisation, family, poverty and inequality, fuel and energy, water, food and agriculture	1.02, 1.03, 3.02, 4.02	1, 2, 3
1.02 Research	Demographic change, biodiversity and ecosystem loss, water, food and agriculture	1.06, 2.02, 3.02, 5.01	1, 2, 3
1.03 Analysis	Digital world, demographic change	1.02, 1.06, 2.02, 3.04, 5.01	1, 2, 3
1.04 Synthesis	Tradition, culture and identity, human rights, sustainable living	1.06, 2.02, 3.04, 4.03, 5.02	1, 2, 3
1.05 Planning	Human rights, sustainable living	1.02, 1.06, 3.03, 3.04	1, 2, 3
1.06 Questioning	Migration, employment, family, trade and aid, water, food and agriculture, digital world	1.02, 1.03, 2.07, 3.03, 4.02	1, 2, 3
Developing information skills	Changing communities	1.01, 1.02, 1.03, 1.04, 1.05, 1.06	2
Establishing information skills	Employment	1.01, 1.02, 1.03, 1.04, 1.05, 1.06	1
Enhancing information skills	Transport systems	1.01, 1.02, 1.03, 1.04, 1.05, 1.06	1
Chapter 2: Critical thinking skills	Topics introduced	Skills links	Assessment links
2.01 Reasoning	Water, food and agriculture, fuel and energy	1.03, 1.04, 1.05, 1.06, 2.02, 3.04, 5.02, 5.04	1, 2
2.02 Evidence	Digital world, biodiversity and ecosystem loss, humans and other species	1.02, 2.01, 2.03, 2.05, 3.04, 5.01, 5.03	1, 2
2.03 Claims	Transport systems, demographic change, sport and recreation	1.03, 2.01, 2.02, 3.04, 5.01, 5.03	1, 2, 3
2.04 Drawing conclusions	Fuel and energy, demographic change, language and communication, conflict and peace, globalisation	1.03, 1.06, 2.01, 2.02, 3.04, 5.01, 5.03, 5.04	1, 2, 3
2.05 Bias and vested interest	Education for all, digital world	1.03, 1.06, 2.02, 2.03, 2.04, 3.04, 5.01, 5.03	1, 2
2.06 Statements of argument	Education for all, employment, humans and other species	1.02, 1.03, 2.02, 2.03, 2.04, 3.04, 5.01, 5.03	1, 2

Chapter 2: Critical thinking skills	Topics introduced	Skills links	Assessment links
2.07 Problem-solving	Transport systems, digital world, changing communities, biodiversity and ecosystem loss,	1.02, 1.03, 1.04, 2.04, 3.03, 4.02, 4.03, 5.03, 5.04	1, 2, 3
2.08 Empathy	Water, food and agriculture, migration, changing communities	1.01, 1.02, 1.06, 3.03, 4.01, 4.03, 5.03	3
Developing critical thinking skills	Globalisation	2.01, 2.02, 2.03, 2.04, 2.05, 2.06, 5.02, 5.04	1
Establishing critical thinking skills	Humans and other species	2.01, 2.02, 2.03, 2.04, 2.05, 2.06, 2.07, 5.02, 5.04	2
Enhancing critical thinking skills	Humans rights	1.03, 2.01, 2.02, 2.03, 2.04, 2.05, 2.06, 2.07, 2.08, 5.01, 5.02, 5.03, 5.04	3

Chapter 3: Independent learning skills	Topics Introduced	Skills links	Assessment links
3.01 Memory	Humans and other species, fuel and energy, family, sport and recreation	1.03, 1.05, 5.01	1, 2, 3
3.02 Note-taking	Digital world, disease and health, water, food and agriculture, humans and other species, human rights, employment, tradition, culture and identity	1.02, 1.05, 3.03, 5.01, 5.03	1, 2, 3
3.03 Reflection	Sustainable living, demographic change	1.03, 3.02, 3.04, 5.01, 5.03	1, 2, 3
3.04 Evaluation	Globalisation, disease and health, education for all	1.02, 1.03, 1.05, 2.04, 3.03	1, 2, 3
Developing independent learning skills	Education for all	3.01, 3.02, 3.03, 3.04	1
Establishing independent learning skills	Poverty and inequality	2.02, 2.03, 3.01, 3.02, 3.03, 3.04, 4.01, 5.04	3
Enhancing independent learning skills	Trade and aid	1.02, 3.01, 3.02, 3.03, 3.04, 5.04	2

Chapter 4: Collaboration skills	Topics Introduced	Skills links	Assessment links
4.01 Team work	Sport and recreation, water, food and agriculture	1.02, 1.05, 5.03, 5.04	3
4.02 Decision-making	Poverty and inequality, water, food and agriculture, tradition, culture and identity, disease and health	1.01, 1.05, 3.03, 3.04, 4.01, 5.03, 5.04	3
4.03 Creativity	Poverty and inequality, digital world, tradition, culture and identity	1.05, 2.02, 2.05, 2.06, 3.03, 5.03, 5.04	2, 3
Developing collaboration skills	Water, food and agriculture	4.01, 4.02, 4.03	3
Establishing collaboration skills	Disease and health	4.01, 4.02, 4.03	3
Enhancing collaboration skills	Language and communication	4.01, 4.02, 4.03	3
Chapter 5: Communication skills	Topics Introduced	Skills links	Assessment links
5.01 Reading	Globalisation, migration	1.02, 1.03, 1.06, 3.02, 3.04	1, 2, 3
5.02 Writing	Sustainable living, humans and other species, fuel and energy	1.04, 1.05, 2.01, 3.02	1, 2, 3
5.03 Listening	Education for all, humans and other species	1.02, 1.03, 3.02, 3.04	1, 2, 3
5.04 Speaking	Sustainable living, changing communities, migration, digital world, humans and other species, fuel and energy, disease and health	1.04, 1.05, 1.06, 2.01	1, 2, 3
Developing communication skills	Family, digital world, migration	5.01, 5.02, 5.03, 5.04	1, 2
Establishing communication skills	Biodiversity and ecosystem loss, transport systems	5.01, 5.02, 5.03, 5.04	1, 2
Enhancing communication skills	Fuel and energy	5.01, 5.02, 5.03, 5.04	1

Chapter 1
Information skills

Learning objectives

By the end of this chapter, you should be able to:

- understand the importance of developing information skills
- identify perspectives and viewpoints from written and spoken sources and use them in your own work
- undertake research to find a variety of relevant information
- analyse and synthesise information found
- plan well, creating SMART plans
- ask and answer a variety of questions.

Introduction

Information is all around us – on television, radio and computers. We can gain information by searching for specific items or by surfing the internet. We constantly use information in our written and spoken work and in interactions with all the people in our lives. It is important to think about how you use information. This chapter focuses on developing the skills you need to cope with the vast amount of information we are subjected to on a daily basis.

In this chapter, you will learn to develop the following information skills:

1.01 Perspectives	**1.02** Research	**1.03** Analysis
1.04 Synthesis	**1.05** Planning	**1.06** Questioning

1.01 Perspectives

 SKILLS LINKS

- Chapter 1: Information skills, 1.02 Research
- Chapter 1: Information skills, 1.03 Analysis
- Chapter 3: Independent learning skills, 3.02 Note-taking
- Chapter 4: Collaboration skills, 4.02 Decision-making

TIP

It is easy to become overwhelmed by the amount of information available so it's important that you are equipped to deal with it.

Understanding that we might see things differently to others is key to understanding what a **perspective** is. Perspectives are based on personal experiences of the world and thinking about them. People see the world differently because experiences and ways of thinking differ. Our views are influenced by many people, including our parents, friends and people we admire.

 KEY TERMS

Perspective: a particular way of regarding something/ a certain world view.

ACTIVITY 1.01

Consider this glass of water. Do you think it is half full or half empty? Ask your classmates what they think.

Figure 1.01 Glass of water

In this section, you will be exploring **global**, **national**, **local**, **cultural** and **personal** perspectives as well as different **viewpoints** within these perspectives, such as those of farmers, scientists, teachers and local politicians.

Considering **issues** from global, national and local perspectives is a requirement for your Individual Report (as described in the Introduction to this book). You will also explore your own personal perspective and whether this has been influenced by other perspectives. For the Team Project (also described in the Introduction), you are required to **collaborate** with team members to research an issue, decide on an aim and plan and carry out a team project on an issue related to one of the global topics. This team project will involve finding out about different cultural perspectives on the chosen issue and these different cultural perspectives should inform the **outcome** and **explanation** you produce for your Team Project.

KEY TERMS

Global: relating to the whole world.

National: related to a particular country/common to a whole country.

Local: related to a particular community or area.

Personal: related to yourself.

Viewpoint: a particular attitude, perspective or way of looking at an issue.

Issue: an important topic or problem for discussion or debate.

Collaborate: work together with others.

Culture: the ideas, customs, and social behaviour of a particular people or society, or a particular group of people within a society.

Outcome: the final product following a period of collaboration to achieve the project aim that shows different cultural perspectives.

Explanation: details about how the outcome meets the project aim and shows different cultural perspectives.

ACTIVITY 1.02

Imagine you are a passenger in a car that stops at some traffic lights. As you are waiting, this limousine pulls up at the lights. Who do you think is in the limousine?

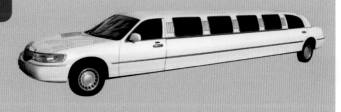
Figure 1.02 Limousine

Discussion point

Share your ideas from Activity 1.02 with a partner.

Chances are some of their ideas were different ideas to yours: they saw it from a different perspective.

Reflection: Why do you think your partner had a different perspective to you?

ACTIVITY 1.03

Imagine you are in the 'Wilderness'. Close your eyes for a couple of minutes – see the wilderness, feel it around you, smell it, and hear it.

Open your eyes and write down all the words and phrase that express what you saw, felt, smelt and heard.

Discussion point

Share your perspective from Activity 1.03 with a partner who is from a different country to your own.

You probably have different words and phrases from your partner, as you have envisaged the 'Wilderness' differently depending on your experiences (what you have already seen, heard and done in your life).

> **Reflection:** Imagine how you might get different lists from people from different cultures and countries. Why do you think this would be?

Different definitions

You might think that certain words mean the same thing to everyone. You would be wrong in this **assumption**, which is why it's important to discuss things and ensure that you know the different perspectives on the same thing.

KEY TERM

Assumption: something that is accepted as true or as certain to happen, without proof.

ACTIVITY 1.04

Here are three words. They are all topics in the IGCSE or O Level Global Perspectives syllabus. What do they mean to you?

Write down a definition for each of the three words before looking at the definitions given in the key terms:

Globalisation
Family
Inequality

Discussion point

Share your definitions for Activity 1.04 with a partner. Do they have the same as you?

Do you have the same definitions as in the key terms box?

KEY TERMS

Globalisation: process by which national and regional economies, societies, and cultures have become integrated through the global network of trade, communication, immigration and transportation.

Family: a basic social unit consisting of parents or guardians and their children, considered as a group, whether living together or not.

Inequality: the unfair situation in society when some people have more opportunities, money, etc. than others.

Thinking about a global perspective

A global perspective asks you to think beyond yourself, your family, your school, your community and your country or the country where you are living. Issues that are in the news are often global in nature, for example an **economic** or **social** issue.

KEY TERMS

Economic: to do with money.

Social: to do with people.

Often, a global issue or problem demands a global **solution**. It would not be possible to solve the global problem of climate change with a local solution, even though local **courses of action** might be taken to help towards a global solution. For the problem of climate change, for example, a local course of action might be a poster campaign aimed at businesses, encouraging them to reduce the amount of fossil fuels they are using.

KEY TERMS

Solution: A means of solving a problem or dealing with a difficult situation.

Course of action: A plan or method used for achieving a specific aim or goal.

ACTIVITY 1.05

Look at this diamond nine grid which ranks some of the global issues that the world is currently facing. The most important one from this person's perspective is unemployment, which is at the top. Of equal importance underneath are population growth and disease. The issue this person thinks is the least important is at the bottom (crime).

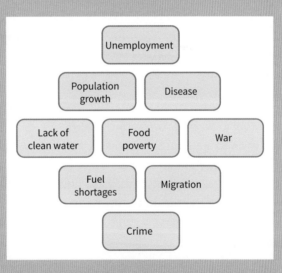

Figure 1.03 Prioritising global issues

Reflection: Do you agree with the priorities in Activity 1.05?

Consider which of these you think will be the most important for you over the next twenty years of your life. How might you change the grid (the order of priority, change of issues)?

5

Discussion point

Discuss the changes you would make to the diagram in Activity 1.05 with a partner.

Listen to your partner's perspective. Do you have the same priorities? Why do you think this might be?

You might have a similar perspective and similar priorities as you have some things in common; you are probably the same age, you might have the same friends and have had similar upbringings. You will also have the same influences in school. If you did this activity with someone in a different country or a different type of school, there may have been more differences.

Global, national, local and personal perspectives

ACTIVITY 1.06

Sometimes a national or local perspective might be different to the global perspective; at other times, it might be the same, depending on the issue.

Read the following issue, which focuses on the use of **Fossil fuels**. Put the different perspectives into your own words and explain each to a partner.

This is a global perspective:

> Globally, we know that climate change is a serious issue and that one of the reasons for this is the overuse of fossil fuels. We also know that if we continue to use fossil fuels at the rate we are doing that they will run out soon. That is the reason we need to consider finding and using renewable sources of energy.

This is a national perspective:

> The perspectives of a country's government, however, might be that they cannot do anything about climate change as it is happening and will continue to happen regardless of whether they stop using fossil fuels or not. Also, the government may say the country needs to use fossil fuels to become as economically developed as other countries who have been using fossil fuels for years.

This is a local perspective:

> Imagine that the community you live in is very globally aware and there is disagreement with the national perspective given above. They think that because there is a lot of wind and sun in the area, there must be alternative ways of generating energy so that fossil fuels are not used for heating and lighting, as they have seen how polluted some of the big cities are becoming and want to protect their environment.

6

Reflection: Which of the perspectives from Activity 1.06 (global, national or local) do you agree with?

You may not agree with any of them and have your own perspective and reasons for this. This is your personal perspective.

It is likely that as you do research about global issues from different perspectives and find new **information**, your personal perspective will change.

This is fine; you just need to ensure that you can give reasons for your personal perspective.

KEY TERM

Information: Facts gathered about something or someone that helps our understanding.

ACTIVITY 1.07

The difference between perspectives and issues

Read the text below to identify the perspectives and the issues and put them under the correct heading in the table that follows.

Why fresh water shortages will cause the next great global crisis

Water is the driving force of all nature, Leonardo da Vinci claimed. Unfortunately for our planet, supplies are now running dry – at an alarming rate. The world's population continues to soar but that rise in numbers has not been matched by an accompanying increase in supplies of fresh water.

The consequences are proving to be profound. Across the globe, reports reveal huge areas in crisis today as reservoirs and aquifers dry up. More than a billion individuals – one in seven people on the planet – now lack access to safe drinking water.

Last week in the Brazilian city of São Paulo, home to 20 million people, and once known as the City of Drizzle, drought got so bad that residents began drilling through basement floors and car parks to try to reach groundwater. City officials warned last week that rationing of supplies was likely soon. Citizens might have access to water for only two days a week, they added.

In California, officials have revealed that the state has entered its fourth year of drought with January this year becoming the driest since meteorological records began. At the same time, per capita water use has continued to rise.

In the Middle East, swathes of countryside have been reduced to desert because of overuse of water. Iran is one of the most severely affected. Heavy overconsumption, coupled with poor rainfall, have ravaged its water resources and devastated its agricultural output. Similarly, the United Arab Emirates is now investing in desalination plants and waste water treatment units because it lacks fresh water.

The global nature of the crisis is underlined in similar reports from other regions. In south Asia, for example, there have been massive losses of groundwater, which has been pumped up with reckless lack of control over the past decade. About 600 million people live on the 2000 sq km area that extends from eastern Pakistan, across the hot dry plains of northern India and into Bangladesh, and the land is the most intensely irrigated in the world. Up to 75% of farmers rely on pumped groundwater to water their crops and water use is intensifying – at the same time that satellite images shows supplies are shrinking alarmingly.

Source: www.theguardian.com

	Perspectives	Issues
1		
2		
3		

You might have identified the following from the text:

Perspectives:

Global

Local – Brazilian city of São Paulo – people that live there; California

National – Middle East; Iran, South Asia, Pakistan, Bangladesh

Viewpoints – Leonardo Da Vinci, City Officials, Farmers

(Although the article deals mainly with the global perspective, it is possible to identify areas that might have their own perspective on the issues below. For example if you were living in Brazil, further research could be done about the Brazilian (national) perspective about water shortages, in comparison to perhaps the perspective of the people in São Paulo or your own home town/local community.)

Issues:

- Increase in population
- Water supplies running low
- Reservoirs and aquifers are drying up
- Lack of access to safe drinking water
- Desert landscape in the Middle East (affecting environment)
- Overuse of water
- Poor amounts of rainfall
- Affecting agriculture
- Need for desalination plants and waste water treatment units
- Loss of groundwater

When talking about perspectives, avoid giving just **information** about the different countries.

Summary

- It is important to understand that people might hold views that are different from yours.

- Having a different perspective does not mean someone is wrong.

- Considering issues from global, national, local and personal perspectives is a requirement for your Individual Report.

- The Team Project focuses on showing understanding of different cultural perspectives.

- A global issue demands a global solution.

- Issues are problems that need resolving; perspectives are the ways different people view the issues.

1.02 Research

 **SKILLS LINKS**

- Chapter 1: Information skills, 1.06 Questioning

- Chapter 2: Critical thinking skills, 2.02 Evidence

- Chapter 3: Independent learning skills, 3.02 Note-taking

- Chapter 5: Communication skills, 5.01 Reading

To gain information that is of use to us and enables us to create **arguments** from different perspectives, we need to be able to do **research**.

 KEY TERMS

Argument: a line of reasoning to support a given perspective, idea, action or issue.

Research: the investigation into and study of materials and sources in order to establish facts and reach new **conclusions**.

Conclusion: a judgement or decision reached.

When undertaking any kind of research, you need to have a clear idea about what you are looking for. For your Individual Report, you will have formulated a question that enables you to consider an issue/issues from different perspectives.

You will be looking for information to support the points you make; allowing you to **analyse** and **synthesise** the **causes** and **consequences** of relevant issue(s) and propose course(s) of action to help resolve the issue(s).

KEY TERMS

Analyse: break down a global topic into issues and explore the causes and consequences of these issues.

Synthesise: the combination of two or more sources of information to form something new and original that might support an argument.

Cause: is responsible for making something happen/is the reason behind something happening.

Consequence: happens because of something else/ is a result or effect of something.

ACTIVITY 1.08

Consider the following question for an Individual Report:

'Should global population growth be restricted?'

What sort of information are you going to look for?

Write down five questions that you think you might need answers to.

Discussion point

Share your five questions from Activity 1.08 with a partner. Do they have the same ideas as you?

Amend your questions if you think you need to (based on the discussion with your partner).

ACTIVITY 1.09

1   List possible **sources of information** relevant to each of the questions you have asked in Activity 1.08, including any **primary data** you may need to collect.

It's important to note that most of the information you will need for an Individual Report will be **secondary data**, but you may need to interview people in your community to find out the local perspectives about the issue(s).

2   Explain how each source of information will help you to answer the questions you have set.

For your Individual Report, you will need to research and analyse a range of different information from different perspectives and evaluate the sources of information you find, considering how well the source of information supports the argument you are making.

KEY TERMS

Sources of information: a publication or type of media where specific information can be obtained, for example reliable websites of government agencies, charities and voluntary organisations, newspapers, books and documentaries.

Primary data: information originally obtained through the direct efforts of the researcher through surveys and interviews.

Secondary data: information obtained from published sources on the internet or in books.

Selecting sources of information

When selecting sources of information to use in your Individual Report, try to use the following diagram.

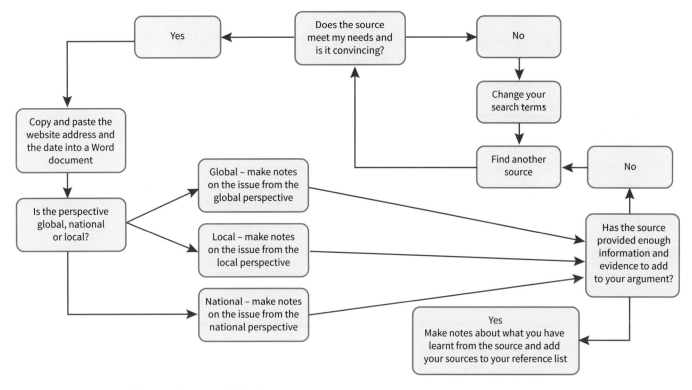

Figure 1.04 Source selection for an Individual Report

Search terms for research

Before you have finalised the question for your Individual Report, you will want to do some general research about the topic to see what sources of information are available. You might start your search with the title of the topic, for example, **Biodiversity and ecosystem loss**. However, you will soon find that it is too broad and will need to be more precise with your search terms. This is when you need to start narrowing down the question(s) you want to answer.

TIP

- You will get too many results if you put in only one or two words into a search engine. Put in between three and six key words to narrow your search.

- Put the main key word first: many search engines think this is the word you are looking for. Also, pay attention to the predictions that come before you type as this might give you further ideas. For example, starting to search 'how loss of biodiversity' returned 'affects humans'.

- The main results always appear in order. Sometimes it might be worth looking beyond the first page, but it is probably more practical for you to change your search terms rather than look at all the results. More precise search terms mean you will find the information you need more quickly.

- Be aware of those results that are sponsored by commercial organisations (such as those on the right-hand side of a Google page). These companies want you to use their sites as they can make money if people do.

ACTIVITY 1.10

1 Enter 'Biodiversity and ecosystem loss' into your search engine. (You don't need to click on any of the websites on the results page, just look at the page of results you get.)

  a How many results do you get? (Quite a lot? Perhaps about two million: certainly too many for you to read!)

  b What sort of sites do you get? (You might have found that some of these are from organisations you have come across before and might use again, for example WWF and WHO; and there will definitely be a **Wikipedia** link.)

2 Enter 'Threats to global biodiversity' into the search engine.

  What sort of results do you get now? (You should notice a change in the types of websites that are showing on the results page).

3 Now enter, 'Human activity threatens global biodiversity' into the search engine.

  You might have noticed that as you refine your search, you are also creating the question for your Individual Report. What might your question be as a result of this activity?

4 Try this activity with another topic from the eight topics for the Individual Report.

Discussion point

Find someone in your class who searched for the same topic as you in Activity 1.10 and compare your results.

Reflection: Can you now formulate a question for an Individual Report for the topic you chose?

KEY TERM

Wikipedia: a free, open-content online encyclopaedia created through the collaborative effort of a community of users known as 'Wikipedians'.

TIP

Wikipedia might be useful as a starting point for further sources of information, as other sources of information are listed at the bottom of a Wikipedia article, However, you should avoid **citing** and **referencing** Wikipedia in your work. This is because it is generally classed as an unreliable source of information as anybody can edit it, so you can't be sure that what you are reading is correct.

KEY TERMS

Citing: quoting from or referencing a particular author or publication, usually in the main body of the work.

Referencing: listing sources of information referred to in a piece of work, usually at the end of the work.

Research for a Team Project

As outlined in the introduction to this book, for your Team Project you will be researching different cultural perspectives about the issue you have decided on as a team. Again, it is useful to start the research process by identifying the information you need. You do not have to include global, national, local and personal perspectives within your Outcome and Explanation, but will need to show understanding of different cultural perspectives.

ACTIVITY 1.11

Imagine the following scenario:

As a team, imagine you have decided on the topic of Water, food and agriculture for your Team Project.

After some initial discussion and looking back at some of the work you have been doing in class about this topic, you decide to focus on the issue of food waste as a solution to food poverty. You want to find out how different countries are dealing with the issue of food poverty and what they do with food waste. As well as using secondary research data from the internet, you also want to do some primary research to find out what the situation is in your community and also in other countries where you have contacts.

You have decided to put together a short video clip as a way of persuading people to produce less food waste, and to donate money or items of food (tins, packets, etc.) to the food bank in your community.

1   What information do you think you need to find out?
2   How are you going to find out this information?

Discussion point
Discuss the ideas you have for Activity 1.11 with a partner.

Primary research

The Team Project asks you to choose a global topic and, in your team, decide how you can narrow down that broad topic to focus on one particular issue. The issue you choose must allow you to explore different cultural perspectives. You might want to undertake some primary research and interact with people from different cultures; either people you know or that live in your community or via links and contacts your teacher has, as well as doing secondary research about different cultures. This primary research will give an additional, very rich source for individual group members to draw on when you each have to write about what you have learned about different cultural perspectives – more so than relying solely on secondary research. You can gain information by creating a questionnaire or survey. Findings from your research should be shown in your outcome and explanation.

Research methods

You need to decide on the **research methods** you are going to use to collect information. This might depend on whether you want **numerical data** or **narrative data**. Common research methods are surveys, questionnaires and interviews.

TIP
You might also want to use primary research for your Individual Report to find out about the local perspective of an issue.

KEY TERMS

Research methods: the methods used to gather data and information that will be used in your work to support the points you make.

Numerical data (quantitative): information about quantities that can be measured and written down with numbers. Examples are your height and your shoe size.

Narrative data (qualitative): descriptive data, usually used to find out what people think about a situation or issue.

Questionnaires and interviewing as primary research

When creating questionnaires and interviewing people to gain information for your Team Project, it's important to discuss what information you need and from whom. For the Team Project, this will depend on the aim, which should allow for different cultural perspectives to be shown in the outcome and explanation. In the scenario in Activity 1.11, you might have drawn up a diagram of ideas to base your questions for your questionnaire/interview on, as in Figure 1.05.

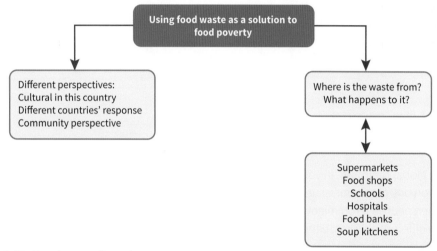

Figure 1.05 Food waste flow chart

From your flow chart, you can focus in on the questions you might want to ask and who you are going to approach, bearing in mind that any primary research needs careful handling.

Ethics in primary research

When interviewing people, it's important that you behave in a way that keeps them from harm, and that you treat all information you gather as confidential. There is no need for you to mention names in the research you do for the Team Project, it is enough that you gain information which shows different cultural perspectives on the issue to include in your outcome and explanation for the Team Project.

In the example in the flow chart in Figure 1.05, you have identified that you want to speak to people who work in supermarkets or food shops to get their perspective about how much perfectly good food is thrown away, and what might be done with it instead. You might also want the perspective of people that work for a charity, such as a food bank or soup kitchen. For another cultural perspective you might find out what other countries do with food waste and find contacts abroad who might be willing to complete your emailed questionnaire.

All the information you get can build towards your video outcome to suggest that food wasted by supermarkets could help reduce food poverty, and to encourage individuals to waste less food and donate to charities that work to get food to people who need it.

TIP

Put the search terms 'ethics in research' into a search engine to find out more about how to conduct primary research.

KEY TERM

Ethics: principles of what is right and wrong that govern a person's behaviour in a particular context, for example when conducting an activity like research.

ACTIVITY 1.12

Primary research steps

Put these steps in the order you think they should go when conducting an interview as primary research for your Team Project:

a   Design your interview questions/questionnaire.

b   Make notes to record key information gained during your interview.

c   Arrange a date, time and place for the interview.

d   Assure interviewees that all information gained will be treated confidentially and no names will be mentioned.

e   Introduce yourself, state the aims of your project and roughly how long the interview will take.

f   Thank people for their time.

g   Ask participants whether they are happy for you to use any information you gain.

h   Contact the people you want to interview beforehand to tell them about your project and how they can help.

i   Get approval for doing the research from your teacher.

Discussion point

Discuss your ideas for the order of steps in Activity 1.12 with a partner to see if they have the same order as you. You might also discuss these steps with your teacher.

TIP

If sending out a questionnaire, make sure you allow enough time for getting responses back and analysing the responses so that they can be used in your project.

Academic honesty

Whether you have done research for your Individual Report or your Team Project, you should ensure that you write the information you have found out in your own words, as it is your work that will be formally assessed. You must not claim someone else's work as your own.

It is possible that you might use the odd quotation, but these should be in quotation marks, cited and referenced. Use quotations sparingly as they are counted in the word limit.

TIP

You must reference all the sources you use in your work. It does not matter which format of referencing you use (Harvard, MLA) but you should use the same one throughout a piece of work. When using a source in class, always copy and paste the website address and add the date to a Word document and then write notes in your own words.

Example website reference from Activity 1.07:

Why fresh water shortages will cause the next great global crisis (2015) McKie, R. [Online] http://www.theguardian.com/environment/2015/mar/08/how-water-shortages-lead-food-crises-conflicts (accessed 11/10/2015).

Summary

- Make sure you know what you are looking for before you start to research.
- You will be mostly using secondary research for your Individual Report.
- The Team Project might require the use of primary research.
- Try to be precise when using search terms.
- Treat people with respect and politeness when interviewing.
- Allow plenty of time for primary research.
- Always cite and reference sources of information.

1.03 Analysis

16

 **SKILLS LINKS**

- Chapter 1: Information skills, 1.02 Research
- Chapter 1: Information skills, 1.06 Questioning
- Chapter 2: Critical thinking skills, 2.02 Evidence
- Chapter 3: Independent learning skills, 3.04 Evaluation
- Chapter 5: Communication skills, 5.01 Reading

In your Individual Report, as well as considering different perspectives about the issue(s) under investigation, you need to be able to analyse them. This involves exploring the causes and consequences of the issues, so that you are able to propose possible courses of action. Analysing and evaluating the quality of the sources of **evidence** you use to support your arguments and answer the question you set as the title of your Individual Report is also part of the assessment criteria. You will be exploring this later in Chapter 2, section 2.02.

 KEY TERM

Evidence: the available facts or information to support an argument, indicating whether something is true.

Reflection: Do you understand the key terms used here (perspective, issue, cause, consequence, course of action and evidence)?

If not, check the glossary now. You have come across these terms before and you need to make sure you understand them before you continue.

Identifying sources

Whilst you are researching during class activities and for your Individual Report, you will come across a number of sources of information that you may think are relevant to the different perspectives: global, national and local. It is important that you analyse what the main perspective of the source is, how it relates to your topic, what the issue is and what the causes and consequences of the issue are. By identifying relevant sources and making notes as you go along, you will quickly see whether you have enough information to explain the issue from different perspectives and have sufficient evidence to back up the points you make.

ACTIVITY 1.13

Read the extract below and identify the following:

- the topic (from the list of eight for the Individual Report)
- the issue
- the perspective
- the cause of the issue
- the consequence(s) of the issue
- the evidence used in the source

Inequality caused by the digital divide

Despite latest figures from the International Telecommunications Union (2015) indicating that global internet usage increased from 6.5 to 43 per cent between 2000 and 2015, at least four billion people in the developing world; Africa, India and parts of Asia, remain offline. This is a clear indication that the digital divide stills exist and causes considerable problems for the nations affected.

Those parts of the world where internet access is not an issue; the United States, Europe and Northern Asia, are all at an advantage both economically, educationally and socially. However, developing countries are often unable to invest in the technology that will enable their citizens to enjoy a reliable internet service. Both the initial start-up costs and the investment needed to maintain the service are too expensive for these countries. Consequently, developing countries are unable to develop. They are put at a competitive and economic disadvantage internationally, because if a country does not have internet access, schools are unable to develop the information and technology skills that pupils need, both for accessing information to help with their education whilst at school, and for future study and employment. Many universities and employers are looking for the ability to be able to use technology for accessing information and services. Businesses are also unable to carry out business online, which puts their companies at a substantial competitive disadvantage within the global market.

Reference

Statistics confirm ICT revolution of the past 15 years (2015) Press Release [Online], http://www.itu.int/net/pressoffice/press_releases/2015/17.aspx#.VhpWQPlVikp (accessed 11/10/2105).

Discussion point

Share the ideas you have for Activity 1.13 with a partner. Did you identify the same things?

Reflection: Imagine that your Individual Report title is: '*Does the digital divide only exist in developing countries?*' Would you consider using the article in Activity 1.13 as a source?

Digital World is the topic. The <u>issue</u> is stated in the title – the digital divide is a cause of inequality. The first paragraph also states that 'the digital divide still exists' and gives <u>evidence</u> of statistics (four billion people in the developing world have no access to the internet). The perspective is a global one as it looks at the situation of internet access across the world. The cause of the issue is the cost for developing countries (start-up costs and maintenance costs). Consequences are economical, educational and social disadvantage, although social disadvantage is not explained. Competitive disadvantage is also referred to with a partial explanation. The source of evidence referred to in the article is recent and considered reliable as the ITU is the United Nations specialised agency for information and communication technologies.

You will need more than one source of information to meet the criteria of *'researches and analyses a balanced range of relevant information from different perspectives'* as stated in the assessment criteria for the Individual Report.

You will need to consider the variety of sources you use as you will want to include different perspectives and viewpoints on the issue(s). You also need to think about how many issues to analyse as the more issues, the less likely you will be able to, *'analyse in depth the causes and consequences of relevant issues'* as required for level 5 of the assessment criteria.

TIP

Consider using two quality sources of information for each perspective; global, national and local. It might be easier to find sources for the global and national perspective, so think about the resources you can use to gain the local perspective such as local and community publications like newspapers and newsletters and websites.

ACTIVITY 1.14

Read the fictional article below, which is a written as if from a national newspaper of a developed country.

Answer the following questions:

1   Is the issue of the digital divide being considered from a global or national perspective?

2   What are the causes, according to this article of a digital divide?

3   What are the consequences of the issues?

4   What evidence is used to support the arguments made?

5   Is this a relevant source for your Individual Report entitled, 'Does the digital divide only exist in developing countries?' Why?/Why not?

The digital divide is happening here

We keep hearing reports about the digital divide in the developing world. Forget the situation in Africa, what about the digital divide that is right under our noses, here in the developed world? According to the Royal Geographic Society (2015), there are approximately four million adults who live in social housing who don't use the internet.

Whilst the wealthy in society have the latest gadgets and are benefitting from advancements in technology, including being able to work from home thanks to technologies that allow for communication and collaboration, those without the means are struggling to pay for a limited connection and cannot afford to renew their technology every couple of years. This limits opportunities as between 75% and 95% of jobs require some use of a computer.

There is an increasing problem with the availability of languages other than English on the internet. This is causing a communication barrier for some communities within our country. This is especially an issue with schools trying to communicate with parents via technology. Often, it is the children who have the more developed English language skills and we cannot always trust they are communicating the right messages to their parents.

Finally, there is the issue of the digital divide between the older and younger generations and this is becoming increasingly an issue in communities where people never really found a use for technology and therefore lack the skills or confidence to use the internet. Hospitals and doctors surgeries are now relying more on technology to communicate with patients, such as informing them when flu jabs are available. Those without the technology are finding it more difficult to access the support and care they need.

Reference
21st Century Challenges (2015) Royal Geographic Society [Online], http://21stcenturychallenges.org/what-is-the-digital-divide/ (accessed 12/10/2015).

Discussion point

Discuss your answers to the questions in Activity 1.14 with a partner.

You will probably have found that this source is from a national perspective, although the issue is the same as the text used in Activity 1.13 – the digital divide and one of the causes is the same (the cost), although this is more about the cost to individuals rather than the cost to a country. Another cause is the use of English, which can cause a language barrier and prevent people using the internet and as a consequence lead to a lack of information about what is happening around them, especially if they have children in school and the school uses a website to keep parents informed. Finally, another cause of the digital divide is that the older generation might not have the skills or confidence to use the internet for services like finding out information from hospitals' or doctors' websites. Evidence is given to support the argument and you can go directly to the source given and perhaps gain further information.

You will probably have decided that yes, you can use this source for your Individual Report.

Once you have found sufficient material and made notes for your Individual Report, you need to think about how you are going to present your ideas to show that you have analysed relevant information from different perspectives and the causes and consequences of identified issues. One way is represented in Figure 1.06.

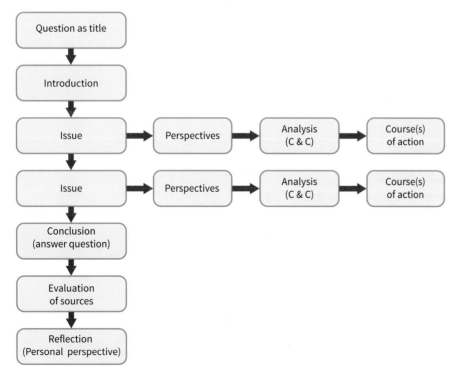

Figure 1.06 Individual Report structure

TIP

Look out for words like *because, since, due to* and *as* when trying to identify causes. These are also words you should be using in your Individual Report when talking about causes.

Look out for words like *as a result, therefore, thus, that's why* and *so* to identify consequences. Use them in your Individual Report when talking about consequences.

Analysing source material

Learning how to analyse sources is not only useful for your Individual Report, it is a useful skill for any written examination where you are given source material to study and are expected to use it to answer the questions. Practising in class will help develop your analytical skills.

ACTIVITY 1.15

Copy out and complete an example form for analysing texts in the form on the next page after reading the article about **Demographic change**. This is an example article (attributed to a fictional author and source), but the citations and footnotes are genuine.

Rapid population growth brings its challenges
By Greeta Birds

The human population is growing at an annual rate of approximately 77 million people per year[1]. The countries responsible for this growth include India, China, Pakistan, Nigeria, Bangladesh and Indonesia and it is expected that by the year 2025, the global population will have reached 8 billion[2]. This is due to improved health care, longer life spans, and reduced infant mortality. Because of opportunities for work, half of the world's population live in cities, which is putting a strain on services such as hospitals and schools. Another major change has been the ageing of the population. In 1999, 10 per cent of the world's population were over 60 years of age[3]. According to the United Nations, this figure will reach almost 2 billion by the year 2025[4]. This change will have extensive social and economic consequences, including issues to do with employment, pensions, and long-term health care. While once restricted to developed countries, concern for the consequences of ageing has now spread to developing countries. According to the Mission for Population Control, which promotes family planning in India, the only solution to what could be drastic environmental consequences if population growth continues, is family planning to control population growth so that standards of living for the poor can be improved.

(Fictional) Reference: Birds, G. (an example article), [Online], https://areallygoodnewspaper.com (accessed 25/11/2015).

[1] http://www.un.org/ga/Istanbul+5/booklet4.pdf
[2] http://www.theguardian.com/global-development-professionals-network/2015/mar/16/2015-challenges-demographic-shifts-population-growth-youth-bulge-ageing
[3] http://www.un.org/esa/population/publications/sixbillion/sixbilpart1.pdf
[4] http://www.un.org/esa/population/publications/bulletin42_43/weinbergermirkin.pdf

The table below shows a form you might consider using for analysing sources during class activities.

Title of source:				
Author:				
Reference:				
Date accessed:				
Issue(s)	**Cause(s) of issue**	**Consequence(s)**	**Supporting evidence**	**Further research to do**

Discussion point

Discuss with a partner to see whether you filled in the form for Activity 1.15 in a similar way.

Reflection: Is using the example form in Activity 1.15 a useful way of analysing a source?

Summary

- When analysing a source, you are looking for causes and consequences.
- You should try to use a range of different sources from different perspectives in your Individual Report.
- Make sure you are clear about the structure of your Individual Report.
- Words like *because, since, due to* and *as* signal causes.
- Words like *as a result, therefore, thus, that's why* and *so* signal consequences.
- The only way to develop your analytical skills is to practice.

1.04 Synthesis

SKILLS LINKS

- Chapter 1: Information skills, 1.06 Questioning
- Chapter 2: Critical thinking skills, 2.02 Evidence
- Chapter 3: Independent learning skills, 3.04 Evaluation
- Chapter 4: Collaboration skills, 4.03 Creativity
- Chapter 5: Communication skills, 5.02 Writing

Once you have analysed sources for information and you feel that you have enough to develop your own argument, either to take part in a discussion or debate in class or to answer the question for your Individual Report, you need to synthesise the information you have. This will then allow you to look for further sources if necessary to fill in any gaps and check that you have sufficient evidence to support the arguments you are making.

TIP

Synthesis does not mean writing a **summary**, a **review** or a **comparison**, but you can use all these to create something new, for example a drama production, a series of posters or a letter to the local council.

KEY TERMS

Summary: a brief statement or account of the main points of something.

Review: a critical appraisal of a book, play, film, hotel or other service or product, published in a newspaper, magazine or on a website.

Comparison: a consideration of the similarities and differences between two things or people.

Reflection: Do you remember what synthesis is? Refer to the definition in the glossary to check. Does Figure 1.07 help?

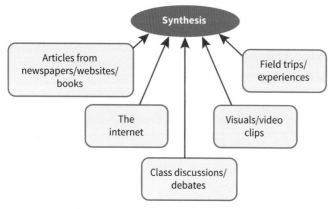

Figure 1.07 Synthesis spider diagram

As the spider diagram in Figure 1.07 shows, synthesis requires you to use a combination of two or more sources to come up with something new and original to support the piece of work you are doing. For example:

- an analysis of issues from different perspectives in order to answer your Individual Report question, build an outcome for your Team Project, or to formulate a line of reasoning to answer a question, as well as to contribute towards all the classwork you will produce
- poems and song lyrics, videos to highlight issues, posters and information leaflets to raise awareness and discussions and debates about global issues.

Using a T-chart

One way of helping you to organise your thinking about a global topic is to use a **graphic organiser** like a spider diagram as in Figure 1.07 or a T-chart. You can find out more about graphic organisers in Chapter 3, section 3.02 when learning about note-taking.

By using a T-chart, you can connect what you already know with what you are learning, and as you do so, can reflect on what else you need to know and questions you want answers to. A T-chart is a two-column list often using 'Notes' and 'Thinking' as the headings to the two columns as in Activity 1.16. A T-chart allows you to write down your observations, questions and reflections from any source, including images and audio and visual texts. Once you have a completed a T-chart, you can use the information gathered for any purpose by synthesising the information in it.

KEY TERM

Graphic organiser: also known as a concept map is a communication tool that enables you to express knowledge, concepts, thoughts, or ideas, and the relationships between them.

ACTIVITY 1.16

Look at the notes/thinking T-chart on the global topic of Culture.

T-chart about culture

Notes	Thinking
1 food	a Many people eat the same kinds of food now.
2 traditions	b Does that mean culture and traditions are disappearing?
3 celebrations	c Does everyone celebrate birthdays in the same way?
4 language	d How many languages are there? Are any languages in danger of extinction? Why?
5 shared history	e Does shared history relate to culture?
6 sense of belonging	f How do people feel if they are moved from where they live because of war?
7 identity	g Can we belong to more than one cultural group?

Put the search term 'culture' into your search engine. Spend five minutes **surfing the internet** to have a look at any images or short texts that come up.

Add another note and another question to the chart.

Discussion point
Share the note and question/observation/reflection you write for Activity 1.16 with a partner.

Reflection: What might you use the information you have gathered in your T-chart in Activity 1.16 for?

TIP

The Team Project asks you to create an outcome and explanation showing different cultural perspectives on an issue. Try to find out about different cultures within your own country by searching for the name of the country you live in and 'different cultures'.

ACTIVITY 1.17

1   Choose one of the global topics listed for the Team Project and search for and note the website addresses of two or three short video clips about the topic, for example, Human rights.

2   Before watching the clips, complete the 'Thinking' part of your T-chart about what you already know about the topic of human rights with any questions/observations you have. You might already have been given a text or some pictures related to the topic and want to know more.

3   While watching the clips, complete the 'Notes' part of your T-chart.

4   After watching the clips, reflect individually on what you have written and what questions you still have.

5   Find someone in your class who has chosen the same topic as you.

6   Share your findings with your partner to gain further information and feedback.

7   Form a small group and discuss what action you could take to inform others about an issue to do with human rights and any other way you might raise awareness of the issue.

Synthesising information for your Individual Report requires you to look through all the notes and summaries you have made on the sources for the topic. Once you have your question, you can then pick out the information you are going to need that shows perspectives, analysis of issues and courses of action.

TIP

You might highlight perspectives; issues; the causes and consequences of an issue and your courses of action in four different colours. Don't forget you need to know where your information has come from as you are expected to evaluate the quality of the sources you have used.

ACTIVITY 1.18

Read this section from an imaginary Individual Report.

'Can reducing greenhouse gas emissions globally help towards sustainable living?'

Here in China, we are becoming more and more worried about air and water pollution, not just for ourselves, but also for future generations. According to the Pew Research Centre (2013), who conducted face-face interviews with 3266 people earlier this year, anxiety about these issues has increased since 2008. Nearly half of those questioned rated air pollution as a significant concern; an increase of 16% since 2008, and 40% now feel that water pollution is a problem; an increase of 12%. Even though the information obtained was from a relatively small sample, considering that the population of China is almost one and half billion, it is a trustworthy source. The concerns are real and the Chinese government has expressed its desire to address them, even though the main cause of both air and water pollution is the Chinese government's preoccupation with economic growth (Balch, 2013).

Economic growth may have helped to reduce poverty, but it has brought with it the problems associated with an increase in carbon emissions; air and water pollution. As a result, the number of people wearing surgical masks has increased due to the thick layer of smog that lies over Beijing every morning and rarely disappears during the day. Many Chinese people are consequently concerned about their health and wearing these masks seems to be one way of breathing in less of the poison from the burning of fossil fuels. As a way of combatting these increasing carbon emissions, China is now considering dropping its rate of growth from 10% to 6%, firstly because a 10% rate of growth is almost impossible to maintain and secondly because these new problems like air and water pollution are dominating news programs across the country.

The global economy is very much dependent on fossil fuels for electricity. However, we need to find new technologies and cleaner, more renewable sources of fuel to cope with the world's energy demands. As well as encouraging businesses to think about the energy sources they use and to consider cutting carbon emissions, encouraging households to use renewable sources of energy like solar power will help protect the environment for future generations. Cash benefits could be given to households to encourage the adoption of solar power for domestic use. All countries need to work together to find ways of addressing the issues arising from the burning of fossil fuels to create a clean energy economy for a healthier world.

References:

Environmental concerns on the rise in China (2013) [Online], http://www.pewglobal.org/2013/09/19/environmental-concerns-on-the-rise-in-china/ (accessed 13/10/2015).

Forget economic growth, we need real prosperity instead (2013), Balch. O. [Online],

http://www.theguardian.com/sustainable-business/forget-economic-growth-real-prosperity-instead (accessed 13/10/2015).

Identify the following from the section:

a   The issues
b   The perspectives
c   Cause(s)
d   Consequences

e   Courses of action
f   Evaluation of sources
g   Evidence
h   References

Discussion point

Share your ideas for Activity 1.18 with a partner.

> **Reflection:** Do you think it is easier to identify information or to produce it?
>
> If you know what you are looking for, it is easier to identify specific details from given information than to synthesise all the information you have to produce something new like sections for an Individual Report. This is why it's important that you start to find sources and make notes early in your course of study. Then it won't be such hard work all at once at the end.

For the section in Activity 1.18, you will possibly have discussed the following:

- The <u>title</u> is clear and allows for the consideration of different perspectives.
- The <u>issues</u> are air and water pollution becoming a more pressing problem due to economic growth.
- The <u>perspectives</u> here are the national (China as the place where this learner lives) and the global.
- <u>Cause</u> is identified by 'brought with it' – economic growth demands the burning of fossil fuels.
- <u>Consequences</u> are smog that lies over the city for most of the day and as a result many people wear surgical masks because they are worried about their health.
- <u>Courses of action</u> are finding new technologies and cleaner, more renewable sources of fuel, encouraging businesses to think about the energy sources they use and to consider cutting carbon emissions, encouraging households to use renewable sources of energy like solar power by offering cash benefits.
- There is evidence of <u>source evaluation</u> – the research done by the Pew Research Centre and the relatively small sample size considering the size of the population.
- There is a <u>reference</u> list which includes references of the sources cited.

Discussion point

Discuss with a partner:

1   How you might improve the section of the imaginary Individual Report in Activity 1.18.

2   What other sections you need to add to create a complete Individual Report.

When synthesising information for your individual Report, you need to be clear about the information you need to include. The table below gives you an example of how you might structure your Individual Report. This is just one idea. You might decide to structure your report differently, and that's fine as long as all the key elements are included as stated in the assessment criteria. These guidelines should help you with what needs including, but the amount of resources and words for each section are approximate and might change, depending on your question.

Guidelines for the Individual Report

SECTION	CONTENT
Title (as a question)	A clear, concise focused global question that can be answered from consideration of different perspectives (global, national and local) and viewpoints within these.
Introduction	A brief explanation of the question and some reason for the choice of topic and question, for example personal interest or local relevance. A brief identification of the issues to be discussed. A short introduction to the perspectives will lead into the next section. Approximately 100–150 words.

SECTION	CONTENT
Issue 1	Analysis of the issue from different perspectives (two sources for each perspective), explaining and comparing causes and consequences. Formulation of possible course(s) of action. Approximately 550–600 words.
Issue 2	Analysis of the issue from different perspectives (two sources for each perspective), explaining and comparing causes and consequences. Formulation of possible course(s) of action. Approximately 550–600 words.
Evaluation of sources of information	Analysis and evaluation of the strengths and weaknesses of the sources in supporting the arguments made. Approximately 275–300 words.
Conclusion	A supported conclusion that clearly answers the question set as the title of the report. Brief consideration of the issues and perspectives and evaluation of the strengths and weaknesses of the course(s) of action to help resolve the issues. Approximately 150–175 words.
Reflection	An outline of what has been learnt by doing the research, changes in personal perspective(s) on the issues and reasons for these changes linked to the evidence presented. Approximately 125–150 words.
Reference List	A list of sources used within the Individual Report.

Summary

- Synthesising is creating something new from all the information you already have.
- You need to be able to synthesise information for all three components of IGCSE and O Level Global Perspectives.
- Using a graphic organiser like a T-chart can help you organise your notes and your thoughts.
- It is harder to synthesise than to analyse but analysing helps with synthesis.
- Synthesis is a skill that you will use throughout your education and future career so it is a skill worth developing.

1.05 Planning

 SKILLS LINKS

- Chapter 1: Information skills, 1.02 Research
- Chapter 1: Information skills, 1.06 Questioning
- Chapter 3: Independent learning skills, 3.03 Reflection
- Chapter 3: Independent learning skills, 3.04 Evaluation

Planning is part of life. We don't do many things without planning. We don't get on a bus without knowing where we are going, or have a party without planning what we are going to eat, drink and who we are going to invite. So, why would you not plan a piece of work, whether a Team Project, your Individual Report or a written answer to a question?

KEY TERMS

Planning: the process of setting goals, developing strategies, and outlining tasks and schedules to accomplish these **goals**.

Goals: aims or the end product to show achievement of something.

Planning is a skill you will use throughout your life, but it needs developing as do all the skills within this book.

Reflection: Think about when you joined a social networking site. You couldn't just access it. You had to go to the website, register and create a password. You needed to then update your profile and decide who to connect with and then invite them. This is planning.

When completing any piece of work, you should get into the habit of following these steps.

PLAN ➡ DO ➡ REVIEW ➡ EVALUATE ➡ PLAN

Figure 1.08 Steps for completing a piece of work

When creating a plan, you should always try to create a **SMART** plan:

KEY TERM

SMART plan: a plan that is specific, measurable, achievable, results-focused, and time- bound.

SMART planning

You should be able to answer the following questions to create a SMART plan.

1 **S**pecific – what are you trying to achieve and how you are going to achieve it?
2 **M**easurable – how are you going to assess whether you have achieved what you set out to achieve?
3 **A**ssignable – what are going to do and do you need help to achieve what you want to achieve?
4 **R**ealistic – do you have the skills (or do others) and the resources (or where are you going to find them) to achieve your aim?
5 **T**imely – when are you going to achieve your aim by and can you really do this in this time frame (if not, you will need to change the time frame)?

ACTIVITY 1.19

Imagine the following Team Project:
Aim: To raise money to send to a charity by holding a cake sale in school.
Answer the questions above to create a SMART plan.

28

Discussion point

Discuss your ideas for Activity 1.19 with a partner. Do you agree?

You might have discussed the following:

1 **S**pecific – You are trying to raise money (you may have a target for the amount you want to raise) and you are going to sell cakes to raise this money.

2 **M**easurable – You will have raised the amount you planned for in Step 1. (Only if it is a sensible amount and you don't try to raise millions!)

3 **A**ssignable – You will need to bake cakes and enlist the help of people to bake cakes and/or provide ingredients.

4 **R**ealistic – you can bake cakes yourself, but possibly not as many as you are going to need, so you will need to get help from family and neighbours and you will to get need the ingredients – you might need help to provide these.

5 **T**imely – you need to decide on a realistic time frame for when you are holding the cake sale and whether you will have enough cakes or not. If not, you might need to reduce the amount you plan to raise (after all anything is better than nothing!)

One way of planning is to imagine the **long-term goal** or outcome and imagine all the **short-term** goals that go towards achieving the long-term goal in a series of steps. You can use a stairway (as in Figure 1.09) to visualise achieving short-term and long-term goals.

KEY TERMS

Long-term goal: an aim that might take a few weeks, months or years to achieve.

Short-term goal: something you want to achieve soon, in the near future. The near future can mean today, this week or this month.

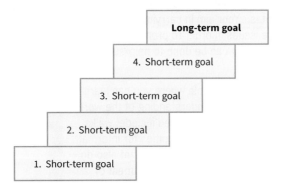

Figure 1.09 Stairway to success

ACTIVITY 1.20

Consider the following long-term goal: To cook a family meal.

Use the stairway to success in Figure 1.09 to identify the four short-term goals to reach your long-term goal.

Discuss your short-term goals with a partner. Do they have the same as you?

Short-term goals might have included: find or ask someone for a recipe, buy the ingredients, set a date and time, enlist a friend to help.

Think of something you want to achieve. Use the stairway to success to identify your long-term goal and the short-term goals to help you achieve your long-term goal.

Discussion point

Share your stairway to success for Activity 1.20 with your partner.

Reflection: Do you think the stairway to success is a good way of planning to achieve a long-term goal?

When planning your Team Project, you need to identify your aim and then plan the following:

1 the outcome and explanation to achieve the aim of your project, which must allow for the representation of different cultural perspectives

2 the tasks that need doing

3 who is going to do what and when

4 the time frame for achieving your goal (the outcome to achieve your aim)

5 how you are going to evaluate your outcome.

Your teacher will want to see that you have a plan for achieving the aim of your Team Project so it's a good idea to get into the habit of planning when doing any team work.

ACTIVITY 1.21

Action planning for Team Projects

Here is a short description of a possible Team Project. Try to complete the Team Project action planning form (with the exception of the teacher comment section) in the table on the next page.

You have decided to investigate the topic of Human rights, in particular, any issues relating to the rights of the **indigenous people** in your country. You want to explore how their different cultural perspective affects/influences their view of the rights they should have and how their perspective differs from yours and your schoolmates. Your aim in carrying out this project is to raise awareness in your school about these issues in order to promote greater understanding of the rights of the indigenous people and what can be done to help/support them.

Research activities include a visit to a community of indigenous people where you can learn more about the rich cultural heritage of the region and develop an understanding of the world view, traditional values and ways of knowing of the people. Activities planned include: walks, a tour of a cultural museum, a kayak trip, weaving workshops, and opportunities for informal discussion. Some primary research such as interviews can be conducted, You might also do some secondary research into government policies/archives, and the rights/treatment of indigenous people elsewhere.

Ideas for active project outcomes might include: the organisation of a Rights Awareness day with various cultural appreciation and human rights' awareness activities; an assembly video screening using footage/interviews from the visit to the community; an interactive lesson for younger pupils; a poster/series of posters to be placed around the school; a collage of pictures/text/poetry, bringing together the issues and what can be done to help.

TEAM PROJECT ACTION PLAN

Name: _____

Team members: _____

TEAM PROJECT IDEA _____

Task (What?)	Action (How?)	Group member (Who?)	Time needed (How long?)	Date for completion (When finished?)

Teacher Comment:

KEY TERM

Indigenous people: groups of people who are native to a particular country and have specific rights as a result their historical ties to a particular area.

!

TIP
Try to have only one aim and one outcome so it's clear what you are trying to do and the project doesn't get too complicated.

Discussion point
Once you have thought about what to write in each section of the form for Activity 1.21, discuss your ideas with a partner.

Reflection: Do you think that the imaginary Team Project in Activity 1.21 is a realistic project? Why? /Why not?

As well as helping you to plan your Team Project, you will also find action planning useful for planning your Individual Report.

ACTIVITY 1.22

Action planning for your Individual Report

Read both example extracts from action plans for example Individual Reports.
Give <u>two</u> strengths and <u>one</u> weakness of each.

Example 1

Name: Hans

Topic: Sustainable living

Question: Can reducing greenhouse gas emissions globally help towards sustainable living?

KEY TASK	ACTIONS	ESTIMATE OF TIME NEEDED	DATE FOR COMPLETION
1. Get Approval for IR title.	1. Draft title based on topic. 2. List reasons for choice of topic and question. 3. Make appointment with teacher to finalise title. 4. Identify possible problems in doing the research.	1. 30 minutes 2. 1 hour 3. 5 minutes; plus 15 minute consultation 4. 15 minutes	1. 2/9 2. 2/9 3. 3/9 for 4/9 4. 2/9
2. Identify local/ national and global perspectives and research relevant sources using internet.	1. Book access to library computers for next two lunch times and check availability at home to shared family PC. 2. Discuss perspectives and issues with teacher. 3. Plan research. 4. Do research	1. 10 minutes 2. 15 minutes 3. 15 minutes 4. ??	1. 3/9 2. 4/9 3. 4/9 4. ??

Example 2

Name: Joanna

Topic: Sustainable living

Question: What are the effects of the growth of cities worldwide?

KEY TASK	ACTIONS	ESTIMATE OF TIME NEEDED	DATE FOR COMPLETION
1. Get Approval	See teacher as soon as possible.		
2. Start Research	Use tablet at home.	4 days	Next month
	Use computer room at school.	4 days	Next month

Discussion point

1 Discuss the strengths and weaknesses of the action plans in Activity 1.22 with a partner.

2 Discuss what you might tell each person if you were the teacher reviewing these action plans.

Planning research

All the research you do also needs planning, otherwise you will find yourself spending hours surfing the internet and not achieving anything. Here is an example of how you might plan your research once you have your question for your Individual Report.

1 Title	Question to guide your research	Should genetically modified crops be used to help solve world food shortages?
2 Research aims	A short paragraph or bullet points outlining what you hope to achieve in the research linked to the question you intend to answer.	The research is about the perspectives (global, national, local) and viewpoints (scientists, politicians, etc) about genetically modified foods and how important they are for food security around the world. The idea is to see if GM foods are a real solution to the problem of food shortages.
3 Context	A description of the background to the research outlining the key issues to be explored which have guided the general approach adopted.	Everybody knows that there is inequality in the world and that although most people in the West have enough food, many people in developing countries do not. It is often shown in the media that many people are dying of hunger.
4 Methods	A description of the methods to be used to gather data and information that will be used as evidence. This should include an explanation of the reasons for the choice of method(s).	I can use the internet to find out global and national perspectives. My teacher has given me a list of useful websites I could explore. I can do interviews and talk with people in my community and in school to see what they think about the issue – this will give me the local perspective. Interviews are good as primary research because you can tell what people really think and ask extra questions.
5 Sources of Data and Evidence	A description of the sources of data and information that will be used as evidence. This should include an explanation of the reasons for the choice of sources. This might include location, types of data, amount of information, and who is involved.	The internet is the easiest for secondary research. I will search for newspaper articles and video clips to get information from different perspectives. I can interview people in school; teachers as well as students. I will also organise interviews with doctors at my local hospital and with members of the local church group.
6 Recording of Data and Evidence	A description of how the information and data will be stored.	What people say will be written down in notes, but I might try to save the interviews to listen to again and compare with others. Some people might not like being recorded but I will explain that I will just summarise what they say for my report and then delete the interview from my phone.
7 Possible Problems	A description of potential difficulties or limitations that might affect the research, for example issues of access, time, cost, ethical considerations, confidentiality, and understanding of other cultures. This might include some explanation of how these difficulties might be overcome.	I might not get enough people to interview for the local perspective. I don't know if it is OK to record the answers but if I ask them for permission they may not tell the truth. Some people may not tell the truth anyway. They could be biased or just make fun of my work.
8 Analysing Data and Evidence	An explanation of how the data and information will be used to answer the research question.	By looking at the notes I will be able to see if people think it is a solution to the issue. I could do a chart and a graph and summarise responses from primary research and synthesise my findings about the global and national perspective.
9 Presentation of information	A description and explanation of how the findings of the research will be presented.	I will need to write up my report so that it can be marked. Charts and tables would be good to show differences of perspective, but I must remember to refer to these in my written work. I must not forget to add my list of references.

ACTIVITY 1.23

Read the information given in the table on the previous page and answer the questions.

1 Is it clear to you what this example Individual Report is about?

2 Do you think this person understands the requirements for the Individual Report? Why? / Why not?

3 Is there anything else you might have included?

Discussion point

Discuss your ideas for Activity 1.23 with a partner.

Summary

- To achieve the best outcome, you need to plan all the work you do.

- Using planning forms and templates helps with planning.

- Plans should be SMART.

- Teams work better together if they plan first.

- Your teacher will want you to plan your Individual Report so that they can guide you.

- Planning your research will help you focus on what you are searching for.

1.06 Questioning

SKILLS LINKS

- Chapter 1: Information skills, 1.02 Research
- Chapter 1: Information skills, 1.03 Analysis
- Chapter 2: Critical thinking skills, 2.07 Problem-solving
- Chapter 3: Independent learning skills, 3.03 Reflection
- Chapter 4: Collaboration skills, 4.02 Decision-making

Gathering information is something we do all the time. It is a basic human activity. We use information for learning about things, about how to do things, for making decisions and for solving any problems we may have. To find **relevant information** and to be able to use this information, we need to be able to ask questions.

KEY TERMS

Relevant information: information that is closely connected or appropriate to the matter in hand or topic you are exploring.

Clarify: to make something clear or easier to understand.

Answering questions

You will be used to answering questions. Your teachers, parents and friends ask you questions all the time. They generally want to obtain information and **clarify** things.

Reflection: Consider some of the common questions you get asked. Do these generally start with: 'what, when, where, which and who/with whom'?

The intention of these questions is to find out or confirm what you are learning, doing, have learnt and done, are expecting to do, etc.

ACTIVITY 1.24

Write down five questions that you have answered recently.

Highlight the key question word at the start of each of these questions.

Discussion point

Discuss your questions from Activity 1.24 with your partner. How many of your questions start with the words why or how?

How and why questions are generally more difficult to answer than questions starting with what, where, who, which and when. This is because you have to think about them and give reasons, which is more difficult to do than answer questions that aim to elicit facts.

Reflection: Which of these questions is the most difficult to answer?

1 What is Migration?

2 Why do people move from one place to another?

You probably decided that question 2 is more difficult to answer as it asks for reasons, whereas question 1 asks for a definition of migration.

TIP

Key question words are:

What? Where? When? Who? Which? Why? How?

You will be answering questions in class or in examinations. Sometimes, rather than a question, you will be given a **command word** to indicate what you need to write by way of an answer.

KEY TERMS

Command word: a command word in a question indicates the type of answer required.

TIP

The following are all command words that your teacher might use or that you might find in a written examination:

Analyse: break something down.

Assess: consider the evidence presented and make an informed judgement.

Compare: look for and state the differences / similarities.

Consider: think about the different choices given.

Explain: a detailed response that gives reasons for how and/or why.

Evaluate: identify strengths and weaknesses.

Identify/Give/State: answer briefly by picking out an answer.

Justify: explain why / give reasons for something.

ACTIVITY 1.25

Read the following text about the global topic of **Employment**. Answer the questions:

1   Give <u>two</u> reasons why it is good to have a job.
2   Explain which of these reasons for having a job is the most important.

> Having a job is the most important way of reducing poverty, as not only does the money from working pay for food and accommodation, decent jobs give people a sense of pride as people feel that they are making a contribution to their family and community. Not having a job can lead to poverty and protests. Unemployment also leads to a rise in crime.

Discussion point

Share your answers to the questions in Activity 1.25 with a partner to see if they agree with you.

Asking questions

As well as answering questions during your course of study for IGCSE or O Level Global Perspectives, you also need to be able to ask questions.

You probably already ask many questions, but have you ever thought about the quality of the questions you ask and whether they actually **elicit** the information you need?

KEY TERM

Elicit: to draw out (information; a reaction, answer, or fact) from someone.

You can get information from different sources; from books and magazines or newspapers, from reading and listening material on the internet and from people that you might interview when conducting primary research. Before creating questions, you need to know the type of information you are looking for.

Here are some of the types of information you might need:

- Perspectives and viewpoints
- Current issues
- Causes and consequences
- Courses of action and solutions
- **Facts, opinions, predictions** and **value judgements**

KEY TERMS

Fact: Something that is known or can be proved to be true.

Opinion: A belief or judgement formed about something, not based on fact or knowledge and which cannot be checked.

Prediction: what someone thinks might happen in the future.

Value judgment: a judgement about whether something is good or bad, right or wrong, depending on someone's standards or priorities.

ACTIVITY 1.26

Let's consider the global topic of **Family**.

Match the question (**a–i**) with what you are trying to find out (**1–9**).

a Do you think an older relative should live with their family or are they better off in a home?

b Should we have to pay for care for an older relative by selling the family home?

c What are the effects on society of people living longer?

d What is the situation globally in relation to older people?

e Are Egyptian families responsible for caring for older relatives?

f How many people over the age of 60 are there globally?

g Why are people living longer?

h What will happen if we all live until we are 100 years old?

i What can be done to help older people live comfortably for the rest of their lives?

Here is what you are trying to find out:

1 National perspective
2 Current issue
3 Cause
4 Consequence
5 Course of action
6 Fact
7 Opinion
8 Prediction
9 Value judgment

Discussion point

Discuss your thoughts about which answer matches each question in Activity 1.26 with a partner.

You may have found that some questions were suitable for finding out different information, for example question **a** could be a suitable question to elicit someone's opinion or a value judgement (because they may think it is wrong that older people should go into homes).

TIP

Try using the key words as search terms. For example, if you are looking for information about the issues to do with older people globally, put 'current issues', 'older people' and 'global'. If you are looking for facts about older people in a specific country, put 'facts,' 'older people' and then the country where you want the information from.

37

Your Individual Report question

When writing your question for your Individual Report, you can use Figure 1.10 to help.

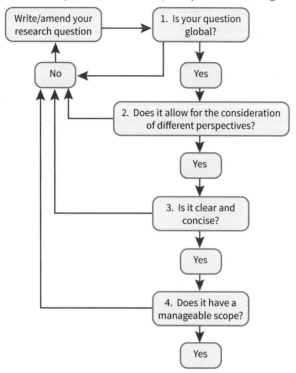

Figure 1.10 Formulating your Individual Report question flow chart

ACTIVITY 1.27

Use the diagram in Figure 1.10 to help you decide which one of the Individual Report questions in each pair is better. Try to give reasons for your decision.

1a Is trade and aid important?
1b Can fair trade help to ensure global food security?
2a Can genetically modified foods help towards sustainable living globally?
2b Are genetically modified foods bad?
3a Is the continued existence of the Amazon rainforest important globally?
3b Why does Indonesia need the rainforest?
4a Has global use of the internet changed the way we communicate?
4b Is digital technology important?

Discussion point

Discuss your thoughts about the example Individual Report questions in Activity 1.27 with a partner.

You might have decided that the following questions in each pair were better:

1b as it has a more manageable scope than **1a** and is a global question
2a as it is a global question and requires more than an opinion as an answer unlike **2b**
3a as **3b** focuses on Indonesia only so is not global, unlike **3a** which is global
4a as **4b** does not have a manageable scope and **4a** is a global question.

All the better questions in each pair allow for the consideration of different perspectives.

However, just having 'global' or 'globally' in the question does not necessarily make it a good question as this example shows: 'What is global sustainable living?'

Summary

- It is as important to be able to ask questions as to answer them.
- How and why questions are generally more demanding than what, where, when, who and which questions.
- Command words are often used instead of direct questions.
- You will need to ask different types of question depending on the information you are looking for.
- Your Individual Report question should be clear and concise, have a manageable scope, be global and allow for the consideration of different perspectives.
- You should be able to answer your Individual Report question in your conclusion.

Summary questions for Chapter 1

1.01 Perspectives

1 Identify one viewpoint within a perspective.
2 Explain the difference between a global and a national perspective.

1.02 Research

3 Identify one method of gaining information from people.
4 Explain the difference between primary and secondary data.

1.03 Analysis

5 Explain the difference between a cause and a consequence.
6 Explain why you think it's important to analyse a range of sources.

1.04 Synthesis

7 Give one example of something you might produce that requires you to synthesise information.
8 Explain the difference between analysis and synthesis.

1.05 Planning

9 Identify two things that need planning in order to carry out a Team Project.
10 Explain why you think planning your research is important.

1.06 Questioning

11 Give one question word that asks for a reason or reasons.
12 Explain why this question is a suitable question for an Individual Report: 'Does humans' relationship with animals benefit the planet?

Practising information skills

In this chapter, you have been looking at developing your ability to deal with the massive amount of information you are exposed to on a daily basis. You should now have a clearer idea about how to deal with this information during your course of study for IGCSE and O Level Global Perspectives. You will so far have been developing your understanding about perspectives, research, analysis, synthesis, planning and questioning. In the following sections of the chapter, you will be taking part in activities to practise what you have learnt.

This section of the chapter is divided into three; developing information skills, establishing information skills and enhancing information skills. Each section is designed to build on the section before. You can either work through each section in turn or choose the section that you feel is at the most appropriate level for you. You should see a progression in difficulty through the three sections.

Developing information skills

This section uses the topic of **Changing communities**, which is one of the eight global topics listed in the IGCSE and O Level Global Perspectives syllabus for the Individual Report (Component 2). You will be using this topic as the vehicle for improving your information skills.

SKILLS LINKS

- Chapter 1: Information skills, 1.01 Perspectives
- Chapter 1: Information skills, 1.02 Research
- Chapter 1: Information skills, 1.03 Analysis
- Chapter 1: Information skills, 1.04 Synthesis
- Chapter 1: Information skills, 1.05 Planning
- Chapter 1: Information skills, 1.06 Questioning

ACTIVITY 1.28

What does the term, 'Changing communities' mean to you? Write down as many words and phrases as you can think of in five minutes. You could do this as a bulleted list.

Discussion point

1 Discuss your ideas about what the term, 'Changing communities' means with different people in your class.

Do they have the same perspective as you?

Were the ideas gathered mostly positive or negative?

2   Look at the two photos in Figures 1.11 and 1.12.

Figure 1.11 Astana – the capital
of Kazakhstan

Figure 1.12 Flooded Bangkok

Which of these images most closely represents how you think that communities
are changing?

Give reasons for your choice.

Do your classmates agree with you? Find out their views.

Does your teacher agree? Find out their views.

ACTIVITY 1.29

1   Consider some of the reasons why communities have changed over the years; improved
    and new technologies, migration, economy, industrialisation, climate change, etc. Which
    of these do you think has had the greatest impact on your community? (It's likely that
    more than one of these has changed your community.)

2   Find one other image that represents how you think communities are changing.

3   Share your image with a partner and discuss both images, identifying how they show
    changes in a community.

ACTIVITY 1.30

Read the text and answer the questions:

1   Do you agree that the issues within this text are considered from a global perspective?
    Give at least one reason for your answer.

2   Give <u>one</u> of the issues discussed within the text.

3   Identify <u>one</u> reason for communities changing.

4   State <u>one</u> consequence of extreme weather conditions from the text.

5   Write down <u>one</u> question you would like an answer to as a result of reading this text.

Changing Communities

Hurricane Katrina was the worst residential disaster in the history of the United States,
amounting to approximately 135 million dollars of damage. This devastation affected
the most vulnerable communities within the region. This is just one example of the impact that
extreme weather conditions due to climate change are having on communities around
the world.

According to the United Nations, unless there is a global effort to reduce carbon emissions,
communities will change forever as a result of climate change. Droughts are affecting
communities globally as people struggle to survive, becoming displaced and losing their jobs

as the land they rely on dries up. Tensions exist between communities who feel that access to clean water is a right and those that are happy to pay for it. In many parts of the world, if you can afford the cost, you can use natural resources like water and heating. However, questions have been asked about whether it is acceptable for some communities to have water to keep their gardens nice and their grass green in a drought when some people do not have enough for their basic needs like washing and cooking. Their gardens are of course the least of their worries and remain dull and brown in times of drought.

Discussion point

Share your answers to the questions in Activity 1.30 with a partner.

ACTIVITY 1.31

Search for a further source of information from your national perspective to find a text about how communities are changing due to extreme weather conditions. This might be a written or spoken source of information.

Once found, use the table below. Copy and paste the website address, and make notes under the headings: perspective, issues, causes and consequences.

Website address:			
Date:			
Perspective	Issues	Causes	Consequences

Reflection: What terms did you use for your search for Activity 1.31?

How long did it take you to find a suitable source?

Do you feel more confident about finding relevant sources of information?

Discussion point

Share your source of information and completed table for Activity 1.31 with a partner or a small group. By doing this you will have different sources of information about the same topic and similar if not exactly the same issues.

ACTIVITY 1.32

1   Use the sources of information you have on the topic of 'Changing communities', to write a short letter (approximately 80–100 words) to go in your community newsletter about how extreme weather due to climate change is affecting the local community and about what can be done locally to cope with the issues arising.

2   Ask a partner in your class to give you some feedback about your letter: two highlights/things that they think are good, and why, and one area where they think you can improve your letter.

ACTIVITY 1.33

Consider the following questions that could be used for the title of an Individual Report:

1 How are communities changing?

2 Is climate change responsible for changing communities globally?

3 What are the reasons for changing communities globally?

Which of these three questions do you think is the best question for an Individual Report? Give reasons for your decision.

(You can use Figure 1.10 to help you decide.)

Discussion point

Share your choice of question for Activity 1.33 with a partner to see if they agree.

Reflection: Can you think of a better question for an Individual Report within the global topic of 'changing communities'?

Check with your teacher to see if your question is a good one.

ACTIVITY 1.34

Imagine you are planning research to complete an Individual Report on the global topic of **Changing communities**. Read through the research planning form below and suggest what might go in the gaps a–h.

1 Title	*Question to guide your research*	(........................**a**........................)
2 Research aims	*A short paragraph or bullet points outlining what you hope to achieve in the research linked to the question you intend to answer.*	The research is about the perspectives (............**b**.........) and viewpoints (.........**c**..........) about (.........**d**.........). The idea is to see (......**e**.............).
3 Context	*A description of the background to the research outlining the key issues to be explored which have guided the general approach adopted.*	Everybody knows that climate changes is causing extreme weather conditions around the world and that it is an individual's as well as a country's responsibility to prevent climate change.
4 Methods	*A description of the methods to be used to gather data and information that will be used as evidence. This should include an explanation of the reasons for the choice of method(s).*	I can (...............**f**.............)
5 Sources of data and evidence	*A description of the sources of data and information that will be used as evidence. This should include an explanation of the reasons for the choice of sources. This might include location, types of data, amount of information, and who is involved.*	The internet is the easiest for secondary research. I will search for newspaper articles and video-clips to get information from different perspectives. I can interview people in school; teachers and other staff as well as students.

(continued)

6 Recording of data and evidence	A description of how the information and data will be stored.	I will copy and paste the website into my online blog and add dates when I find sources. I will (..........g............) and then create summaries from the notes I make.
7 Possible problems	A description of potential difficulties or limitations that might affect the research, for example issues of access, time, cost, ethical considerations, confidentiality, and understanding of other cultures. This might include some explanation of how these difficulties might be overcome.	I might not get enough people to interview for the local perspective.
8 Analysing data and evidence	An explanation of how the data and information will be used to answer the research question.	By looking at my notes I will be able to see if whether I have enough information to answer my question. If not, (............h...............)
9 Presentation of information	A description and explanation of how the findings of the research will be presented.	I will need to write up my report so that it can be marked. I must not forget to add my list of references.

Discussion point

Share your ideas for Activity 1.34 with a partner.

Establishing information skills

This section uses the topic of **Employment** to establish your information skills. This topic is one of the eight global topics listed in the IGCSE and O Level Global Perspectives syllabus for the Written Examination (Component 1). Your teacher can tell you what these are. You will build on the skills you have acquired so far so that you start to feel more confident about finding and using information from different sources.

SKILLS LINKS

- Chapter 1: Information skills, 1.01 Perspectives
- Chapter 1: Information skills, 1.02 Research
- Chapter 1: Information skills, 1.03 Analysis
- Chapter 1: Information skills, 1.04 Synthesis
- Chapter 1: Information skills, 1.05 Planning
- Chapter 1: Information skills, 1.06 Questioning

ACTIVITY 1.35

Work with a partner to break down the global topic of 'Employment' into sub-topics, for example motivation, pay, hours...

Reflection: Do you have a job? If so, what tasks does your job require you to do?

ACTIVITY 1.36

1 Which of these questions would give you information from a <u>global</u>, a <u>national</u>, a <u>local</u> or a <u>personal</u> perspective?

   a What work do you see yourself doing in ten years' time?

   b What causes unemployment?

   c What is being done locally to help the unemployed?

   d What are the main things you consider when looking for a job?

   e Why has the level of unemployment increased in recent years?

   f Why is it important to be employed?

2 Write the answers to these questions by finding out any information you didn't already know. Don't forget to note down websites that give you the information needed for the activity.

Discussion point

Share your answers to Activity 1.36 (b, c, e, and f) with a partner to see if they have the same information as you. Discuss also the search terms you used to find the answers and any useful websites you wrote down.

ACTIVITY 1.37

Read the text about why people work, then answer the questions.

1 Identify two reasons why people work.

2 Which one of these reasons do you think is most important? Explain your answer.

Why do people work?

We all have different reasons for working. At face value, you might think that this is a straightforward question that has a straightforward answer, which is 'for money'. However, nothing is ever straightforward, is it? Have you ever considered what motivates you? Ask around and you will find that the reasons people work are different. Generally we all work because we get something we need from working. That something affects our quality of life and our general well-being.

Consider the following: Some people work because they love what they do, others like to achieve certain goals that they set themselves. Some feel that they are contributing to something bigger than themselves and that they have a responsibility to society to work, which may be one explanation why people do voluntary work for charities. Some work because they like the contact with other people; customers, fellow workers, etc. Others wouldn't know what to do with their time otherwise. Motivation is what drives people to work and motivation is complex. What motivates some does not motivate others. The importance of money, however, should not be underestimated. It is the main benefit of working, but people don't just work for the money itself, they work for what it can provide – basic needs like food and accommodation, sending children to school and college, nice holidays, etc. These are motivational.

So, what motivates you?

Discussion point

Discuss your answers to Activity 1.37 with a partner and then ask your teacher how many marks your answers might have scored.

Reflection: How would you answer the question posed at the end of the text for Activity 1.37: '*So, what motivates you?*'

ACTIVITY 1.38 PART A

Imagine you want to do some primary research to find out what motivates different people, what they think about work, why they work and how important motivation is for them to do a good job. The aim of the activity will be to produce a poster to persuade people about the importance of motivation for better performance at work. Answer the following questions:

1   Who are you going to ask?
2   How many people are you going to ask?
3   What information do you want?
4   What methods are you going to use?
5   How are you going to collect information?
6   How are you going to record information?
7   What are you going to do with the information you collect?

Discussion point

Discuss your ideas for Part A of Activity 1.38 with a partner.

ACTIVITY 1.38 PART B

For this part of the activity, you are going to conduct some primary research. Limit the number of people you are going to ask to ten, and they should be people at your school (students, teachers, and other school staff), parents and relatives and/or neighbours.

1   Decide on asking them to complete a questionnaire with ten questions about what motivates them, what they think about work, why they work and how important motivation is for them to do a good job… You can have a mixture of questions that ask for narrative and numerical data.
2   Work with your partner to design your questionnaire.
3   Ask your teacher for feedback so that you can improve your questionnaire.
4   Give your questionnaire to the ten people you have chosen.
5   Collect your questionnaires (after about one week, which you need to tell them when you hand them out).
6   Analyse the information you have gathered.
7   Design a poster to persuade people that being well-motivated leads to better performance at work.
8   Ask your teacher to give you feedback on your poster – does it show your primary research findings and does it persuade of the importance of being well-motivated for better performance at work?

ACTIVITY 1.39

For this activity, you will be considering the issue of youth unemployment. Don't forget that when researching, you can look for written and spoken texts.

1 Put the search terms 'youth unemployment globally' into your search engine and find one article from a newspaper that you might be able to use to find out more about this topic. (You will see that there are still a lot of websites so will need to narrow your search.) Make a note of this website.

2 Put the search terms 'causes of youth unemployment globally' in your search engine. Find one website that gives you information about the causes of youth unemployment from a global perspective. Make a note of this website.

3 Now put 'consequences of youth unemployment globally' into your search engine and choose one website that gives you information about the consequences of youth unemployment from a global perspective. Make a note of this website.

4 For each of your sources, make notes about the current situation regarding youth unemployment around the world and the main causes and consequences of youth unemployment globally.

5 Repeat steps 1, 2, 3 and 4. This time replace the term, 'globally' with the name of the country you live in.

6 Write one paragraph addressing the current situation regarding youth unemployment globally, its causes and consequences and another for the situation where you live. Try to include words like **because, since, due to** and **as** when writing about **causes** and *as a result, therefore, thus, that's why* and *so* when writing about **consequences**. Make sure that you use your own words from your notes. (When you copy and paste one of your sentences into your search engine, the search should not bring up the website where the information originally came from.)

7 Put the websites you found in a reference list at the end of your work.

Discussion point

Share the work you have done for Activity 1.39 with a partner or with your teacher to gain some feedback. Ask them to comment on what they think is one of the strengths of the work, and one area that they think needs improvement.

Reflection: Use the feedback gained from sharing the work done for Activity 1.39 to go back and improve your work.

ACTIVITY 1.40

Work with a partner or in a small group for this activity.

Using the sources of information gathered throughout this section on the global topic of Employment, produce some song lyrics. You can use a well-known tune to perform your lyrics to, and either perform live in front of your class or make a recording of yourself performing it. You might make a plan of action to include the following:

1 The aim of your song.

2 The audience for your song.

3 The issue(s).

4 The words and phrases you want to include.

You can use the template below for your plan and get some feedback from your teacher when your plan is complete, before you write your lyrics.

Group activity: to produce song lyrics for the global topic of 'Employment'				
Aim:				
Audience:				
Issue:				
Task (What?)	Action (How?)	Group member (Who?)	Time needed (How long?)	Date for completion (When finished?)
Teacher Comment:				
Strength(s):				
Area(s) for improvement:				

Enhancing information skills

This section uses the topic of **Transport systems** to enhance your information skills. This topic is one of the eight global topics listed in the IGCSE Global and O Level Perspectives syllabus for the Written Examination (Component 1). By working through the activities in this section, you will continue to build on the information skills you have acquired so far.

SKILLS LINKS

- Chapter 1: Information skills, 1.01 Perspectives
- Chapter 1: Information skills, 1.02 Research
- Chapter 1: Information skills, 1.03 Analysis
- Chapter 1: Information skills, 1.04 Synthesis
- Chapter 1: Information skills, 1.05 Planning
- Chapter 1: Information skills, 1.06 Questioning

ACTIVITY 1.41

Here are two questions that you might want to ask when looking at issues to do with transport systems from a national perspective:

- How have transport systems in my country changed in recent years and why?
- What improvements could be made to the public transport system in my country and why?

Write down two questions to look at issues to do with transport systems from a global perspective.

Discussion point

Discuss the questions you have written for Activity 1.41 with a partner. Decide which are the best two out of the four questions and why.

ACTIVITY 1.42

Use key words from the questions you have written for Activity 1.41 to search for the information you need to find information about transport systems from both a national and global perspective. You might share the work with a partner and take two questions (one global and one national) each.

For your questions, write down each question, the website where you find the information to answer each question and a short answer to each question in your own words.

Discussion point

Discuss the answers to your questions in Activity 1.42 with your partner.

Reflection: What have you learnt about the global topic of transport systems that you didn't know before you started Activities 1.41 and 1.42?

What do you now think about issues to do with transport systems (this is your personal perspective)?

ACTIVITY 1.43

1 When analysing a text for information, what are you generally looking for? Try to think of at least three things.

2 Analyse the following text to gain information for these three things.

Traffic congestion around the world

Many cities in the world have to cope with thousands of cars going through them every day. Traffic congestion is, therefore, a major problem, as is air pollution from car and lorry fumes. The reasons why traffic congestion is such an issue is that there are more vehicles on the road because the adult population is increasing and adults need and want to be able to get around easily. Bad driving causes accidents, which leads to roads being out of action as the police and ambulance services are called and accidents are dealt with. Poor road quality and management mean that roadworks also cause congestion and disruption.

Added to this is a lack of adequate infrastructure. Local governments do not act to prevent traffic congestion; instead they try to deal with problems as they arise and often don't have the manpower or resources including cash to respond immediately. As cities don't expand with the population, many streets become gridlocked as cars are parked outside houses on either side of the road, with little room for other vehicles to pass.

3   Add a paragraph that explains traffic congestion from a national or local perspective (what you write will depend on where you live).

For the national perspective, you will need to do some secondary research, and for the local perspective, you might need to do some primary research).

Discussion point

Share your national or local perspective from Activity 1.43 with a partner.

- Do you have the same information?

- Are there any viewpoints expressed within your national or local perspective?

- Does your information reflect a national or local perspective, or is it just factual information about your country?

Reflection: Consider the difference between giving information *from a perspective* and giving information *about a country*.

What words might you use to ensure that you give information *from a perspective*?

ACTIVITY 1.44

1   Use a Notes/Thinking T-chart to record what you already know about the global topic of transport systems. Write the issues as notes in one column, and questions and observations in the thinking column.

Notes	Thinking

2   Add to these notes by finding three different sources of information about traffic congestion: newspaper article, video clip, charity website, etc.

3   Once you have made your notes, write out these sources as if for a reference list.

4   Depending on which referencing system you have used, check you have written your references out correctly by visiting a website about that referencing system.

5   Make any changes to your references that you need to as a result of any further information you have gained about referencing.

6   Ask your teacher to confirm that your references are correct.

ACTIVITY 1.45

1   Read the text and write six questions, one for each of the question words: what, where, when, which, how and why. (Make sure you know the answers.)

2   Swap your questions with a partner for them to answer using the text.

Traffic congestion

Solutions to traffic congestion should be the responsibility of employers, local governments and individuals. Traffic congestion is always at its worst at what has become known as the typical start and finish times to the working day; that is at 9.00 a.m. and at 5.00 p.m. This is because everyone travels to and from work at the same time of the day, every day. It is not, however, suggested that employers make people redundant, thereby creating unemployment, but that there must be alternative working practices that can be adopted. Examples include staggering the start and finish times and encouraging home-working. Improving public transport could also help ease traffic congestion as people travel to and from work not only on buses but also on underground systems and trains. Increasing the cost of parking whilst reducing the fares for public transport might also be a solution to traffic congestion. What about banning cars from the city centre? Is this a realistic solution to the problem of traffic congestion in this country?

Discussion point

1   Discuss with your partner whether it was easy or difficult to answer your partner's questions in Activity 1.45 (which ones were easier and why do you think this was, etc.).

2   Assess the quality of the questions; did they extract the key information from the text about the perspective(s), issue(s), causes, consequences, courses of action/solutions?

ACTIVITY 1.46

Read the text and answer the questions that follow.

There are currently over one billion cars on the planet, which are responsible for almost 15% of global fossil fuel carbon emissions. Despite this, there has been a 20% reduction in the number of cars entering the centre of the European city of Lyon in France since 2005. Bicycle share schemes are on the increase, more city centre streets are closed off to vehicles, public transport continues to grow, main roads are being replaced by cycle paths. So, the question is, do we need cars in cities at all?

This is still a dream in many cities globally, but in some European cities, there is a real move towards car-free city centres, as one resident of Hamburg in Germany tells us.

'I live in Hamburg in Germany and got rid of my car three years ago. I don't really miss it at all, but then I live and work in the city centre. I use a combination of bicycle, trains, and taxis. If I actually need a car to go further afield than work or out socially, I use a car from a car-share scheme, but this doesn't happen very often as I can get to most places by other means. As well as being environmentally friendly, not having a car has saved me a lot of money as there is no insurance or car tax to pay and I don't need to buy petrol.'

1   Identify the trend in the number of cars entering Lyon city centre since 2005.

2   Give two reasons why people might not be using cars so much in city centres.

3   Explain one global consequence of reducing the number of cars in city centres.

4   Opinion is divided about the need to stop cars entering the city centre. The chairperson of the local transport committee suggests collecting evidence of public opinion by stopping people in the city centre to ask them some questions. How effective do you think this method is? Give reasons for your opinion.

Discussion point

Discuss your answers to the questions in Activity 1.46 with a partner. As a pair, write out the four answers to the questions.

ACTIVITY 1.47

When answering longer questions, it is important to plan your answer. You should read the question carefully so you know what is being asked of you.

Consider the following question:

Do you think getting rid of cars from city centres should be a priority for all countries?

In your answer you should:

- state your conclusion
- give reasons for your opinion
- use the material in the sources and your own experience and evidence
- show that you have considered different perspectives.

The word 'should' is very important here as it means that you _must_ cover all the points mentioned. If the question said 'may', then the things that follow are suggestions only and you won't be penalised for not including them.

Here's a useful checklist for your answer.

	Criteria	Yes
1	There is a clear introduction.	
2	All points in the question have been included and are clear .	
3	All material is relevant.	
4	Sentences are short and to the point.	
5	Different perspectives have been considered.	
6	Information from the source material has been included.	
7	There is a clear conclusion.	
8	There is an answer to the question.	

Write your answer to the question using the source material from this section on transport systems. Before you start, ask your teacher for a copy of the mark scheme.

Reflection: Have you answered 'yes' to the eight points in the checklist for the work produced for Activity 1.47? If not, go through your answer and check it.

Discussion point

Share your answer to Activity 1.47 with a partner, together with the mark scheme , to get some feedback to improve your answer.

Chapter 2
Critical thinking skills

Learning objectives

By the end of this chapter, you should be able to:

- understand the importance of developing critical thinking skills
- develop a clear and sensible line of reasoning
- evaluate a line of reasoning, evidence, claims and conclusions
- draw conclusions from information given
- recognise bias and vested interest
- identify and explain what facts, opinions, predictions and value judgements are
- apply problem-solving techniques to issues that arise
- increase your empathy.

Introduction

As with all the skills in this book, studying IGCSE or O Level Global Perspectives enables you to develop your critical thinking skills. Thinking critically does not just mean thinking a lot, it's about thinking better. It's about equipping you to deal with information and problems that arise during the time you are studying and beyond.

In this chapter, you will learn to develop your critical thinking skills by focusing on the following:

2.01 Reasoning	**2.02** Evidence	**2.03** Claims	**2.04** Drawing conclusions
2.05 Bias and vested interest	**2.06** Statements of argument; fact, opinion, prediction and value judgement	**2.07** Problem-solving	**2.08** Empathy

2.01 Reasoning

SKILLS LINKS

- Chapter 1: Information skills, 1.03 Analysis
- Chapter 1: Information skills, 1.04 Synthesis
- Chapter 1: Information skills, 1.05 Planning
- Chapter 1: Information skills, 1.06 Questioning
- Chapter 2: Critical thinking skills, 2.02 Evidence
- Chapter 3: Independent learning skills, 3.04 Evaluation
- Chapter 5: Communication skills, 5.02 Writing
- Chapter 5: Communication skills, 5.04 Speaking

ACTIVITY 2.01

Find a short video-clip that tells you about the importance of **critical thinking**.

The best way of understanding something ourselves is to try to explain it to others. See if you can tell someone else what critical thinking is and why it's important.

KEY TERM

Critical thinking: actively applying, analysing, synthesising, and/or evaluating information gathered from observation, experience, reflection, reasoning, or communication.

TIP

There are many websites that explain what critical thinking is. As well as knowing what it is, it is useful to search for 'why critical thinking is important'.

Whilst searching for information about critical thinking, you will have discovered that critical thinking also includes the ability to deal with information. Some of the sections in Chapter 1: Information skills are, therefore, also relevant to critical thinking. For example, the ability to ask and answer questions not only enables us to deal with information, it is also classed as a critical thinking skill as asking and answering questions gets us to think better. Don't worry about this overlap. Critical thinking teaches us that things are not always back or white and there is bound to be some overlap or 'grey' areas at times.

TIP

You will need to understand the terms given to some critical thinking skills so that if asked to evaluate a claim, or draw a conclusion, for example, you know what you are expected to do.

It will become clear which terms you need to know as the chapter progresses.

The first section of this chapter focuses on your ability to give reasons for your opinions and any action you want to take. Developing your **reasoning** skills will enable you to draw **inferences** and make **deductions**, using appropriate language to explain your perspective, and using evidence to support the points you make.

KEY TERMS

Reasoning: thinking about something in a clear and sensible way.

Inference: an idea or conclusion reached based on evidence and reasoning.

Deduction: the process of reaching a decision or answer by thinking about the known evidence.

ACTIVITY 2.02A

Read the text about **Water** and answer the questions.

Turn off the water whilst brushing your teeth

Why should I have to turn off the water while I clean my teeth because someone tells us that there are water shortages and water should be saved? In the first place, I take no pleasure in brushing my teeth. Secondly, it's really annoying that I'm told that I have to turn off the water. Everyone else in my family turns the water off when they brush their teeth, so it shouldn't matter if I do or not, since I'm only one person.

Figure 2.01 Water turned on

1 How good do you think this argument is?
2 What reasoning is used for the argument?
3 Does the author give any evidence to support the reasoning?

Discussion point

Discuss your answers to the questions in Activity 2.02A with a partner.

This is not a very good argument. The reasons for not turning off the tap have nothing to do with the use of water. They are the author's opinion about cleaning their teeth and being told to do something. The reasoning does not have any evidence to support it.

Reflection: How could the author have made the argument in the text in Activity 2.02A stronger?

ACTIVITY 2.02B

Now read the following text and answer the same three questions as you did for Activity 2.02A.

Turn off the water whilst brushing your teeth

You really need to start turning the tap off when you brush your teeth. Firstly, there is no reason for leaving the water running, because when you're brushing your teeth, you're not using the water, so it's simply being wasted. Another reason for turning the water off when brushing your teeth is that you could save three litres of water every time you brush your teeth as the average amount of running water from a tap is five litres of water per minute and you only need two litres if you turn off the tap in between brushing. By turning the water off while you brush your teeth, you would consequently help save water in our town, which needs it, because it rains so little here.

Figure 2.02 Water turned off

Discussion point

Discuss your answers to the questions in Activity 2.02B with your partner.

You should have noticed that this is a better argument as the reasoning is stronger. The reasoning is supported by evidence – the amount of water saved and used for the activities mentioned. The evidence is also relevant as it relates to the argument of saving water by turning it off when not being used for the teeth brushing activity.

TIP

An **argument** is generally made up of two or more lines of reasoning which try to persuade us to accept a proposal or an opinion. If the reasoning is strong, then we will be more convinced by that argument than by an argument that has weak reasoning.

If an argument makes sense, the reasoning is considered *sound*. If an argument does not have solid reasons and evidence to support the point it is trying to make, or if it uses reasons and evidence that do not make sense, it is considered to have *unsound* reasoning.

KEY TERMS

Logical: reasonable and makes sense.

When evaluating any argument, you should always check to see whether the argument contains the following:

- reasons in favour of the argument that are relevant, and contribute to it
- ideas that follow on from each other in a **logical** way
- evidence, which can be in the form of statistics, examples, findings from research, personal stories and experiences.

ACTIVITY 2.03A

You may be asked to explain how well the reasoning within an argument works, or to compare one person's reasoning with another's.

Read the following section (Section A) of a text on the topic of **Fuel and energy** and answer the questions.

> **Section A text**
>
> We know that fossil fuels are going to run out soon, and that we need to find alternatives. We need to be thinking about these alternatives now. Nuclear power is the best alternative because nuclear power produces more energy than fossil fuels. Research shows that a pound of nuclear fuel carries about one million times the energy as a pound of fossil fuel.

1 What do you think the main argument of the whole text is (you only have a short section here)?
2 What is the reasoning presented here?
3 Is there any evidence to support the reasoning?

Discussion point

Discuss your answers to the questions in Activity 2.03A with a partner.

You should have realised that the text is arguing for alternatives to using fossil fuels for energy (because fossil fuels will run out) and that this section presents reasoning for the use of nuclear power, because more energy is obtained from nuclear power than from burning fossil fuels. Evidence from research supports the reasoning but it could be stronger as it doesn't specify which research and when.

 KEY TERM

Counter-argument: an argument or set of reasons presented to oppose an idea, action, proposal, perspective, or opinion developed in another argument.

ACTIVITY 2.03B

Now read the reasoning for a **counter-argument** to the use of nuclear power and answer the questions.

> **Section B text**
>
> Nuclear power cannot be an alternative to fossil fuels for energy as it's not safe. Just look at the nuclear disasters that have happened around the world! Surely, it would be safer to replace fossil fuels with wind and solar power, wouldn't it?

1 What is the reasoning presented in Section B?
2 Is there any evidence to support the reasoning?
3 Do you think the reasoning in Section B is better or worse than the reasoning in Section A? Explain your answer.

Discussion point

Discuss your answers to the questions in Activity 2.03B with your partner.

You probably decided that the reasoning in the Section B text was not as strong as in the Section A text as there is not as much evidence to support the reasoning. The reason given for not using nuclear energy is that it's not safe but no examples of where it has been unsafe are stated, just 'around the world'. There is also no reasoning given for the statement about using wind and solar power.

ACTIVITY 2.03C

Do some research for evidence to support the reasoning in the Section B text in Activity 2.03B.

Reflection: How easy was it to find evidence to support the reasoning in the Section B text in Activity 2.03B?

What search terms did you use?

Does the reasoning in the Section B text in Activity 2.03B now seem stronger than the reasoning in the Section A text?

Different lines of reasoning make up an argument. When developing an argument, you need to organise your thoughts and ideas and put them into some sort of structure.

Figure 2.03 gives a visual of the things to consider when developing an argument.

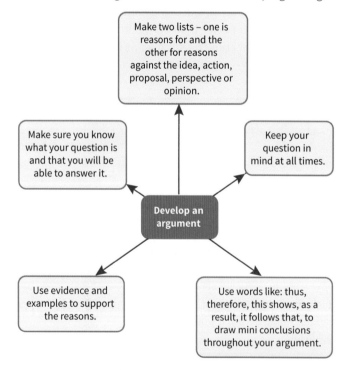

Figure 2.03 Developing an argument

As well as being able to develop lines of reasoning for formal study, you will also benefit from being able to hold your own in a discussion about what is happening in the world, what you think about this and why. The more you think of reasons for your arguments and support these reasons with evidence, the more you will be listened to and respected in whatever line of work you eventually undertake.

ACTIVITY 2.04

Using the material about fuel and energy, consider the question: '*Is it better to replace fossil fuels with nuclear power than with wind or solar power?*'

Use the diagram in Figure 2.03 to plan one side of the argument to answer this question (you can either agree or disagree with the question but should search for evidence to support your reasoning).

Discussion point

Find someone in your class with the opposing viewpoint to the one you have developed in Activity 2.04 and hold the discussion to try to answer the question: '*Is it better to replace fossil fuels with nuclear power than with wind or solar power?*'

Reflection: Whose argument (yours or your partners) do you think was stronger in Activity 2.04?

Why do you think this?

Summary

- An argument is made up of different lines of reasoning.
- A line of reasoning needs relevant evidence to support it.
- If reasoning in an argument is strong then we are more likely to be convinced by the argument.
- You are expected to evaluate the quality of reasoning.
- You are expected to be able to develop a line of reasoning in all the IGCSE and O Level Global Perspectives components.
- Evaluating reasoning is good practice for developing your own lines of reasoning.

59

2.02 Evidence

 **SKILLS LINKS**

- Chapter 1: Information skills, 1.02 Research
- Chapter 2: Critical thinking skills, 2.01 Reasoning
- Chapter 2: Critical thinking skills, 2.03 Claims
- Chapter 2: Critical thinking skills, 2.05 Bias and vested interest
- Chapter 3: Independent learning skills, 3.04 Evaluation
- Chapter 5: Communication skills, 5.01 Reading
- Chapter 5: Communication skills, 5.03 Listening

While working on the previous section about reasoning, you will have realised the importance of using evidence to support your reasoning for any argument. This section explores the types of evidence you will come across during your Global Perspectives studies and the evidence you should be looking for to support any **claims** and arguments you make.

> **KEY TERM**
>
> **Claim:** statement of something being true.

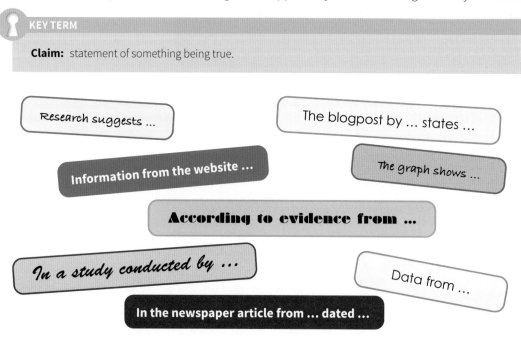

Figure 2.04 Evidence

> **ACTIVITY 2.05**
>
> Complete the Wall of Sources in Figure 2.05 with as many types of sources of information as you can. The first is done for you.
>
>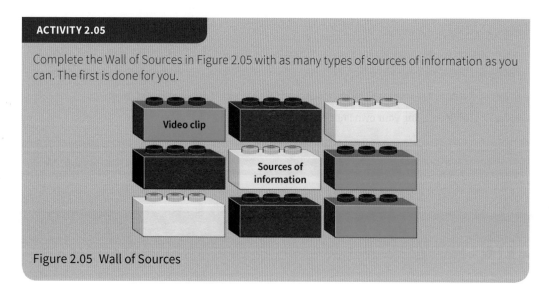
>
> Figure 2.05 Wall of Sources

Discussion point

Discuss your Wall of Sources from Activity 2.05 with a partner and add any further building blocks with other sources of information to your wall.

ACTIVITY 2.06

Answer the following questions.

1   What does a **reliable** source of information mean to you?
2   How do you know if a source is reliable or not?
3   Why is it important to identify reliable sources of information?
4   List two reliable sources of information you have found recently. Why do you think they are reliable?

Discussion point

Do you and your partner agree on the answers to the questions 1–4 in Activity 2.06?

Reflection: Which of the questions in Activity 2.06 (1–4) are you still not sure about?

All will become clearer: read on!

KEY TERMS

Reliable: able to be trusted/ believed.

Face value: to take something someone is saying at face value is to believe that it is the truth, rather than looking for evidence, any hidden meaning or the bigger picture.

When researching for information, it's important that you do not accept things at **face value**.

We get information from first-hand experiences, what people tell us, what we read, and by observation and experimentation.

Reflection: Consider the following **anecdote**:

A carpenter, a school teacher, and scientist were travelling by train through Scotland when they saw a black sheep through the window of the train.

'Aha,' said the carpenter with a smile. 'I see that Scottish sheep are black.'

'Hmm,' said the school teacher. 'You mean that some Scottish sheep are black.'

'No,' said the scientist glumly. 'All we know is that there is at least one sheep in Scotland, and that at least one side of that one sheep is black.'

What does this anecdote teach you?

KEY TERM

Anecdote: short story, usually to make the listeners laugh or think about a topic.

Discussion

Discuss your ideas about the anecdote in the reflection point with a partner.

If you want to know if something you read is true, it's a good idea to check where the information has come from. You might even want to see if the information can be checked in more than one source.

When choosing a source of information, you will want to check it against the features in Figure 2.06.

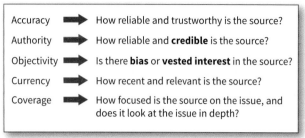

Figure 2.06 Choosing a source of information

You do not need to remember all the terms in Figure 2.06, although you do need to understand what bias and vested interest are. These are the focus of Section 2.05. You will also need to be able to refer to the reliability and credibility of a source.

KEY TERMS

Credible: how convincing or believable something is.

Bias: prejudice for or against one person or group, especially in a way considered to be unfair.

Vested interest: a personal reason for involvement or interest, especially an expectation of a financial or other gain.

Prejudice: opinion that is not based on reason or actual experience.

ACTIVITY 2.07

Imagine you have been doing some research for your Individual Report entitled:
'Has the internet changed the world we live in?' which falls under the topic **Digital world**.
When searching for information, you come across three different websites:

a a blog for and by people aged over fifty in the United Kingdom

b a newspaper article dated four years ago

c an article from a magazine about the impact of technology written in the current year.

Answer the following questions:

1 Which of these three sources do you think might be the most reliable? Why?

2 Which of these three sources do you think might be the least reliable? Why?

3 Which of these three resources do you think is the most credible? Why?

Discussion point
Discuss your ideas for Activity 2.07 with a partner. Do they agree with you?

Reflection: Did you find Activity 2.07 easy or difficult to do?

You probably were able to decide that the most reliable source is **c**, as this is an article from a credible source, which answers questions 1 and 3. We suppose that whoever wrote this article is an expert on the topic. However, they may also have a vested interest (as they get paid to write for the magazine) and it may be biased in that it only mentions the positives about the impact of the internet on society. As source **a** is a blog it is not classed as reliable and also gives a narrow perspective as it only includes opinions of some people aged over fifty in the UK. Source **b** might be a credible and reliable source, depending on the newspaper the article appeared in. However as it is dated four years ago, you might want to check that the information is still relevant.

If you thought differently, that's fine. Often we need to discuss these things with others to clarify our own thoughts. The purpose of the activity was to get you to think about questioning the sources that you use.

Sometimes you will find information from what you think is an authoritative (reliable and credible) source, but the only way of **verifying** the information is to **cross-reference** it by looking for the same information in other sources.

KEY TERMS

Verifying: making sure that something is true, accurate, or justified.

Cross-reference: reference to another source that gives the same or similar information, or elaborates on the original.

ACTIVITY 2.08

1   Search for 'endangered species, wild tigers', which relates to the global topic of **Biodiversity and ecosystem loss**, to find a source that tells you the current situation with wild tigers.

2   Copy and paste any facts you find out about wild tigers into your search engine to find other sources that have the same information.

63

Reflection: Did you find more than one source of information with the same details for Activity 2.08?

TIP
It is likely that you will be able to check whether or not information is correct as it will appear in different types of sources that can be classed as credible and reliable, for example charity websites and newspaper articles. If you can only find information in blogs or sites that can be edited by anyone, such as Wikipedia, you need to be careful – they may not be reliable.

You might want to use a checklist of questions like the one in the table below to evaluate any sources you use.

Criteria	Printed sources	Web sources
Accuracy	How reliable and free from error is the source?	Is the information free from errors in spelling, grammar, etc.?
	Is there reference to verifiable primary evidence?	Are charts and graphs clearly labelled and easy to read?
	Is there a reference list?	Are there links to other sources?
Authority	Is the author an expert?	Who is responsible for the web page?
	Is the publisher well thought of?	Is the person responsible for the web page an expert in their field?

(continued)

Criteria	Printed sources	Web sources
Objectivity	Is the information presented free of bias?	Is advertising clearly differentiated from the content of the website?
	How is the information trying to influence the reader?	Are opinion pieces clearly labelled as such?
Currency	Is the content up to date?	Is there a date to show when the web page was written?
	Is the publication date clearly indicated?	Are there signs that the work is kept up to date?
Coverage	What topics are included in the work?	Is the page complete or under construction?
	How much depth is there for each topic?	Is the entire source on the web or only part of it?

ACTIVITY 2.09

Do a search for a source of information that you might use for an Individual Report that falls within the global topic of **Humans and other species**, entitled: 'Are humans responsible for animal extinction?'

Use the questions in the checklist in the table above to establish whether the source you find is reliable and/or credible.

Discussion point

Discuss the source you found for Activity 2.09 with a partner. Explain why you think the source is reliable and/or credible. Does your partner agree?

Summary

- You should use evidence to support lines of reasoning for arguments and claims.
- You should try to use different sources of evidence during your course of study.
- It's important not to take information at face value.
- Try to use sources of information that are reliable and credible.
- Make sure you can explain why you think a source of information is biased.
- You are expected to be able to evaluate sources.

2.03 Claims

SKILLS LINKS

- Chapter 1: Information skills, 1.03 Analysis
- Chapter 2: Critical thinking skills, 2.01 Reasoning
- Chapter 2: Critical thinking skills, 2.02 Evidence
- Chapter 3: Independent learning skills, 3.04 Evaluation
- Chapter 5: Communication skills, 5.01 Reading
- Chapter 5: Communication skills, 5.03 Listening

Figure 2.07   Claims related to global topics

As well as using evidence to support a line of reasoning for an argument, evidence will help you to justify a claim.

ACTIVITY 2.10A

1   Remind yourself about the definition of 'claim' – you can look in the glossary.
2   Consider the following claims from the topic of **Transport systems**:
    a   Globally, more than twice as many men die in motor vehicle crashes than women.
    b   More fatal motor vehicle crashes occur when it's raining than when it's snowing or sleeting.
    c   Fewer older people die in motor vehicle crashes than younger people.

Which of the claims (**a–c**) do you think is the most believable? Why do you think this?

Discussion point

Share your thoughts about the claims in Activity 2.10A with a partner.

When discussing the claims, it is likely that you thought that **b** was not as believable as the other two claims and it would be difficult to check these facts as it's difficult to distinguish between rain, sleet and snow. It's likely that you think one claim is more believable than another, because you might have read something in a newspaper, seen it on the television or you might have heard others (friends, family) talking about it. 'I heard it somewhere,' is the reason generally given for people believing claims. Did you both think that **c** was more believable than the other claims? This is probably because you have heard more about this than the other two.

ACTIVITY 2.10B

1   Choose one of the claims from Activity 2.10A (**a–c**) and try to find evidence to support it. Spend about fifteen minutes on this task.
2   Share your findings with someone who chose a different claim to the one you chose.

Reflection: What has doing activities 2.10A and 2.10B taught you?

Why people believe claims

People believe claims for the following reasons.

- It sounds believable.
- They trust the source.
- They hear the claim made from various sources.
- The claim is supported by experimental data (evidence).

TIP

The global topics for the Written Examination are:

- Demographic change
- Education for all
- Employment
- Fuel and energy
- Globalisation
- Law and criminality
- Migration
- Transport systems

ACTIVITY 2.11

1   Choose one of the eight global topics for the Written Examination.
2   Find a partner who is interested in the same topic as you.
3   Do some research to find some evidence to make claims.
4   List five claims and state the web address where the evidence is. Complete the Making Claims table below.
5   Once complete, give your table to another pair for them to find the evidence for the claim from the web address given. When found, the 'yes' box can be checked.
6   If the 'yes' box for the claim is not checked, find another web address that gives evidence for the claim.

Global Topic:			
	Claim	**Evidence**	**Yes**
1			
2			
3			
4			
5			

Discussion point

As a pair, discuss the quality of your sources of evidence for the claims made in Activity 2.11. You can refer back to the sources checklist.

Reflection: Are all the sources of evidence you used in Activity 2.11 reliable and credible?

Sometimes, the evidence used to support a claim might be in the form of a chart or table of **statistics** as is the case in Activity 2.12.

KEY TERM

Statistics: the collection and analysis of numerical data for the purpose of evidence in support of claims for arguments.

ACTIVITY 2.12

Look at the table below. Answer the following questions to do with the global topic of **Demographic change**:

1 What evidence is there to support the claim that '*the global population is more than 6 billion*'?

2 What is the evidence to support the claim that '*the world population is continuing to grow*'?

3 What evidence is there to support the claim that '*the population of Nigeria in 2050 will be more than double that of 2015*'?

Demographic change from 2015 to 2050

According to the United Nations, the population of the world in 2015 stood at 7.3 billion. The predicted world population for 2050 is 9.8 billion – an increase of 2.5 billion. The tables below show predicted demographic change from 2015 to 2050.

The most populated countries in 2015	
Country	*Population (millions)*
China	1372
India	1314
United States	321
Indonesia	256
Brazil	205
Pakistan	199
Nigeria	182
Bangladesh	160
Russia	144
Mexico	127

The predicted most populated countries in 2050	
Country	*Population (millions)*
India	1660
China	1366
United States	398
Nigeria	397
Indonesia	366
Pakistan	344
Brazil	226
Bangladesh	202
Congo, Dem. Rep.	194
Ethiopia	165

Discussion point

Discuss your answers to the questions in Activity 2.12 with a partner. Do they agree with you?

The source gives evidence that the population of the world in 2015 stood at 7.3 billion, which is more than 6 billion. The predicted world population for 2050 is 9.8 billion – an increase of 2.5 billion, which is evidence for the claim that the population of the world is increasing. The figure given for Nigeria in 2050 (397 million) is more than double that given for 2015 (182 million).

> **Reflection:** What other claims could you make using data from the tables in Activity 2.12?

TIP

When making a claim, it's a good idea to have more than one source of evidence to support it. Using your search engine, see if you can find further evidence to support the claims made in Activity 2.12 about demographic change (1–3).

ACTIVITY 2.13

Imagine that you want to make the claim that a specific **Sports** team is the best in the world. You can choose any sports team you like, for example a football or rugby team.

1 Find some evidence to support your claim.

2 Cross-reference this evidence with another source of evidence.

3 Write a short paragraph to answer the questions:

   a Who are the best team in the world?

   b Why are they the best team in the world?

   c What evidence is there to support your claim?

   d How reliable is this evidence?

Discussion point

Share your paragraph from answering the questions in Activity 2.13 with a partner. Does the evidence you have found convince them about your claim? Are you convinced about their claim? Why/Why not?

> **Reflection:** Consider how many times you make claims that are unsupported and expect people to believe them. Try supporting claims you make to see if there is a difference in the way people respond to you.

Testing claims

As well as supporting the claims you make with evidence, you will need to be able to show how you might test a claim that someone makes. When testing claims, you will want to consider the use of different types of:

- information
- sources of evidence
- methods.

The questions to ask yourself for each are indicated in Figure 2.08.

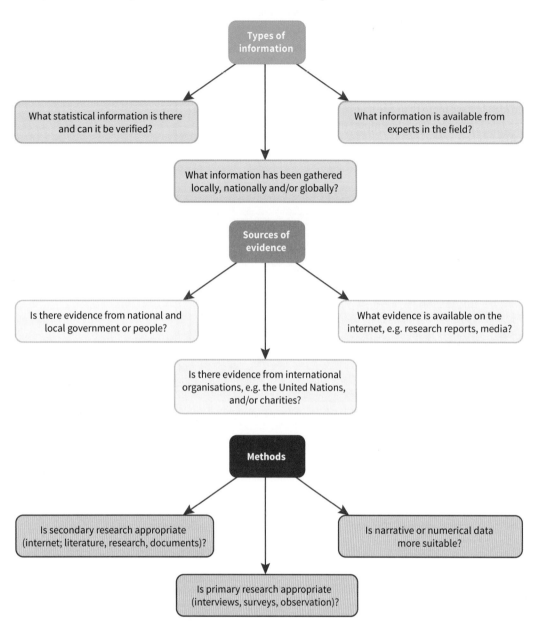

Figure 2.08 Testing claims

ACTIVITY 2.14

Read the following claim:

'*Travelling by train costs more now than it did twenty years ago.*'

Write down how you might test this claim.

Discussion point

Share your ideas about testing the claim in Activity 2.14 with a partner. Do they have the same ideas as you? Agree on the best way of testing this claim.

You might have found out how much a train ticket was for a particular journey twenty years ago and what percentage of the average wage this was, and the current figures and then compared them. You could do this by searching on the internet. This is probably more reliable than asking your parents or grandparents as they may not remember the exact figures.

Summary

- Evidence helps you to justify a claim.
- People believe claims because they sound believable, and they trust the sources of evidence.
- The more reliable and credible the source, the more believable the claim is.
- More than one source of evidence makes a claim more believable.
- Testing claims involves considering using different types of information, sources of evidence and methods.

2.04 Drawing conclusions

SKILLS LINKS

- Chapter 1: Information skills, 1.03 Analysis
- Chapter 1: Information skills, 1.06 Questioning
- Chapter 2: Critical thinking skills, 2.01 Reasoning
- Chapter 2: Critical thinking skills, 2.02 Evidence
- Chapter 3: Independent learning skills, 3.04 Evaluation
- Chapter 5: Communication skills, 5.01 Reading
- Chapter 5: Communication skills, 5.02 Writing
- Chapter 5: Communication skills, 5.03 Listening

For any activity that involves research such as those you will do during your Global Perspectives course, drawing **conclusions** is often the final, and most important, part of the process, done after you have found your evidence.

- For your Individual Report, you will draw conclusions to answer the question you set as the title of your report.
- For your Team Project, you will draw conclusions from your research to create your outcome and explanation.
- In the Written Examination, you will draw conclusions from the source material provided to answer the questions set.

GLOBAL WARMING IS CAUSED BY HUMAN ACTIVITY

More people in the world speak Chinese than any other language

Climate change is the result of global warming

FOSSIL FUELS WILL RUN OUT ONE DAY

Overpopulation will impact on available resources

Figure 2.09 Drawing conclusions

Conclusions are different from claims in that a claim can be made without reference to any evidence, whereas a conclusion is made as a result of research and the evidence discovered.

In this section, we explore what it means to draw conclusions and how you can draw conclusions from different types of source material.

KEY TERM

Conclusion: a judgment or decision reached by reasoning.

Reflection: What does the term 'to draw conclusions' mean to you?

You will find a definition in the glossary to remind yourself if you are not sure.

Discussion point

Work with a partner to choose one of the global topics you have both done some research about and discuss three conclusions that each of you made about that topic.

Did you come up with the same conclusions?

Why do you think this was?

You might have discussed similar conclusions as you could have looked at similar sources and found the same or similar evidence.

Reflection: Think about a time you listened in on someone else's conversation (perhaps when you were in a coffee shop). You probably drew some conclusions by observing body language and listening to bits of what was being said.

For example, Tina says, 'Let's stay in this evening and watch television instead of going out to eat', and Miriam says, 'Fine'. However, the way Miriam says it in an annoyed tone of voice, with crossed arms, **indicates** that actually it isn't what she would like to do. In this case, you could certainly draw the conclusion that Miriam would have preferred to go out even if you didn't know these people. She didn't clearly state that she wanted to go out, but it was certainly **implied.**

Indicates: shows/demonstrates something.

Implied: suggested or pointed towards something.

Jump to conclusions: to assume something without using any evidence that might suggest otherwise.

TIP

It is easy to **jump to conclusions** without enough evidence.

Global Perspectives is not about jumping to conclusions, it's about drawing conclusions based on evidence from different sources that come from different perspectives and looking at the viewpoints within these perspectives.

ACTIVITY 2.15

Read the text below on the topic of **Language and communication** and draw at least one conclusion.

If the world were one hundred people …

12 would speak Chinese	3 would speak Bengali
5 would speak Spanish	3 would speak Portuguese
5 would speak English	2 would speak Russian
3 would speak Arabic	2 would speak Japanese
3 would speak Hindi	62 would speak other languages

Source: 100people.org

73

Discussion point

Share your conclusion from Activity 2.15 with your partner and discuss other conclusions you may have drawn.

TIP

When drawing conclusions you don't repeat the information that you have been given, you read between the lines and **infer meaning.**

Infer meaning: to suggest or point towards something, similar to imply.

ACTIVITY 2.16

Read the text on the topic of **Conflict and peace** and identify which of the following conclusions are appropriate to how Sam is feeling.

a Sam is a proud citizen of his country.

b Sam is looking forward to going abroad to fight.

c Sam is frightened of going to war.

d Sam wishes he had never joined the military.

> Sam had a strong sense of loyalty and patriotism. He had always wanted to serve his country, but this was crazy. He was being sent to fight a war he knew very little about in a country a long way from home. He was supposed to help protect people he didn't even know and fight against an enemy he was terrified of. He was worried about being blown up by a bomb, and feared that he might never see his friends and family again.

Discussion point

Discuss your choice of conclusions for Activity 2.16 with a partner. Did you both identify conclusions **a** and **c** as the correct conclusions?

Reflection: What other conclusions might you draw from the information given in the text in Activity 2.16?

ACTIVITY 2.17

1 Look at the images in Figure 2.10 related to the global topic of **Globalisation**.

    a Draw one conclusion about the setting of the images (where is this happening?)

    b Draw one conclusion about the relationships of the people in the pictures (who are the people in the images and how are they related?)

    c Draw one conclusion about the feelings of each person in the images (what are they feeling? What are they thinking?)

2 Write a summary of your conclusions.

Discussion point

Share your summary from Activity 2.17 with a partner.

Do they agree with your conclusions?

Are their conclusions different? If so, why do you think this is?

Figure 2.10 Some consequences of globalisation

You might have discussed whether any of your conclusions lacked enough support to be likely. You might need to find more (text-based) evidence before you can draw a reliable conclusion from an image. You might have been able to understand more clearly what was happening in the images by drawing conclusions. You might simply have jumped to conclusions without enough evidence.

Reflection: Consider an image that you have seen recently and the conclusion you made. Did you make the right conclusion once you found out more about the **context** of the image?

KEY TERM

Context: background or circumstances that form the setting for an event, statement, or idea.

ACTIVITY 2.18

1 Find a short text about an issue related to any one of the global topics. Highlight the sections that give information to draw conclusions from. Write three conclusions.

2 Give your text to a partner and ask them to draw three conclusions from the information in the highlighted sections.

3 Compare the conclusions that you and your partner have written.

4 Find another source of information (an image or a short video-clip) that supports one of the best conclusions you and your partner have drawn from the information in the text.

Summary

- Global Perspectives asks you to draw conclusions from evidence rather than jump to conclusions based on little or no evidence.

- Conclusions can be drawn from different sources of information.

- Conclusions are the final part of any research.

- You will draw conclusions in all three of the Global Perspectives components.

- To draw a conclusion you need to be able to infer meaning from given information.

2.05 Bias and vested interest

SKILLS LINKS

- Chapter 1: Information skills, 1.03 Analysis
- Chapter 1: Information skills, 1.06 Questioning
- Chapter 2: Critical thinking skills, 2.02 Evidence
- Chapter 2: Critical thinking skills, 2.03 Claims
- Chapter 2: Critical thinking skills, 2.04 Drawing conclusions
- Chapter 3: Independent learning skills, 3.04 Evaluation
- Chapter 5: Communication skills, 5.01 Reading
- Chapter 5: Communication skills, 5.03 Listening

When drawing conclusions, it's important that you gain the evidence for conclusions from different sources and perspectives to try to minimise bias and/or vested interest and remain **objective**.

Figure 2.11 Statements of bias and vested interest

KEY TERM

Objective: remaining unbiased and neutral.

Discussion point

Discuss the terms 'bias' and 'vested interest' with a partner. Try to agree on a definition for each and give an example of where you might find each.

You might refer back to Section 2.02 about evidence, or to the glossary, where you will find definitions for bias and vested interest.

You will find bias on government websites or in governmental publications. Most advertisements for products to buy will say how wonderful the products are as companies have a vested interest in you buying their products, for example gaining more profits, employing more people or people keeping their jobs.

Reflection: Consider the restaurant sign in Figure 2.12 – the kind of sign you might see on a main road between two towns.

Would you go to this restaurant if you were on holiday? Why?

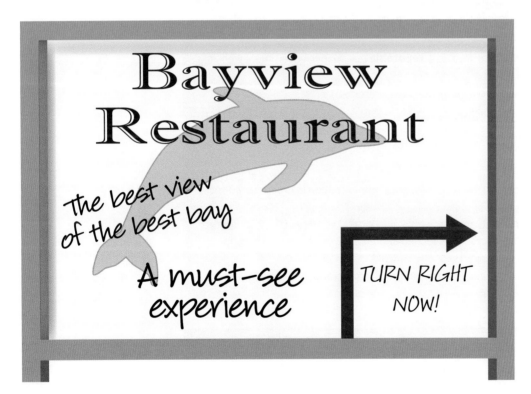

Figure 2.12 Restaurant sign

Discussion point

- Discuss the restaurant sign (Figure 2.12) with a partner and the reason(s) why you might turn right.

- Discuss also how this sign shows bias and/or vested interest.

77

ACTIVITY 2.19

Read the text on the global topic of **Education for all** and answer the following question:
Why might this statement be biased?

> The school has a really good reputation and some famous people have graduated from there
> – politicians and business people. It has an amazing history. It is also set in beautiful grounds
> and the sports' facilities are excellent, but there are many other good schools that provide a
> decent standard of education. This school really just caters for local families. I wouldn't try
> applying if you don't live locally as competition is fierce. As we live nearby, my son should get
> a place there next year.

Discussion point

Discuss your answer to the question in Activity 2.19 with a partner. Do you think that you
have both understood what bias is?

ACTIVITY 2.20

Consider the following claim:
'**Technology** brings only benefits with it.'

1 Find one source of information that supports this claim.
2 For this source of information, answer the questions **a–g**.
   a How recent is the information in the source?
   b Where does the information come from (e.g. **reputable** newspaper, government website,
      NGO website or publication)?
   c How is the information presented (inform, persuade, describe)?
   d Is the author presenting a perspective or point of view? If so, how do they use information
      to support it?
   e Does the author present and/or support different/opposing viewpoints?
   f Is the author biased? If so, how?
   g Does the author have a vested interest for providing the information in the source? If so,
      what is it?
3 Share your source of information and answers with a partner. Make a note of the web address
   for their source of information when you have looked at their answers to the questions for
   their source.
4 Find other sources that help verify what you are being told in the source you found for task 1.

KEY TERMS

Reputable: well thought of.
NGO: non-governmental organisation.

TIP

Do not believe everything you read or hear. Many sources of information are biased, which is why it's a good idea not to rely on only one source of information. You can still use information from government websites, which may contain political bias, but try to support the claims you make with more than this one source of information. For example, you might use a mixture of government and non-government websites and reputable newspapers as well as original research papers, although these can be difficult to understand as they are intended for specialists.

Looking for bias

When looking for bias, ask yourself the questions in Figure 2.13.

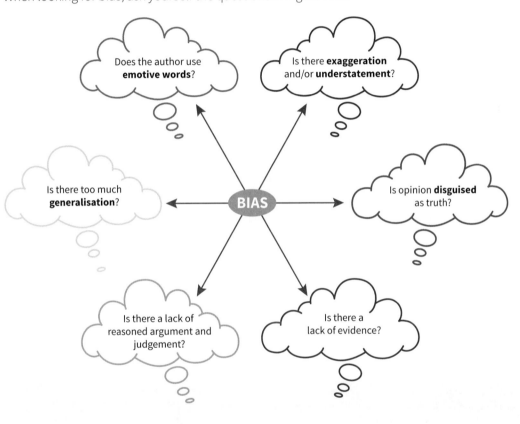

Figure 2.13 Looking for bias

KEY TERMS

Exaggeration: too much emphasis on something.

Understatement: too little emphasis on something.

Emotive words: moving language, used by the writer or speaker to try make us feel something.

Generalisation: an overview, lacking specific evidence or details.

Disguised: hidden, camouflaged or covered up.

ACTIVITY 2.21

Use the questions in Figure 2.13 to evaluate the following statements in terms of bias:

1   Technology has got us into this mess and technology will get us out of it.
2   Statistics show that more students are going into higher education than ever before.
3   In the last decade, the popularity of reality television has coincided with the fall in intelligence of the population.
4   Everyone is just out to make as much money as they can.
5   Culture is completely disappearing due to globalisation.
6   Flooding is causing massive devastation in parts of Europe.

Discussion point

Discuss your thoughts about the statements in Activity 2.21 with a partner.

Summary

- When looking for evidence, try to search for information from a variety of sources to minimise the incidence of bias and vested interest.

- When searching for information, always keep in mind that there might be bias and/or vested interest in a source.

- You might be asked about bias and/or vested interest.

- Remember to look for exaggeration, understatement, emotive language, opinion disguised as truth, generalisations and lack of evidence when looking for bias.

2.06 Statements of argument

SKILLS LINKS

- Chapter 1: Information skills, 1.02 Research
- Chapter 1: Information skills, 1.03 Analysis
- Chapter 2: Critical thinking skills, 2.02 Evidence
- Chapter 2: Critical thinking skills, 2.03 Claims
- Chapter 2: Critical thinking skills, 2.04 Drawing conclusions
- Chapter 3: Independent learning skills, 3.04 Evaluation
- Chapter 5: Communication skills, 5.01 Reading
- Chapter 5: Communication skills, 5.03 Listening

FACT: It's 32 degrees Celsius outside.

OPINION: It's too hot outside.

VALUE JUDGEMENT: It's too hot outside – I could get heatstroke.

PREDICTION: It will get cooler this evening.

Figure 2.14 Statements of argument

A lot of what we read and listen to is a mixture of fact and opinion. Being able to tell the difference between fact and opinion is important for evaluating written and spoken texts and developing persuasive arguments.

As a general rule, a fact can be proven. A fact within the global topic of Education for all, for example is: *'Educating girls helps to **alleviate** poverty'*.

KEY TERM

Alleviate: ease, lessen, reduce.

This is a fact because evidence shows that basic education improves girls' employment opportunities, improves their health and the health of their children and leads to an increase in the age that girls get married. The statement: *'All girls should stay at home and help their families'* is someone's opinion and cannot be proven to be true as there is no evidence to suggest it is true; it is simply someone's belief or what someone thinks or feels.

ACTIVITY 2.22

Which of these are facts and which are opinions?
a The planet's climate has been warming over the past century.
b We can do something about climate change.
c Young people are almost three times as likely as adults to be unemployed.
d The global recession has affected young people the most all over the world.
e It's easy to get to places.
f Some international charities are excellent.

Discussion point
Share your thoughts about which of the statements in Activity 2.22 are facts and which are opinions with a partner.

Reflection: Do you understand the difference between fact and opinion?

> **TIP**
>
> When debating an issue or presenting a spoken argument, there are many facts that most people take as given, such as the fact that the planet's climate has been warming over the past century, so you won't need to persuade people by finding a reliable source of information to prove this fact.
>
> When writing an argument, however, such as when you write your Individual Report, it is good practice to support each fact you quote with a reliable source of evidence – and don't forget to reference it.

Whilst an opinion is what someone thinks, feels or believes, a value judgement is a little more. Value judgements consider the reasons why someone might think of something as right or wrong, or as good or bad.

The following is an example of a value judgement, because as well as an opinion (*I don't think there should be major sporting events*), the statement considers fairness. Here, fairness is seen as a good thing and moving people from their homes is seen as unfair, therefore bad.

'*I don't think there should be major sporting events. It is just not fair to move people from their homes simply to accommodate a global sporting event like the Olympic Games.*'

During your Global Perspectives course, you will be identifying, giving and explaining facts, opinions, value judgements and predictions.

ACTIVITY 2.23

Do you agree that a value judgment can be used to answer each of the following questions?
1   Who has a better education system, New Zealand or America?
2   Should we wear a school uniform?
3   Is it appropriate to work on Saturdays?

Discussion point

Share your thoughts about the statements in Activity 2.23 with a partner.

At face value, these questions are asking for opinions, but it depends on what you value. For example, for question 1, it is difficult to know unless you have experience of both systems or have done some research. If one of the education systems is better at providing more opportunities for creating global citizens and encouraging critical thinking skills, then it is likely that you would feel that this was the better of the two; or if the education system ensured that girls and boys were given equal opportunities, then you might consider this the better system as it's morally right to promote gender equality.

Reflection: Are you starting to look beyond a seemingly straightforward question and think differently about the types of answers that can be given?

ACTIVITY 2.24

Read the text and identify the following:

- one fact
- one opinion
- one prediction
- one value judgement.

Once you have identified each, write a sentence to explain why you think your chosen text part is a fact, opinion, prediction or value judgement.

Health education

Most people would agree that health and education are the two most important services a country can provide. In recent years, many countries have been successful in reducing some of the most serious risks to children's health. Nowadays, children live longer and are healthier than in the past. This means that 2.5 million fewer children die every year now than did in 1990.

However, ill health still stops many children from going to school, and often it's because of a lack of health education within families. If we don't educate people in local communities about personal hygiene, they are more likely to become ill.

We need to ensure that health education is available for all families, and not just for those that can afford it. Health education is a basic human right, and not to provide it for the most vulnerable in society is not acceptable.

Discussion point

Discuss your responses to Activity 2.24 with a partner. Did you agree?

Remember that sometimes there is more than one correct answer in a text of this length. As well as being able to identify a statement of argument, it's important that you can explain why you think a statement is a fact, opinion, value judgement or prediction, as your work will be credited for the reasoning you give.

Reflection: Did you correctly identify the prediction within the text in Activity 2.24?

Remember that a prediction is an **assertion** or statement about something that will or might happen at some point in the future.

KEY TERM

Assertion: another word for a statement or claim.

ACTIVITY 2.25

1 Read the following questions that might fall within the global topic of **Humans and other species**. Which of these questions do you think will result in an answer that is: a fact, an opinion, a prediction or a value judgement?

   a Why is it unacceptable to use animals for experimentation?

   b How many species of monk seal exist in the world?

   c What will happen if humans continue to hunt and poach endangered species?

   d Do you think that humans can enjoy a meat-free diet?

   e Which is the largest ocean?

   f Is it okay to wear a fur coat?

   g What will happen to the amount of available fish if overfishing continues?

   h Are some animals more important than others?

2 Write down your answers to these questions. You may need to do some research for some of them.

3 Look at your answers and revisit part 1 of this activity to make any changes to the answers you originally gave for part 1.

4 Create one further question to gain a fact, an opinion, a value judgement and a prediction within the topic of humans and other species.

Discussion

Share your responses to the questions (**a–h**) in Activity 2.25 with a partner. Try to explain why you think a certain question will get a certain type of information.

Reflection: Are you getting better at understanding the types of question you need to ask to get certain types of information?

TIP

It's okay to change your opinion as you think about issues you haven't previously considered. You just need to ask yourself some key questions:

- What do I think?

- Why do I think this?

- What has influenced my thinking?

- How has my thinking changed? Why? / Why not?

It's also okay for others to have different opinions to you. You might not agree, but you should still respect their opinion. After all, life would be pretty boring if we all thought the same thing, wouldn't it?

ACTIVITY 2.26

1   Use a global topic of your choice to create a short news article that contains four different statements of argument (fact, opinion, value judgement, prediction). Your text should be no longer than 150 words and you may need to do some research.

2   Write down four questions for a partner to answer (one for each of the statements of argument). Make sure that you know the answers to your questions.

3   Give your partner your text and questions and ask them to try to answer them. You will be answering their questions from their text at the same time.

Discussion point

Discuss the answers to both sets of questions created in Activity 2.26 with the partner you worked with for the activity.

Reflection: Which part of Activity 2.26 did you find most difficult; creating your text, creating your questions, or answering your partner's questions?

Try to think about why this was the most difficult part of the activity so that you know where you need to develop further skills.

Summary

- Facts can be proven and opinions are what someone thinks, feels or believes.
- A value judgement considers whether something is right or wrong, good or bad, fair or unfair.
- Prediction is forecasting what is likely to happen at some time in the future.
- You should support facts in written work with reliable and credible evidence.
- Certain types of question lead to gaining certain types of information.
- You might be asked to identify and explain facts, opinions, value judgements and predictions.

2.07 Problem-solving

SKILLS LINKS

- Chapter 1: Information skills, 1.02 Research
- Chapter 1: Information skills, 1.03 Analysis
- Chapter 1: Information skills, 1.04 Synthesis
- Chapter 2: Critical Thinking, 2.04 Drawing conclusions
- Chapter 3: Independent learning skills, 3.03 Reflection
- Chapter 4: Collaboration skills, 4.02 Decision-making
- Chapter 4: Collaboration skills, 4.03 Creativity
- Chapter 5: Communication skills, 5.03 Listening
- Chapter 5: Communication skills, 5.04 Speaking

Good **problem**-solving skills can benefit everyone as we all face problems and **challenges** every day. Some of the problems we face are more challenging than others, but having good problem-solving skills can help you cope with the daily challenges of life.

Figure 2.15 Problem-solving

KEY TERMS

Problem: a difficult issue needing a course of action or solution to improve or resolve it.

Challenges: things that need thinking about and dealing with.

However well prepared we think we are for problem-solving, there is always a certain amount of the unexpected, which means that planning and goal setting are important (as you explored in Section 1.05).

During your Global Perspectives course, once you have analysed and evaluated an issue, you need to think about any courses of action you might take to improve the situation or resolve the issue, whether as a team or independently.

The Team Project asks you to investigate an issue to produce an outcome and explanation for a course of action to, for example, raise awareness of or help to resolve an identified issue, according to the aim of your project. For your Individual Report, you will need to propose courses of action to help resolve or improve an issue you have analysed and evaluated. In written work you may be asked to identify, explain or propose a course of action based on the source material given.

Figure 2.16 shows some questions to consider when planning to take action.

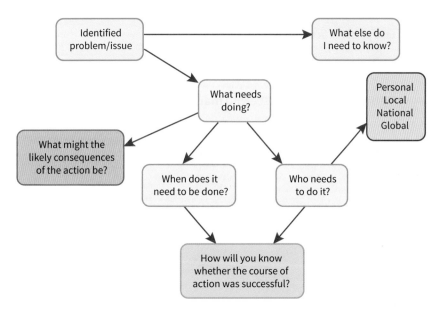

Figure 2.16 Questions for taking action

TIP

Some problems need personal action. For example, your team will be working on your Team Project this week and you have fallen ill. Do you stay off school? If you do, they will have to manage without your input, but if you go in, they may catch what you have and also become ill, which might mean the team has to **reschedule** some tasks and fall behind in the work.

KEY TERM

Reschedule: to do the tasks/what needs doing another time.

ACTIVITY 2.27

Work with a partner for this activity.

1 Decide what sort of action you both think is needed for the following imaginary problems/
issues (personal, local, national or global).

 a The village hall where you live is in desperate need of a new roof.

 b The train service across the country cannot cope with the number of people using it.
 Trains are often overcrowded and never on time.

 c Identity theft via the internet is on the increase.

 d Your elderly neighbour has had a fall and become temporarily housebound.

2 Choose one of the global topics and write imaginary problems/issues that need global,
national, local and personal action.

Reflection: Do you know when you need to take personal action or do you rely on others to tell
you?

Using the questions in Figure 2.16 is one way of breaking down an issue into **manageable**
parts so that you can take action.

KEY TERM

Manageable: to deal with easily.

Another way is to work with a couple of other people in a team to follow the steps in
Figure 2.17.

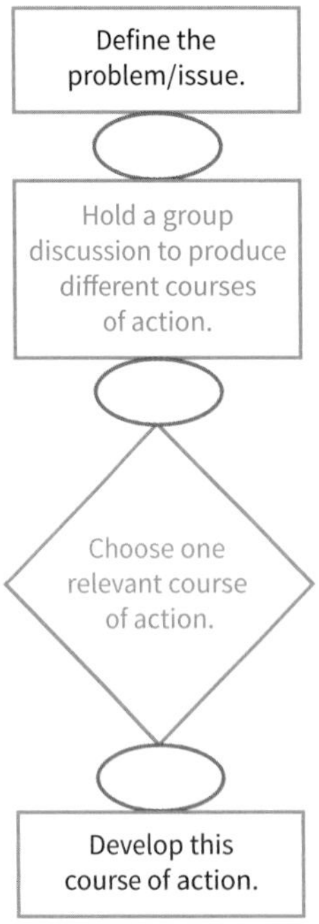

Define the
problem/issue.

Hold a group
discussion to produce
different courses
of action.

Choose one
relevant course
of action.

Develop this
course of action.

Figure 2.17 Developing a course of action

ACTIVITY 2.28

For your Individual Report, you need to develop the courses of action you propose.

Imagine the following issue within the global topic of **Biodiversity and ecosystem loss**:

Issue: Loss of habitat for different species.

This is an extract that might have come from an Individual Report entitled:

*How important is it to improve **biodiversity** and prevent **ecosystem** loss?*

Read the extract and answer the questions:

1   Is a global course of action proposed? If so, is it developed?
2   Is a national or local course of action proposed? If so, is it developed?
3   Is a personal course of action proposed? If so, is it developed?

It is clear that there needs to be a focus on improving biodiversity globally. There are many international non-governmental organisations such as The World Wide Fund for Nature that are trying to prevent biodiversity and ecosystem loss. However, the conservation of biodiversity, for example reforestation, can be expensive, and in poorer or less developed countries where biodiversity loss is an issue, it isn't a priority because producing food is more important.

In the developed world, however, although still limited for this issue, money is more readily available so it should be easier to take action to prevent biodiversity and ecosystem loss. A local initiative to encourage people to do something to enhance biodiversity could be provided by lottery funding. The aim could be to help biodiversity and create new ecosystems by planting new types of trees and hedges. This would help attract bees, bats, birds, butterflies, invertebrates and mammals as well as replace older varieties of trees that are nearing the end of their life. Not only will this course of action considerably help biodiversity by introducing additional ecosystems into the area, it will also provide an attraction for the community and other people who visit it. Thus it will have a dual role; a beautiful place to visit and a home to many animals.

Some of the things that could be done to contribute to the reduction of biodiversity and ecosystem loss include actions such setting up and giving a regular donation to a charity. A small amount per month would be all that is needed and this would soon add up if many people contributed. Advertising through social media would highlight the issue and encourage more people to donate. It is also possible to support these charities through other means (such as purchasing their products, for example gifts) to help reduce deforestation, and help save threatened animals like giant pandas and rhinos. Another course of action would be to work as a volunteer to assist on projects, such as tree planting. As well as taking action for a good cause, you could meet like-minded people who are also concerned about the state of the planet and would join you in gaining sponsorship for charitable events to raise money to support the cause of a particular charity (e.g. a sponsored run/walk).

Discussion point

Discuss your answers to the three questions in Activity 2.28 with a partner. Did they notice everything you did?

You will have noticed that a global course of action is suggested (reforestation) but not really developed, although reasons are given as to why global action might not be the most appropriate for this issue. Local action is emphasised as money from the lottery can be sought to plant trees and hedges, etc. This course of action is developed, as are the personal courses of action proposed.

Reflection: Can you see how to develop your courses of action for your Individual Report a little better now?

KEY TERMS

Biodiversity: the variety of plant and animal life in the world or in a particular habitat.

Ecosystem: the living things, from plants and animals to microscopic organisms that share an environment.

In Figure 2.16 one of the questions asks you to identify further information that you might need using the question, 'What else do I need to know?'

You might need further information before you can propose courses of action, for example information about what is already being done to resolve or improve an issue you have analysed.

ACTIVITY 2.29

Read these short sections from the extract in Activity 2.28. What questions might you ask to close any gaps in your knowledge?

'There are many international non-governmental organisations such as The World Wide Fund for Nature that are trying to prevent biodiversity and ecosystem loss.'

'A small amount per month would be all that is needed and this would soon add up if many people contributed.'

Discussion point

Discuss your ideas for the questions you might ask in Activity 2.29 with a partner.

You might have asked the following questions:

- How many international non-governmental organisations are trying to prevent biodiversity and ecosystem loss and who are they?
- What are these organisations doing?
- How much is a 'small amount'?
- How many people would need to donate?

It's important that you get into the habit of identifying the gaps in the information you find and are given. After all, you wouldn't get to a concert or sports match without finding out what time it started and where it was, would you?

TIP

Being able to identify gaps in your knowledge is a skill that will help with problem solving as the more you know, the easier it will be to come up with a suitable course of action.

Summary

- Good problem-solving skills help you take action to help resolve or improve issues.
- Planning and setting goals help with problem-solving.
- You need to propose courses of action in your Individual Report.
- Courses of action in your Individual Report can be global, national, local and/or personal and should be developed.
- It's important to ask questions to find information to close the gaps in your knowledge.

2.08 Empathy

 **SKILLS LINKS**

- Chapter 1: Information skills, 1.01 Perspectives
- Chapter 1: Information skills, 1.02 Research
- Chapter 1: Information skills, 1.06 Questioning
- Chapter 3: Independent learning skills, 3.03 Reflection
- Chapter 4: Collaboration skills, 4.01 Teamwork
- Chapter 4: Collaboration skills, 4.03 Creativity
- Chapter 5: Communication skills, 5.03 Listening

We often see things on the television, in **documentary films** or via social media and feel shocked at what we see, but because it isn't affecting us, we may not really take it in. We may quickly forget it to get back to our daily lives.

However, to get the most out of your Global Perspectives course and to be able to build and maintain close friendships and develop strong communities, you need **empathy**. As with all the skills within this book, empathy is one that can be developed.

Empathy is a word you may never have come across before. If you have come across it, you may think it means something other than what it actually does. Often, people confuse empathy with sympathy.

 KEY TERMS

Documentary films: factual films/programmes about real-life issues.

Empathy: the experience of understanding and sharing another person's feelings from their perspective. You place yourself 'in their shoes' and imagine what they are feeling.

> **Reflection:** Consider the definition of empathy (given in the key term box).
>
> How does empathy differ from sympathy?

Discussion

Discuss your ideas about the differences between empathy and sympathy with a partner. Did your partner agree with your thoughts?

ACTIVITY 2.30

Are you empathetic?

Respond yes/no to the statements below to see how empathetic you already are. (Try to be as honest as you can.) Give an example to support the responses you have given 'yes' to.

	Statement	Yes	No	Example
1	I often think about other people's feelings.			
2	I listen to others talk about what they are experiencing.			
3	I try to understand other people's points of view.			
4	I'm aware that not everybody reacts to experiences the same way as I do.			
5	I don't make fun of other people as I can imagine how it feels to be in their shoes.			

Discussion point

Share your responses and examples of empathy from Activity 2.30 with a partner (someone in your class who knows you quite well).

- Do they agree with the responses you have given?

- Do they think that you are as empathetic as you think you are?

If you responded 'yes' to all the statements, then you are already showing signs of empathy. The examples you have given are probably personal; they relate to family and friends rather than local, national or global. Developing your empathy further will enable you to relate to others better within your community and country and as a global citizen.

Five steps to develop empathy

Figure 2.18 highlights five steps you could use to develop your ability to empathise.

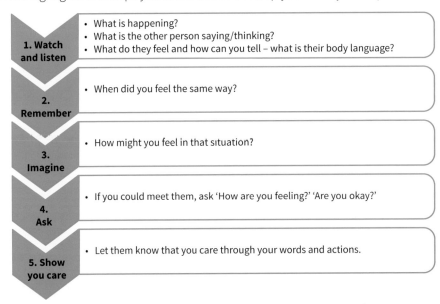

Figure 2.18 Developing empathy

TIP

There is an expression which suggests that you shouldn't criticise someone until you have walked a mile in their shoes. Putting yourself in someone else's shoes is a good way of developing empathy. One way of imagining what it feels like being in someone else's shoes is to ask yourself, 'How would I feel in this situation?'

ACTIVITY 2.31

This activity uses the global topic of **Water, food and agriculture** to develop your empathy.

Imagine you are the boy in the image in Figure 2.19.

1   Using Figure 2.18, write answers to respond to the first three steps.

2   Work with a partner. One of you takes on the role of the boy in the image. Then role-play the dialogue that might take place for steps four and five of Figure 2.18.

3   Do some research to find another image (from any global topic) where empathy might be needed.

4   Do steps 1–3 of Figure 2.18 independently and then do a role-play for steps 4 and 5 of Figure 2.18. This time, the partner that did not take the role of the boy takes on the role of someone needing empathy.

5   You should now decide on one of the images each and write a short paragraph to show empathy for the person in the image.

6   Swap your paragraphs and give feedback to your partner about how empathetic their paragraph is.

Figure 2.19 Boy fetching water

Empathy and your Team Project

When doing the work for your Team Project, you will need to treat people with empathy for their situation. Empathy will help you to gain their respect and trust and encourage them to answer the questions you have designed as part of the primary research you might be carrying out.

> **TIP**
>
> Always ask your teacher first about the type of Team Project you want to carry out: some topics are not suitable for a Team Project. You should also check with your teacher about the questions you want to ask to get the information you need.

ACTIVITY 2.32

1   Find a short interview between a reporter and a migrant or refugee from a war-torn country. (You could try the search terms: 'clips' 'interview' 'migrants' 'refugees'.)

2   Listen to what the interviewer says. Write down examples of empathy that the interviewer demonstrates.

3   Answer the following questions:

    a   Overall, how empathetic do you think the interviewer is to the situation of the person being interviewed?

    b   How do you think that the interviewer could be more empathetic?

Discussion point

Find a partner who has a different interview to yours for Activity 2.32. Share your interview and your thoughts about how empathetic the interviewer is with a partner. Which of the two interviewers do you think is more empathetic to the situation of the person being interviewed and why do you think this?

> **TIP**
>
> When you listen to others, making eye contact, not interrupting the speaker, and asking follow-up questions can show that you're making a real effort to understand what the person is going through. Using 'you' questions rather than 'I' statements also enables you to show empathy. These are things to look for when watching others to consider whether they are being empathetic or not.

ACTIVITY 2.33

1 Read the following email. Highlight the areas that show empathy.

Send   Chat   Attach   Address   Fonts   Colours   Save As Draft

Dear Jonas,

I am writing to say how very sorry I am to hear of your terrible loss on Sunday evening. None of us could have been prepared for what happened, and it was such a shock to find out how much damage was done to our small community, and particularly to your home by that tornado. Even though your home suffered such awful damage, you still supported and comforted all of us around you. You are an inspiration to us all, and I am truly grateful for the support you gave me – knowing that I am not alone really helped. If there is anything I can do to help you, please do not hesitate to ask, and once we get back to some sort of normal life, please feel free to call on me for anything you need,

My very best wishes,

Michael

Figure 2.20 Email showing empathy

2 Share your ideas with a partner to see if you agree.
3 Choose one of the global topics and find a song or poem that shows empathy.

95

Discussion point
Share your song or poem from Activity 2.33 with a partner and discuss how it shows empathy.

Reflection: Do you think that you are more empathetic now than when you started this section of the book?

Summary

- Empathy is different from sympathy.
- Empathy helps us to build and maintain close friendships and develop strong communities.
- It's important to show empathy if doing any primary research for your Team Project.
- Empathy can be developed like any other skill.
- Imagine 'walking in another person's shoes' to develop your empathy.

Summary questions for Chapter 2

2.01 Reasoning

1 Give one reason why being able to develop a line of reasoning is a useful skill.

2 Explain why it is important to support reasoning with evidence.

2.02 Evidence

3 Identify one thing you should consider when choosing sources of information from the internet.

4 Explain why you might need to cross-reference information.

2.03 Claims

5 Identify two ways of testing a claim.

6 Explain why it is important to support claims with evidence.

2.04 Drawing conclusions

7 Explain the difference between a claim and a conclusion.

8 What conclusion can you draw from the following information:
'If the world were 100 people, 50 would be male and 50 would be female'?

2.05 Bias and vested interest

9 Identify one source of information that might be biased.

10 Give an example of vested interest and explain why it is vested interest.

2.06 Statements of argument

11 Give one opinion from a global topic of your choice and explain why it's an opinion.

12 Explain how a value judgement differs from a prediction.

2.07 Problem-solving

13 Identify one personal course of action presented in this section of the book.

14 Explain why problem-solving is an important skill to develop.

2.08 Empathy

15 Identify one way of showing empathy to the situation of someone else.

16 Explain why it's important to have empathy.

Practising critical thinking skills

In this chapter, you have been looking at how to develop your critical thinking skills. You should now understand not only what the term 'critical thinking' means, but also be able to apply what you have learnt to your Global Perspectives studies, perhaps by thinking a little differently to how you did before you started this chapter.

Learning about what makes good reasoning and how claims and conclusions need supporting with evidence is all part of critical thinking. Different statements of argument like fact, opinion, prediction and value judgement can help your understanding of perspectives and issues, and it's important to realise that some of the information you read and hear might be subject to bias and vested interest.

In the following sections of this chapter, you will be taking part in activities to practise what you have learnt.

There are three sections; developing critical thinking skills, establishing critical thinking skills and enhancing critical thinking skills. Each section is designed to build on the section before. You can either work through each section in turn or choose the section that you feel is at the most appropriate level for you. You should see a progression in difficulty through the three sections.

Developing critical thinking skills

This section uses the topic of **Globalisation**, which is one of the eight global topics listed in the IGCSE and O Level Global Perspectives syllabus for the Written Examination (Component 1). You will be using this topic as the vehicle for improving your critical thinking skills.

SKILLS LINKS

- Chapter 2: Critical thinking skills, 2.01 Reasoning
- Chapter 2: Critical thinking skills, 2.02 Evidence
- Chapter 2: Critical thinking skills, 2.03 Claims
- Chapter 2: Critical thinking skills, 2.04 Drawing conclusions
- Chapter 2: Critical thinking skills, 2.05 Bias and vested interest
- Chapter 2: Critical thinking skills, 2.06 Statements of argument
- Chapter 5: Communication, 5. 02 Writing
- Chapter 5: Communication, 5. 04 Speaking

ACTIVITY 2.34

On your own and then with a partner, decide which one of the definitions (**a–c**) most accurately explains what globalisation is.

a thinking about everyone in the world and being able to connect with people via social media

b removing barriers to international trade and encouraging investment in worldwide markets

c being able to speak more than one foreign language and have the same traditions as the rest of the world

Discussion point

Ask your classmates what they think globalisation means and make notes to come up with a definition.

Reflection: How do you think globalisation might affect you in the future?

ACTIVITY 2.35

Read the short text about globalisation and answer the questions.

1 What do you think the main argument of the text is?

2 How good do you think this argument is?

3 What reasoning is used for the argument?

4 Does the author give any evidence to support the reasoning?

Globalisation

Globalisation has more drawbacks than benefits. This is because in the developing world globalisation has failed to make the lives of people better, as it has failed to reduce poverty. Many people in the developing world are still living on less than one dollar a day. Despite the United Nations (2015) reporting that there has been a gradual reduction in poverty across the world, they state that 2.2 billion people are still living in poverty.

Globalisation has meant an increase in international trade, which has led to an increase in the number of people employed. This has not been a good thing as in the developing world so-called sweatshops mean that many employees of large, mostly western, companies work in appalling conditions, which are often dangerous and can be fatal. The collapse of a sweatshop in Bangladesh in 2013 is one such example that claimed people's lives.

Additionally, the growth in competition has forced some companies to reduce their workforce so that they can cut costs and increase profits. For example, in China, which has experienced a strong economic growth in the last years, unemployment has started to become a real issue, especially in towns and cities.

Reference:

United Nations, *Human Development Report* (2014, p.3), [Online], http://hdr.undp.org/sites/default/files/hdr14-report-en-1.pdf (accessed 19/11/2015).

Discussion point
Discuss your answers to the questions (**1–4**) in Activity 2.35 with a partner. Did you agree?

Reflection: How might you make the main argument in the text for Activity 2.35 stronger?

ACTIVITY 2.36

Read a possible counter argument (below) to the argument in the text in Activity 2.35.

Do you agree that the reasoning in this counterargument is not as good as the reasoning in the argument in Activity 2.35? Give reasons for your opinion.

Globalisation

Some argue, however, that sweatshops in the developing world have generally been a good thing. Working conditions in clothes factories may often seem pretty awful, but they are better than a life of work in agriculture or having no job at all.

Many of the three million people working in sweatshops in Bangladesh are women, who, reportedly, have become more empowered than ever before. Although the minimum wage paid to workers in the clothes industry in Bangladesh may still seem low by standards in the western world, in 2010 it was still nearly double that from 2006. The Bangladeshi economy has been growing every year, so we can conclude that life is getting better for people in Bangladesh.

Reference:
International Labour Organization, *Bangladesh: Seeking better employment conditions for better socioeconomic outcomes* (2013), [Online], http://www.ilo.org/wcmsp5/groups/public/---dgreports/---dcomm/documents/publication/wcms_229105.pdf (accessed 19/11/2015).

Discussion point
Discuss your opinion about the strength of the reasoning in the counterargument in the text in Activity 2.36 with a partner. Do they give the same reasons as you?

ACTIVITY 2.37

1 Choose one of the two arguments:
   a Globalisation has more drawbacks than benefits.
   b Globalisation has more benefits than drawbacks.
2 Do some research to find either some of the drawbacks or the benefits of globalisation (aim for two drawbacks or two benefits).
3 Once you have your benefits or drawbacks, write them down and explain why you think they are drawbacks or benefits.
4 Do another search to find some evidence to support your explanations.
5 You should now have two short paragraphs (you can use Figure 2.03: Developing an argument and Section 5.02 about writing to help you).
6 Find someone in your class who has chosen the same argument as you (**a** or **b**).

Discussion point

Share your two paragraphs from Activity 2.37 and give feedback to your partner:

Are the paragraphs clear, are reasons and evidence to support the reasoning given?

Reflection: How easy or difficult did you find it to do Activity 2.37?

Don't worry if you found it difficult: with practice it will get easier.

ACTIVITY 2.38

1   In a small team – with your partner from Activity 2.37 and two other members of your class who chose the other argument (**a** or **b**) – compare what you have all written.

   You should now find that you have two lines of reasoning that emphasise the benefits and two that emphasise the drawbacks of globalisation.

2   Working together in a small team, use the information you have to try start to formulate a response to the question:

   'Are the benefits of globalisation greater than the drawbacks?'

   You don't need to draw any conclusions yet, just organise the lines of reasoning you have in a logical way.

Discussion point

Ask your teacher for some feedback about the work you have produced for Activity 2.38:

- Is each line of reasoning clear, explained and does it have supporting evidence?

- Do the lines of reasoning follow on logically?

Reflection: Can you now draw a mini-conclusion that might go some way towards answering the question:

'Are the benefits of globalisation greater than the drawbacks?'

ACTIVITY 2.39

Here is a list of sources of evidence that might be suitable to include in an Individual Report entitled: *'How has globalisation affected family life?'*

- Blog
- Women's magazine
- Video-clip
- Interview with mum
- Newspaper article
- Documentary film
- Government website
- NGO website
- Data from a survey asked in the local community
- Business and Trade magazine

1   Which of these sources do you think might be the most reliable?
2   Which of these sources do you think might be the most credible?
3   Which of these sources might be subject to bias and/or vested interest?

Discussion point

Discuss your ideas for Activity 2.39 with a partner.

Reflection: Refer back to the work you did for Activities 2.37 and 2.38. Reflect on whether the sources of evidence you have used are reliable, credible or biased.

ACTIVITY 2.40

1   What conclusions can you draw (linked to the topic of **Globalisation**) from looking at these two images?

Figure 2.21 Drawing conclusions A

Figure 2.22 Drawing conclusions B

2   For each image:

a   Draw one conclusion about the setting of the images (where is this happening?)

b   Draw one conclusion about the relationships of the people in the pictures (who are the people in the images and how are they related?)

c   Draw one conclusion about the feelings of each person in the images (what are they feeling? What are they thinking?)

Write a summary of your conclusions.

Discussion point

Discuss your ideas for Activity 2.40 with a partner.

Reflection: Is it getting easier to draw conclusions?

ACTIVITY 2.41

1   Choose one of the images from Activity 2.40.

2   Do some research to find out more about the issues (sweatshops and going to a western university) and make two claims. Remember to support your claims with evidence (one piece of evidence for each claim).

Discussion point

Share the claims you made for Activity 2.41 with a partner. Do they believe them?

Reflection: Why do you think people do not always believe the claims you make?

ACTIVITY 2.42

Read the text and identify the following:

- one fact
- one opinion
- one prediction.

> Some people believe that globalisation has made it easier to find out about other cultures by searching on the internet and by travelling more easily to other countries and cultures.
>
> Despite these benefits, the principal argument against what has been known as cultural globalisation is that it has caused loss of cultural identity and languages. According to UNESCO, 600 languages disappeared in the last century. UNESCO also reports that languages continue to disappear at a rate of one language every two weeks. It has been estimated that up to 90 percent of the world's languages will disappear before the end of the 21st Century if current trends continue. Nowadays, many people think that pop and westernised culture have destroyed the individuality of many other cultures. So maybe it's time to protect other languages and cultures if we don't want them to disappear.
>
> **Reference:**
> UNESCO, *Linguistic Diversity: 3,000 Languages In Danger*, [Online], http://www.unesco.org/bpi/eng/unescopress/2002/02-07e.shtml (accessed 19/11/2015).

Discussion point

Share your fact, opinion and prediction from Activity 2.42 with a partner.

Reflection: Do you now feel confident about identifying facts, opinions and predictions?

If not, refer back to Section 2.06 about statements of argument and look in the glossary for a definition of each. There is also further practice in the following section: Establishing critical thinking skills.

Establishing critical thinking skills

This section uses the topic of **Humans and other species** to establish your critical thinking skills. This topic is one of the eight global topics listed in the IGCSE and O Level Global Perspectives syllabus for the Individual Report (Component 2). You will build on the skills you have acquired so far so that you start to feel more confident when developing an argument using appropriate sources of evidence.

SKILLS LINKS

- Chapter 2: Critical thinking skills, 2.01 Reasoning
- Chapter 2: Critical thinking skills, 2.02 Evidence
- Chapter 2: Critical thinking skills, 2.03 Claims
- Chapter 2: Critical thinking skills, 2.04 Drawing conclusions
- Chapter 2: Critical thinking skills, 2.05 Bias and vested interest
- Chapter 2: Critical thinking skills, 2.06 Statements of argument
- Chapter 2: Critical thinking skills, 2.07 Problem-solving
- Chapter 5: Communication skills, 5.02 Writing
- Chapter 5: Communication skills, 5.04 Speaking

ACTIVITY 2.43

Look at the example of how the topic of **Humans and other species** might be broken down in Figure 2.23. Answer the questions.

1 What issues to do with the global topic of humans and other species have been identified in the diagram?

2 What type of information might you be looking for to answer the question, 'how many endangered species?' (fact, opinion, value judgement or prediction)

3 Might the answer to the question, 'Is vegetarianism a healthy alternative to meat?' elicit a fact, opinion or value judgement? Give reasons for your answer.

4 What further issues to do with humans and other species might you put in boxes A and B?

5 What questions connected to the issues (A and B boxes) might you put in boxes C and D?

6 Which issue from the whole diagram interests you the most?

7 For your chosen issue from question **6**, write down a question that needs a fact, a question that needs an opinion, a question that needs a value judgement and a question that needs a prediction.

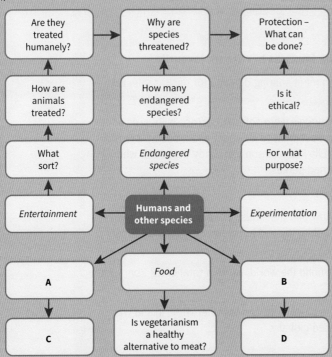

Figure 2.23 Humans and other species

Discussion point

Discuss your responses to Activity 2.43 questions **1–5** with a partner.

Reflection: Did your partner have some interesting responses to questions **4** and **5** in Activity 2.43?

Had you thought of their ideas?

Discussion point

Find someone in your class who has chosen the same issue as you from the global topic of humans and other species for question **7** of Activity 2.43. Compare the questions you have formulated to elicit facts, opinions, value judgements and predictions.

Reflection: Does the issue you chose in response to Activity 2.43 question **6** still interest you as much, or are you more interested in another issue to do with the topic?

If so, why do you think this is?

ACTIVITY 2.44

Read the text and answer the questions:

1. How good do you think the argument for wearing fur is in this text?
2. What reasoning is used for the argument?
3. Does the author give any evidence to support the reasoning?
4. Are there any gaps? What else might you need to find out before agreeing with the argument for wearing fur?

Fur trade booming after swing from fashion faux pas to catwalk favourite

Figures show farmers stepping up production to meet soaring demand for mink, sable, fox and ferret pelts.

In 1994, four of the world's most famous supermodels were splashed across billboards under the slogan 'We'd rather go naked than wear fur'. Fast-forward 21 years and it seems it is now another story for Naomi Campbell, Kate Moss, Elle Macpherson and Cindy Crawford, who have been pictured in fur coats, gilets and trimmed parkas.

They are not alone in falling off the anti-fur wagon.

Figures from the International Fur Federation show that the industry is enjoying another year of considerable growth. The demand for mink, sable, fox and ferret has soared and farmers have stepped up production.

In 2013/14, 87.2m mink pelts were produced around the world, worth a total of £2.2bn, with 35m produced by China alone.

China also remains one of the biggest producers of fox pelt, and together with Finland was responsible for 91% of the 7.8m fox furs produced globally.

The figures – the first to show a breakdown of different pelts – follow on from research by the IFF last year which valued the global fur trade at more than £26bn.

On the British catwalks last year, more than 60% of shows featured fur, and at New York fashion week the figure topped 70%. While luxury labels such as Fendi have a long history of featuring real fur in their shows, fur is increasingly being used by newer brands as well. In New York, the up-and-coming label Cushnie Et Ochs said fur was its favourite material of the season, adding that it was 'not ashamed'.

This month Karl Largerfeld said he would be putting on a special 'couture fur' show to mark his 50th anniversary of working for Fendi. 'For me, fur is Fendi and Fendi is fur, fun furs' he said. 'Fendi is my Italian version of creativity. The Fendi haute fourrure fashion show is the opportunity to stage the royal furs of furs.'

He told the New York Times: 'For me, as long as people eat meat and wear leather, I don't get the message. It's very easy to say no fur, no fur, no fur, but it's an industry. Who will pay for all the unemployment of the people if you suppress the industry of the fur?'

Source: http://www.theguardian.com/uk

Discussion point

Discuss your answers to Activity 2.44 questions **1–4** with a partner.

Reflection: Is the argument in the text for Activity 2.44 strong enough to encourage you to wear fur?

ACTIVITY 2.45

Now, consider the counterargument – not wearing fur.

1   Write down four questions to guide you to find information to produce an argument against wearing fur. These four questions can be designed to search for one fact, one opinion, one value judgement and one prediction.

2   Use these four questions for your initial search for information to use in your argument. *(You can always edit/change your questions if you are unable to find suitable information.)*

3   Using the answers to your questions, put together a paragraph that argues against wearing fur.

Discussion point

Share the paragraph you wrote for Activity 2.45 with a partner to gain feedback; do they think your argument is strong enough to persuade someone not to wear fur?

Reflection: Taking the feedback your partner gave you for the paragraph you wrote for Activity 2.45 into account, how might you make your argument stronger?

ACTIVITY 2.46

Use the search terms 'human nutrition' 'beef' 'benefits' 'video' to find a video-clip from a magazine about beef. Watch the video-clip.

1   What is the main argument?
2   Do you think the reasoning in the argument is strong? Why?/ Why not?
3   Why might you need to cross check the information given?

Discussion point
Discuss your answers to questions **1–3** in Activity 2.46 with a partner.

ACTIVITY 2.47

Read the following claims and search for one piece of evidence to support each claim.

a   We don't need to eat animals to be healthy.
b   It is not always clear whether companies test their products on animals.
c   Animal research helps save human lives.
d   Fake fur is better for the planet than real fur.
e   Animals are no longer used in some circuses.

Discussion point
Share the evidence you have found for each of the claims in Activity 2.47 with a partner.

ACTIVITY 2.48

1   Do some research on some of the issues to do with the global topic of **humans and other species**. Complete the table by writing down five claims (these can come from different perspectives) and put the web address where you have found evidence to support each claim.
2   Once complete, give your table to a partner for them to find the evidence for the claim from the web address given. When found, the 'yes' box can be checked.
3   If the 'yes' box for the claim is not checked, find another web address that gives evidence for the claim.

Global Topic: Humans and other species			
	Claim	**Evidence**	**Yes**
1			
2			
3			
4			
5			

Discussion point

Work with a partner to choose one of the claims within either of the tables you produced for Activity 2.48. Using Figure 2.08: Testing claims, discuss how you might test the claim you have chosen.

ACTIVITY 2.49

Imagine you have been doing research, analysing and synthesising information for your Individual Report entitled:

How important is the continued existence of the Amazon rainforest?

1 You found this cartoon. What conclusion can you draw?

"It says, 'Get back on the tour bus'."

Figure 2.24 Drawing conclusions

2 Now do further research to help you draw conclusions for an imaginary Individual Report entitled: *How important is the continued existence of the Amazon Rainforest?*

3 Once you have completed your research and found evidence to support your arguments (from global, national and local perspectives), you reach the conclusion that it is very important that the Amazon rainforest continues to exist. You now need to propose courses of action. (*The cartoon might help you to think of at least one course of action.*)

For each of the perspectives (global, national, local and personal), suggest a suitable course of action (you may need to do some research to see what is already being done to protect the Amazon rainforest).

Discussion point

Discuss the conclusions you have drawn and your courses of action proposed in Activity 2.49 with a partner or in a small team. Decide on the best course of action for each of the perspectives (global, national, local and personal).

Reflection: What might you now need to do to develop the courses of action chosen in Activity 2.49?

Enhancing critical thinking skills

This section uses the topic of **Human rights** to enhance your critical thinking skills. This topic is one of the eight global topics listed in the IGCSE and O Level Global Perspectives syllabus for the Team Project (Component 3). By working through the activities in this section, you will continue to build on the critical thinking skills you have acquired so far.

SKILLS LINKS

- Chapter 1: Information skills, 1.03 Analysis
- Chapter 2: Critical thinking skills, 2.01 Reasoning
- Chapter 2: Critical thinking skills, 2.02 Evidence
- Chapter 2: Critical thinking skills, 2.03 Claims
- Chapter 2: Critical thinking skills, 2.04 Drawing conclusions
- Chapter 2: Critical thinking skills, 2.05 Bias and vested interest
- Chapter 2: Critical thinking skills, 2.06 Statements of argument
- Chapter 2: Critical thinking skills, 2.07 Problem-solving
- Chapter 2: Critical thinking skills, 2.08 Empathy
- Chapter 5: Communication skills, 5.01 Reading
- Chapter 5: Communication skills, 5.02 Writing
- Chapter 5: Communication skills, 5.03 Listening
- Chapter 5: Communication, 5.04 Speaking

ACTIVITY 2.50

Work with a partner to create a diagram to break down the global topic of **Human rights** into issues and questions, as you did for the global topic of humans and other species in Activity 2.43.

You might keep adding to this diagram as you work through this section and do further research about the topic.

Reflection: Having completed Activity 2.50, do you now have a better idea about what the global topic 'Human rights' includes and the types of issues you might investigate?

If not, you might need to do further research to identify the issues. Continuing to work through this section should also help.

ACTIVITY 2.51

1 Write down each question and the type of information you need in order to be able to answer each of the questions (**a–d**).

   a How many indigenous people in the world are there?

   b How are indigenous people around the world treated?

   c Is the way that indigenous people are treated just and fair?

   d What will happen to the indigenous people of the world in the future?

2 Do some research to try to answer the questions (**a–d**).

Discussion point

Share the type of information required by each question (**a–d**) in Activity 2.51 with a partner.

ACTIVITY 2.52

Work with a partner for this activity.

1 Read the text. Copy and complete the table below with three reasons for the claim and supporting evidence and references.

2 Once you have completed all three rows (or as much of this as you can) in your table, share your information with a partner to see if you have the same information or can add to the information you have.

3 Looking at the information you now both have, decide whether you think the argument in the text is convincing.

Claim: Indigenous people are among the most disadvantaged in society			
	Reason for claim	*Supporting Evidence*	*Citation/Reference*
1			
2			
3			

Indigenous people are among the most disadvantaged in society

There are approximately 370 million indigenous people living in more than seventy different countries in the world. They are among the most disadvantaged people in society. Examples include the Adivasi of India, the Ashaninka people of South America and the Inuit people of the Arctic.

Another example are the Aboriginals of Australia. Today, more than half the population of Aboriginals live in towns, mostly on the outskirts in awful conditions because of extreme poverty (2015a). These poor living conditions result in a lower life expectancy than for the rest of the population of Australia, estimated by an Australian government department (2015b) at roughly 10 years lower for both males and females.

The Australian government is aiming to improve Aboriginal health by attempting to deal with the social problems within their communities (2008). Nevertheless, there are still higher incidences of diabetes, heart disease and kidney failure among the indigenous populations than have been reported for the non-indigenous population.

Many Aboriginals work as labourers on cattle ranches that have taken over the land the Aboriginals once owned. They suffer from racist attitudes and sometimes violent behaviour.

Although a High Court judgment in 1992 recognised the existence of Aboriginal right over large parts of Australia, some Aboriginal groups are still displaced, failing to gain back land due to the Australian government's land rights legislation.

These are just some of the reasons why indigenous people are among the most disadvantaged people in society.

References:

Australian Institute of Family Matters (2015a), *Aboriginal Australians and Poverty*, [Online], https://aifs. gov.au/publications/family-matters/issue-35/aboriginal-australians-and-poverty (accessed 21/11/2015).

Australian Institute of Health and Welfare (2015b), *Life Expectancy*, [Online], http://www.aihw.gov.au/deaths/life-expectancy/ (accessed 21/11/2015).

World Health Organisation (2008) *Australia's disturbing health disparities set Aboriginals apart,* [Online] http://www.who.int/bulletin/volumes/86/4/08-020408/en/ (accessed 21/11/2015).

ACTIVITY 2.53

1   Working with a partner, choose one of the other examples of indigenous people from the text in Activity 2.52 (the Adivasi of India, the Ashaninka of South America, the Inuit of the Arctic).

2   Use appropriate terms to search for information to further support the claim that:

    'Indigenous people are among the most disadvantaged in society.'

3   Add the information to the table you completed in Activity 2.52 by adding a further row (or two if you find more reasons and evidence).

Discussion point

Find someone in your class who chose a different indigenous people to the one you chose for Activity 2.53. Discuss the information you found to support the claim that *'Indigenous people are among the most disadvantaged in society'*. Continue adding to the table produced for Activity 2.52 as you find and discuss additional information.

Reflection: Can you now see that the more evidence there is, the more believable a claim is?

If not, then carry on reading and practising or go back over section 2.03 about claims.

ACTIVITY 2.54

Choose one of the websites listed in the references at the end of the text for Activity 2.52. Use the table in below to evaluate the source.

Criteria	Web sources	Yes/No	Notes
Accuracy	Is the information free from errors in spelling, grammar, etc.?		
	Are charts and graphs clearly labelled and easy to read?		
	Are there links to other sources?		
Authority	Who is responsible for the web page?		
	Is the person responsible for the web page an expert in their field?		
Objectivity	Is advertising clearly differentiated from the content of the website?		
	Are opinion pieces clearly labelled as such?		
Currency	Is there a date to show when the web page was written?		
	Are there signs that the work is kept up to date?		
Coverage	Is the page complete or under construction?		
	Is the entire source on the web or only part of it?		

111

Discussion point

Find someone in your class who has chosen the same web source from the list of references as you have for Activity 2.54 and discuss each of the criteria.

Reflection: Overall, do you think the web source that you have chosen from Activity 2.54 is a reliable and credible source of information? Give reasons for your answer.

ACTIVITY 2.55

Using the search terms, 'poverty' 'Orissa' 'India' and 'video' find a short video-clip about the landless people in Orissa, India.

Answer the following questions:

1   Do you think the source is reliable and credible? Give reasons for your answer.

2   What conclusions can be drawn from the video-clip?

3   Are there any examples of bias and/or vested interest in the clip?

4   What course of action is suggested to help resolve the situation?

Discussion point

Discuss your answers to the questions (**1–4**) in Activity 2.55 with a partner.

Reflection: Are your critical thinking skills continuing to improve? How do you know?

ACTIVITY 2.56

1   Imagine you are one of the indigenous people in the image.

2   Using the five steps in Section 2.08 about empathy, Figure 2.18: developing empathy, write answers to respond to the first three questions.

3   Work with a partner. One of you takes on the role of the person in the image and the other is the interviewer. Role play the dialogue that might take place for all five steps of Figure 2.18: developing empathy.

4   Swap roles and conduct the role play again (or find a similar image – perhaps from another indigenous people). Make sure you have both had a chance to play the role of the empathetic interviewer and the person in the image.

Figure 2.25 Indigenous people

Reflection:

- As the interviewer in Activity 2.56, which of you (you or your partner) showed more empathy?

- Why do you think this was?

ACTIVITY 2.57

1 Find a short interview between a reporter and someone from an indigenous people.
(You could try the search terms: 'interview' 'indigenous people')

2 Listen to what the interviewer says. Write down examples of empathy that the interviewer uses.

3 Answer the following questions:

a Overall, how empathetic do you think the interviewer is to the situation of the person being interviewed?

b How do you think that the interviewer could be more empathetic?

Discussion point

Find a partner who has a different interview to yours for Activity 2.57. Share your interview and your thoughts about how empathetic the interviewer is with your partner. Which of the two interviewers do you think is more empathetic to the situation of the person being interviewed and why do you think this?

ACTIVITY 2.58

Write a proposal to persuade a government (for example, Australian, Indian, Canadian) to take action to help indigenous people of the country – make sure that you show empathy in your proposal and use the information you have found out whilst studying this section of the book.

Discussion point

Share your proposal from Activity 2.58 with a partner to gain feedback.

Ideas for the feedback discussion include:

- Are all claims made supported with reliable and credible evidence?

- Is empathy for the Indigenous people shown in the proposal?

You can also share your proposal with your teacher for feedback.

Reflection: Are you more confident that you can show empathy when the need arises? If not, read through Section 2.08 about empathy again and practise being empathetic with your friends.

Chapter 3
Independent learning skills

Learning objectives

By the end of this chapter, you should be able to:

- understand a little more about how your brain works
- remember more easily what you have done, seen and heard
- make useful notes to aid your understanding of what you have done, seen and heard
- reflect on what you have done, seen and heard
- evaluate what you have done, seen and heard.

Introduction

As well as enabling you to work collaboratively with others in pairs and teams, studying IGCSE or O Level Global Perspectives helps you to develop your independent learning skills so that you will be able to work confidently on your own. You will be able to transfer these skills to other subject areas. They will also be useful for any learning you do in the future.

This chapter focuses on developing the following independent learning skills:

3.01 Memory   **3.02** Note-taking
3.03 Reflection   **3.04** Evaluation

3.01 Memory

SKILLS LINKS

- Chapter 1: Information skills, 1.02 Research
- Chapter 1: Information skills, 1.05 Planning
- Chapter 5: Communication skills, 5.02 Writing

How our brain works

To begin thinking about developing memory skills, we need to take a brief look at how our brain works.

Scientists are now beginning to recognise that anyone can learn at any time in their life. Our brain helps us to take in information and remember it for future use. To allow you to do that, you may need to change the way you do things so that you can remember things better. Changing the way you do things, including how you learn, is what this section on memory is about.

Brain facts

Your brain grows and develops throughout your life. This means that you never stop learning. No two brains are the same, and the whole brain is active all the time. This brain activity is made up of messages sent by billions of brain cells called neurons – messages that affect everything you do. The neurons communicate by a process known as neuronal firing.

TIP
Type 'how your brain works' into your search engine to find out more about your brain.

The more we learn, the better we get at learning. It is a bit like exercise; the more we do, the fitter we get.

> **Reflection:** Think about how you learnt to ride a bicycle. You had to get on it and pedal. You would not have learnt how to ride a bicycle by reading a book about it.

Linking learning to memory

Let us now consider what **memory** is and how it links to learning.

Neuroscientists define learning as the process whereby neurons that fire together (cells that work together to carry messages between the brain and other parts of the body to help us remember things) in response to a situation or experience are changed in a way that means they will fire again in the future. It is this repeated firing of neurons that helps us remember things. The process of remembering something means that the neurons that fired together are more likely to do so again in the future, which helps us continue to remember things.

KEY TERMS

Memory: the ability of the mind to store and remember learning.

Reflection: Consider a new language you are learning.

It is only by recalling words you have learnt that you can speak or write them or understand something that others say. We need to learn something before we can remember it. We also need to remember past learning in order to associate it with new learning to commit both old and new learning to our memory.

TIP

So how do we remember?

By repeatedly doing things.

It is not just facts and information that we need to remember throughout our lives, but also how to do things. Being able to remember how to do things, such as riding a bicycle or speaking a new language, is probably more important than remembering facts. We can always look up facts and information.

Improve your memory to improve your learning

Pictures and images help us to remember things for longer. Funny things also stick in our minds. Look for pictures, cartoons and photos to help you remember key ideas and issues.

ACTIVITY 3.01

1   Search the internet to find an image to help you remember what independent learning looks like.

2   Find an image that sums up an issue to do with the Individual Report topic of **Humans and other species**.

Consider these questions:

a   What issue(s) does the picture represent?

b   Why have you chosen this picture?

c   If you see this picture in the future, will you remember the issue(s)?

3   When looking at Figure 3.01, what issue(s) do you think of?

Figure 3.01 City skyline

When looking at Figure 3.01, it is likely that you thought of burning fossil fuels and the pollution that results. You might also have considered globalisation or sustainable living. All of these are relevant global issues to consider when studying IGCSE or O Level Global Perspectives. As well as helping us remember key issues and ideas, pictures can evoke emotion and empathy, something to consider when thinking about the Team Project component of IGCSE or O Level Global Perspectives.

Keeping focused

When learning, it is important to focus on the task in hand. This gives your brain time to **encode** the information properly so that you can remember it. Multi-tasking does not facilitate this. Spending longer at your computer will not help you to remember more. Even an adult can only concentrate for a maximum of fifteen minutes at any one time so have a break when you need to. Getting up and doing something different for a couple of minutes will help you to refocus when you return to your work. Physical activity not only helps keep your body fit, it also helps keep your brain fit and aids memory.

KEY TERMS

Encode: translate into understanding.
Association: linking groups of ideas to each other.

Making connections

When we learn something new, we should try to make **associations** and connections, linking information and ideas to aid our memory. Try to link key terms with other key terms to build a spider diagram to use as a memory aid.

ACTIVITY 3.02

Figure 3.02 shows a spider diagram for the Individual Report topic of **Family**. Copy the diagram and add your own associations.

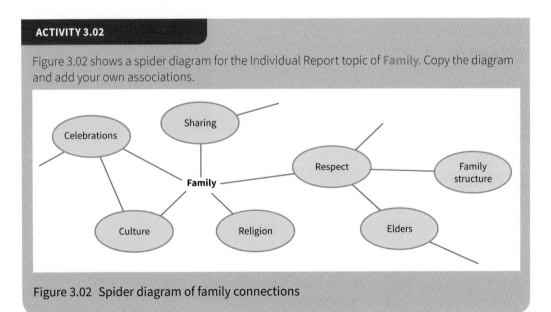

Figure 3.02 Spider diagram of family connections

TIP
Find out more by typing 'spider diagrams' into your search engine. See Section 3.02 for more information about them, plus other forms of visual notes.

Once you have associations and connections, you can start to think about questions for your Individual Report, in this case, on the topic of **Family**. For example, 'How does culture affect family structure?' or 'What is the impact of religion on family life?' might be suitable questions to focus on in an Individual Report for this topic.

Discussion point

Discuss with your partner to come up with two further suggestions for Individual Report questions for the topic of **Family**.

Although you do not have to remember specific facts for any parts of the IGCSE and O Level Global Perspectives course, as you might do for other subjects like History, for example, developing memory skills is still useful, especially when researching information. You will need to remember relevant information from what you have researched and write it down in your own words. Memory skills will help with this. As you develop your memory skills, you will also be able to develop your note-taking, summarising skills and, in the long term, your essay skills to complete the Individual Report.

Organisation

You will remember more if you are organised. Our brains like order which is why this text book is set out with chapters, sections and headings, and why planning is an essential skill (see Chapter 1 Section 1.05).

TIP

You will need to organise information for your Individual Report, which you write in class. It is a good idea to signpost your work, perhaps by using sub-headings, so that the organisation of your work is clear.

How much information?

Research into memory suggests that the maximum number of different pieces of information that the brain can deal with at any one time is seven. It can also only hold these seven pieces of information for less than 30 seconds. If you want to lengthen the 30 seconds to a few minutes or even an hour, you need to continually review the information.

Chunking

If you have a large amount of information, you should try **chunking** – breaking it into smaller chunks, then focusing on trying to remember those chunks as individual pieces of information.

For example, *to be able to understand this sentence, the beginning of the sentence must be held in mind while you read the rest*. Our short-term memory is responsible for this level of remembering. Another example of short-term memory is trying to remember a persuasive argument until the other person stops talking. This is why the other person should repeat what the argument is, continuing to persuade until the end so that we do not forget what the argument is about.

KEY TERM

Chunking: breaking down information into smaller, more manageable pieces.

ACTIVITY 3.03

1   Ask your partner to read paragraph 1 of the short article below to themselves first.

Next, ask them to read it aloud to you. Do not look at it yourself yet. Do not write anything down.

After your partner has read it aloud once only, answer the following question:

What is Sports Worldwide looking for?

2   Next, read paragraph 2 to your partner and then ask them the following question:

Will you need to pay for meals?

Paragraph 1	**Paragraph 2**
Sports Worldwide is looking for volunteers to help at sporting events this Summer. As a volunteer you will be making a difference to thousands of people who share a common interest – sport. The services that volunteers provide are essential to all the individuals and organisations they support.	We are looking for volunteers to help out at sporting events across the country during the Summer holidays. Accommodation and travel will be organised for you but you will need to pay for meals. We will, however, provide you with a uniform that you can keep and which cannot be bought in the shops.

You could probably answer question 1 without looking at the text, but you might have had to look at the text to answer question 2. Information we hear or see quickly disappears unless we help ourselves to remember it by repeating it and writing it down. Section 3.02 on note-taking skills will help with this.

Making sense of it all

Using all five senses can also aid memory and help understanding. Sometimes it is not enough just to see and hear it; we need to smell, taste and touch it too.

ACTIVITY 3.04

Imagine you live in a world without aeroplanes. What would the consequences be? Use your imagination. Close your eyes and use your senses to think about what that world would be like. Use the following questions as prompts:

- What can you see?
- What can you hear?
- What can you smell?
- What can you taste?
- What can you touch?

You are more likely to remember the consequences of a world without aeroplanes now that you have visualised them than if you had simply written them down.

This section has focused on developing memory skills, which you will find useful when researching and using information, both for the Individual Report and the Team Project. You will also find memory skills useful for any examinations. Remembering what you read in source material that is provided will make answering the questions easier, even though you can keep referring to the source material throughout the examination.

Summary

- Learning is the process whereby brain cells called neurons fire together in response to a situation or experience and are changed in a way that means they will fire again in the future.

- Memory is the repeated firing of neurons in response to a situation or experience.

- We need to learn something before we can remember it.

- Pictures, images, associations and connections help us remember ideas and issues.

- You are more likely to remember something if you do not multi-task while trying to learn something new.

- You will remember more if you are organised because our brains like order.

- You need to break down large amounts of information into more manageable pieces.

- Using all five senses will help you remember more.

3.02 Note-taking

SKILLS LINKS

- Chapter 1: Information skills, 1.02 Research
- Chapter 1: Information skills, 1.05 Planning
- Chapter 3: Independent learning skills, 3.03 Reflection
- Chapter 5: Communication skills, 5.01 Reading
- Chapter 5: Communication skills, 5.03 Listening

As you discovered in Section 3.01 about developing memory skills, it is not possible to remember everything you have done, seen and heard all the time. This is why note-taking is a useful skill. With any subject you study, you usually need information, and there is a lot of information available to you from books, your teacher and from the internet.

Good note-taking does not just happen naturally; you have to develop the skill of note-taking, recording key information and being able to find it when you need to use it.

Good note-taking helps you focus on the important parts of what you read or hear. By focusing on the important parts, you are more likely to understand and remember what you have read or heard. Good note-taking helps you structure your written work and enables you to avoid **plagiarism**.

KEY TERM

Plagiarism: intentionally or unintentionally copying the words and phrases of someone else and passing these off as your own work.

TIP

For further information about note-taking, try searching for a video clip using a search engine. You could use the terms: 'How to: Take the BEST Notes! + Study Tips!'

Note-taking steps

Note-taking is a form of learning. Taking notes does not mean writing down everything the teacher says or everything you read and then going away to make sense of what you have written down. Once you have finished listening and reading, you should already understand what you have read and heard. Here are three easy steps you can use to take good notes.

Step 1: Questions

Don't write down facts; write down conclusions. It is important that as you listen and read you try to understand. It is a good idea to format notes as a series of questions which you can then answer. If you need to record data, facts or direct quotations, add them as evidence under each question.

ACTIVITY 3.05

Read the following text relevant to the Individual Report topic of **Digital world** and write down three questions.

The internet enables us to find information, but the information is usually in small pieces and the internet does not connect facts together or give us the context we necessarily want. We get distracted following links so that we often find ourselves on social networking sites rather than doing what we intended. We generally forget what we were originally looking for. Therefore, we lose our ability to concentrate and to think about important issues in detail. Knowledge is important but it comes in different forms. Having information is only one kind of knowledge. There is also knowledge about how to do things, like driving a car or baking a cake. Whilst we can follow instructions about how to do these things, we cannot experience them like we can in real life.

Figure 3.03 Using the Internet

The text about the internet is a short text, but writing down questions about it should have helped you to retrieve the key information from the text. Using this method should enable you to understand and remember the key points from any text.

Just remember that you don't need every piece of information, and writing in your own words is better than copying the words in the text. What's important is that, when explaining anything identified from a text, your reasoning is coherent and logical.

Discussion point
Discuss the questions you have written with your partner for Activity 3.05. Are your questions similar?

Here are some suggestions – you will have different questions, which is fine.

1   How is information presented on the Internet? (answer – fragmented, in small chunks, not connected, out of context, lacking meaning)

2   What happens when we follow the links? (answer – can lose focus, get easily distracted, start looking at other websites, lose concentration)

3   As well as having information, what other knowledge is there? (answer – how to do practical things like drive a car or bake a cake)

Step 2: Visual aids
You can use coloured pens as a visual aid for remembering key information from a text. If you get into the habit of using the same colour each time for the same information, you will find it easier to organise your notes and find what you are looking for once you come to structure the information you have gathered.

> **TIP**
> Try different colours for different types of notes:
>
> **Red** = Questions
> **Blue** = Conclusions (answers to questions)
> **Green** = Supporting information (data/facts/direct quotations to back up your conclusions)

ACTIVITY 3.06

Imagine you have found this text whilst researching the topic of **Disease and Health** for your Team Project.

Make notes of **five questions**, **five conclusions** and **five supporting pieces of information** in the suggested colours.

> **Some worrying news about the eating habits of teenagers in America**
>
> A recent study conducted in America has found that more than two thirds of all teenagers drink sweet fizzy drinks like lemonade every day and that almost half of all those asked eat fast food daily. In contrast to this, many teenagers do not eat enough fruit and vegetables. Less than a quarter of those asked ate five portions of fruit and vegetables per day, which is the recommended amount. Fruit and vegetables are low in calories and high in fibre, vitamins and minerals, so according to researchers, eating a diet high in fruit and vegetables helps to prevent health problems such as diabetes, heart disease and cancer. On the other hand, fast foods are high in fat and calories. Consuming fast food and fizzy drinks increases the number

of calories teenagers eat which, without increased activity, can cause obesity, which leads to disease.

Researchers say that one aim of the study was to provide information to those people responsible for creating health policy. For example, the findings about fizzy drinks and fast food may help policymakers decide whether to ban sales of these items on school campuses.

Figure 3.04 Eating habits of teenagers

Here are some suggestions, although you may have different questions, conclusions and supporting pieces of information.

1   **Who were the subjects of the study? Teenagers in the US** 'study conducted in America', 'two thirds of all teenagers'

2   **Why was the study done? To have an impact on health policy** decide whether to ban fizzy drinks and fast food on school campuses

3   **What was the study about? Teenagers' eating and drinking habits (healthy/ unhealthy food and drink)** almost half eat fast food every day / two thirds drink fizzy drinks every day

4   **Why is it important to eat fruit and vegetables? Low in calories and high in fibre, vitamins and minerals** can prevent diseases – cancer, diabetes

5   **Why is fast food unhealthy? High in fat and calories** can cause obesity

Considering the length of the text, these **notes** are brief and they are **selective**. If you keep them well spaced, you can add more details later if you want to.

Sometimes you will want more detailed notes and will be looking for **specific details** from a text. In this case, you will want to write down the questions you want answers to first. Then you will search for the answers and relevant supporting information.

At other times, you will just want to know the **gist** of a text. In this case, you will skim read the text (see Section 5.01 on reading).

 KEY TERMS

Notes: a short record of key points or ideas written down to aid memory.

Selective: carefully choosing information as the best or most suitable for your purpose.

Specific detail: the detail required to answer a question.

Gist: the general meaning of a piece of text.

Step 3: Understanding

Once you have your notes, you need to spend some time organising them and your thoughts. In general, ten minutes should be enough to look over them, reviewing them to ensure you understand what you have written. For example, do you have a piece of evidence to support a conclusion you have made? If not, you may need to go back to the text to find one. If there is anything you do not understand, you can have another look at the text and check your notes or you can discard this information. There is no point having notes you do not understand.

One of the best ways of checking your own understanding is to try to explain or teach the topic to someone else. You will know you have good notes when you try to use them to tell your partner about the text you read or listened to.

ACTIVITY 3.07

Using the three steps, read and make notes about the extract below to help you explain the main content of the text about the topic of **Water** to your partner.

Water

One third of the world's population is living in either water-short or water-scarce regions.

The World Health Organisation already reports that, at any one time, up to half of humanity has one of six main diseases associated with poor drinking water and inadequate sanitation. They report that about 5 million people die each year from poor drinking water, poor sanitation, or a dirty home environment, often resulting from water shortage. One solution for cleaning water is to use advanced technology. However, this technology is expensive so the cost of this would need to be passed on to customers.

There should be an international body setting prices and ensuring that clean drinking water is available everywhere and for everyone.

Figure 3.05 Water – a crucial resource

Note-taking using other strategies

As well as the three steps discussed above, there are other ways of taking notes. You need to find one that suits you and that you will use regularly.

'Five things' is one way. You simply write down five short pieces of information from the text (in no more than five words).

ACTIVITY 3.08

Try the 'five things' strategy with this text from the Individual Report topic **Humans and other species**.

The threats to cheetahs

Mankind is the main threat to the existence of the cheetah. This is because people hunt and poach cheetahs. Another threat to the cheetah's survival is the loss of its habitat. National Parks have been set up to help to keep a constant population of cheetahs in the wild, but more needs to be done. One of the problems is that drought and disease cause serious problems to the already limited cheetah population within these National Parks. The cheetah population continues to decline due to the trapping and shooting of cheetahs by farmers. They do this because cheetahs are notorious for killing farmers' livestock, damaging their livelihood. Namibia has the largest cheetah population in the world but the cheetah population has been reduced from 6000 animals in 1980 to fewer than 2500 animals today.

Figure 3.06 Cheetahs are under threat

TIP

When working on a computer, use virtual 'stickies' to make notes on key information using the 'five things' strategy.

Visual notes

As well as the note-taking strategies you have tried so far in this section, you can add labels to a diagram or use diagrams to record information – for example, spidergrams, timelines, mind maps and flow charts.

Timelines

Timelines are a useful way of organising notes to make sense of when things happen.

In this example, the timeline shows some of the significant events to do with global human rights from 1990 to 2000.

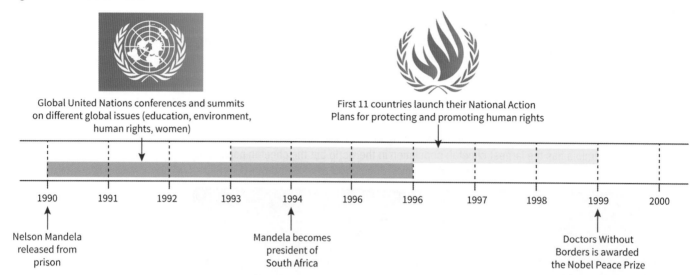

Figure 3.07 Timeline of significant human rights events 1990–2000

Advantages

- A timeline gives you a visual image of a series of important events in date order.
- You can use a timeline to make notes about the causes of an issue and when these happened, for example, the causes of the uprising in Syria. Search for 'Syria timeline 2015' to see some examples.
- You can easily add events to a timeline.

Mind maps

A mind map is different from a timeline in that it is generally not used for putting things in date order, but more for organising information visually around a single idea or issue. Often it uses colours and pictures, as in Figure 3.08.

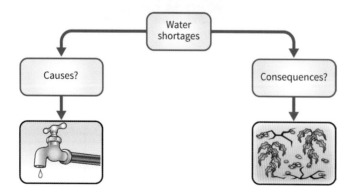

Figure 3.08 Example of a mind map

Advantages

- Mind maps can use words and images and are often colourful.
- Mind maps help you to record what you already know about a topic or issue, connecting prior to new learning,

126

- Mind maps allow you to add words and images connected to the central idea or issue or any branches off that central idea or issue.

Flow charts

A flow chart is a diagram that can be used to represent a process. The steps are shown in boxes and are connected with arrows.

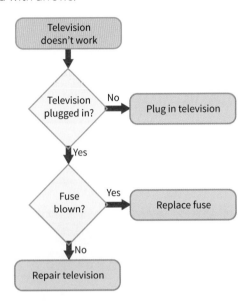

Figure 3.09 Example of a flow chart

Advantages:
- Flow charts help you to gain an idea of the steps you need to take to complete something, for example a Team Project or an Individual Report. You can find a flow chart for the structure of an Individual Report in Chapter 1.
- You can easily add in information as you think of further steps in the process.

Spidergrams

A spider diagram or spidergram is a simple plan with lines and circles for organising information so that it's easier to use or remember.

A spidergram is similar to a mind map except that a mind map uses colour and pictures whereas a spidergram uses mainly words, although you can adapt it to suit your needs.

Both can help with note-taking.

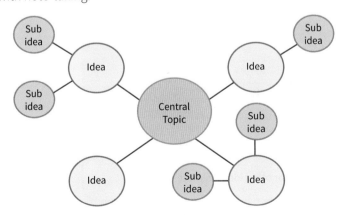

Figure 3.10 Example of a spidergram

Advantages

- All your notes are on one page so you are less likely to write irrelevant information.
- You can see the main points straightaway.
- You can connect key points and ideas, which is good for structuring a report or essay.
- You can clearly see where there are gaps where you need to do more research.

Making a spidergram

A spidergram starts with a central idea and branches out. You should use a whole sheet of A4 paper and put the main idea in the centre. You can then draw branches pointing outwards. You should use one branch per point. By adding smaller branches, you can add detail and examples.

TIP

Explore the use of spidergrams by putting the word 'spidergrams' into your search engine.

ACTIVITY 3.09

Read this text and produce a spidergram of the key points.

Employment

Getting paid for working in a job is one of the best ways to get out of poverty. Good jobs play a vital role in giving people a sense of well-being and confidence. Having a job makes a person feel as if they are making a contribution to their family and their community.

However, unemployment is rising across the world, and is becoming a serious global issue. There have already been protests and riots in places like Brazil and Greece, because people are not able to earn a living to feed themselves or their families. Another effect of unemployment is the increased population within towns and cities as people move from the countryside to where the work is. Overpopulation leads to overcrowding and poor-quality housing in many large cities. Poorly heated or damp housing can cause serious health issues, resulting in illness such as pneumonia. Another serious consequence of overcrowding is rising crime as poor living conditions can lead young people to turn to crime or drugs.

'The more people are employed, the better the living standards and the healthier and happier the community,' states Henry Gold from the World Bank.

You do not need to record everything in your diagram. You might find it easier to write some headings after reading the text once, for example:

- benefits of a job
- effects of unemployment
- consequences of rural unemployment
- consequences of overpopulated towns.

TIP

Try searching for 'word clouds', 'wall of ideas' and 'timeline' for other ideas for note-taking.

Graphic organisers

Graphic organisers enable you to do as their title suggests: organise your notes graphically, in a table for example.

> **TIP**
>
> There are many different kinds of graphic organiser for different uses and subjects.
>
> Explore some of them by typing 'graphic organisers' into your search engine.

KWL Charts

One popular graphic organiser that your teacher may have asked you to use before is the **KWL chart** (see Activity 3.10).

KWL charts help you to collect and organise information related to a topic you are researching.

KEY TERM

KWL chart: a graphic organiser that helps people organise information in three columns:

K   what you **K**now.

W   what you **W**ant to know.

L   what you have **L**earnt.

ACTIVITY 3.10

For the Team Project topic of **Tradition, culture and identity**, use the five questions given below to complete a KWL chart. Fill in the **K** column with what you know (short answers to the questions) and the **W** column with what you still need to find out.

You should write notes using key phrases, words and question words rather than entire sentences; that way, when you use your notes to write up your research, you will have the content for your piece and be more likely to write in your own words.

Questions about tradition, culture and identity

1   In what country is there a different culture to yours and how is it different?

2   What does this different culture celebrate?

3   What do people from this different culture wear and why?

4   Why do you think different cultures exist?

5   Why is it important to have different cultures?

Once you have completed the first two columns of your chart, you have an idea of what you need to find out, which is what you will record in the **L**earnt column.

You can use library and internet resources to search for the information you need to add to the **L**earnt column. Once you have the necessary information, add this in note form to your **L**earnt column .

Use the information from your note-taking template to tell you partner about what you now know about the topic of 'culture'.

	K	W	L
1			
2			
3			
4			
5			

Reflection: Now you have explored a selection of ways to take notes, consider which you think you might use regularly and start to use it to gather relevant information in your own words.

Summary

- You do not need to write down everything when making notes – only key words/ideas/questions.

- It is useful to know what you are looking for before you start to search for relevant information (ask yourself what questions you want answers to).

- Use a strategy to make notes and stick with it so that it becomes second nature.

- Ignore any information that does not answer the questions you want answers to. This gets easier the more you do it.

- Copying and pasting is plagiarism and is not a useful use of time. Making notes is more productive in the long term.

3.03 Reflection

 SKILLS LINKS

- Chapter 1: Information skills, 1.02 Research
- Chapter 3: Independent learning skills, 3.02 Note-taking
- Chapter 3: Independent learning skills, 3.04 Evaluation skills
- Chapter 5: Communication skills, 5.01 Reading
- Chapter 5: Communication skills, 5.03 Listening

You learnt about the importance of good note-taking in Section 3.02, so you know that good notes help you to understand and remember the information you find. Good notes also enable you to talk and write about what you have discovered to someone else, but using your own words. In the last section we looked at how to take notes effectively from written sources. This section looks at taking notes in other situations, such as when working in teams, and then how to use these notes to reflect effectively on the experience of working in a team. Once you have completed something as a team, you reflect on how it went, which is a different type of note-taking called **reflection**.

 KEY TERM

Reflection: serious thought or consideration about something you have done or something that has happened.

The importance of reflection

Experiences, ideas and events occur throughout our lives and, unless we reflect on them, we forget them. Reflecting on experiences enables us to remember experiences better and for longer, and allows us to develop personally and professionally. Reflection also helps us to analyse and discuss our feelings with others, so that we can consider them from different perspectives.

Reflection is also a way of 'learning from experience'. You do something, you think about what you did, and what happened, and you then decide what you would do differently next time. It is a useful skill for your study of IGCSE or O Level Global Perspectives as the Personal Element of the Team Project involves completing an individual Reflective Paper after you have completed your Team Project (see Chapter 4 for more about the Team Project).

In a Reflective Paper, you think carefully about the **benefits** and **challenges** of working as a team and your own performance as a team member. You analyse and evaluate the **strengths** and **limitations** of the project outcome in achieving the project aim. You also explain what you have learnt about different **cultural perspectives** and your own learning from the project.

KEY TERMS

Benefits: advantages of doing something.

Challenges: difficulties that arise that need to be overcome.

Strengths: the benefits or good points about something.

Limitations: what is not done well and could be improved upon.

Cultural perspectives: the way that individuals are shaped by their environment as well as social and cultural factors, such as nationality, race and gender, which affect their viewpoint.

Reflection is also a useful life-long skill to help you make better choices and decisions. If you are a reflective learner, you are more likely to be more of an independent learner, someone who is **self-aware** and motivated to continue learning.

KEY TERM

Self-aware: aware of your own character, feelings, motives and desires.

Reflection: Ask yourself the following question: Am I already a reflective learner?

If the answer is yes, then well done, but keep reading as you can always get better at reflection. If the answer is no, then don't worry. This section gives you some activities and tips to help you on your way to becoming a more reflective learner.

You might say that you are too busy studying to reflect. However, being able to reflect will improve your learning, so you need to find time to do it. You might also say that you are always thinking anyway, but it is not enough just to think, you have to communicate your thoughts to someone else.

So, although reflection itself is an independent activity, you will only deepen your learning if you share these reflections, either in written or spoken form. The easiest option is to write down your reflections.

TIP

Start a blog to write down your reflections as you work through your IGCSE or O Level Global Perspectives course. You can give access to friends and teachers who can make comments on your blog as they would on a social networking site. In this way, you get some feedback and can deepen your learning.

Many blogs are free and easy to set up. Try typing 'blogging' into your search engine to find one that you think you could use.

The reflective learning process

To begin the process of reflection, you should consider everyday activities and events, and write down what happened. You then reflect on what happened to consider what you learnt, and what you could have or have done differently, and this is where learning happens.

The 'five key questions' strategy

The 'five key questions' strategy is a useful, fairly quick way of reflecting. By answering the five key questions below, you are not only describing what happened but also reflecting on the experience in a meaningful way.

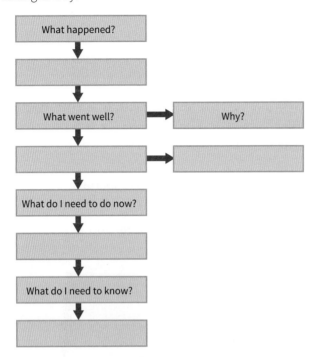

Figure 3.11 'The five key questions' strategy

ACTIVITY 3.11

Read the blog entry below and identify which part of the blog answers each of the five questions above:

Blog entry

For our Team Project we decided to create and deliver a presentation to make other people aware of the problem of global warming. We wanted to start with Grade 7 students and inform them that they too had a responsibility to help slow down global warming. We knew that they were not aware of the things they could do, so we wanted to show them how every individual can help in some way.

We had a group meeting and shared our initial ideas about what should be in the presentation.

This initial brainstorming discussion went well as everyone seemed prepared to contribute their ideas.

However, I was sometimes a bit reluctant to voice my opinion as I didn't feel that I had done enough research and I thought the others in my group would think my suggestions were silly.

I feel that, before our next meeting, I need to do some more research so that I am knowledgeable about the main causes of global warming.

I will ask Ms Chad if there are a couple of good websites she can suggest that focus on the causes of global warming. Then I will be able to think about possible solutions and be ready with my ideas at our next team meeting.

Discussion point

Discuss the answers to the five key questions for Activity 3.11 with your partner.

You should have got a clue to the answers from the way the text was set out.

The 'five key questions' strategy is a good way to start developing your reflection skills. It can be used for any experience.

To develop your reflection skills further, you can use the 'four prompts' strategy. This strategy can be used for experiences and for activities that involve researching information, either by reading or by listening.

Four prompts to develop your reflections

1 Identify one important idea, piece of information or research finding that you learnt while doing an activity.

2 Ask yourself why you think this idea, piece of information or research finding is important.

3 Think about how what you have learnt connects with your own life.

4 Consider the questions you now want answers to and why these questions are important to you.

ACTIVITY 3.12

Using the four prompts strategy

1 Read the text about China's one-child policy, which relates to the topic **Demographic change**.

2 Answer the four prompts.

3 Record your answers in your blog.

4 Share your answers with a partner.

5 Add any further thoughts to your blog after discussion with your partner.

China's one-child policy

When China declared it was relaxing its one-child policy in late 2013, marketing director Kang Lu talked to her husband about whether they wanted a second baby. 'But given our current circumstances, we quickly abandoned the idea,' she said. 'It wasn't a tough decision.'

They weren't alone. So far, a good number of Chinese families have been less than enthusiastic about the partial relaxation of the policy, choosing to stick with one child, often for practical and economic reasons, but also because decades of government propaganda have convinced them that one child really is best.

Experts say this only underlines a looming demographic crisis in China: low fertility rates, a rapidly ageing population and a shrinking labour force will inevitably put immense strains on the economy in the decades ahead, and on the government's ability to pay people's pensions.

Yet for many urban couples in modern China, having a second child is not an attractive option. There are no kindergartens for children under three. Kang's parents had moved to Beijing for three years to help look after their daughter, but now felt too old to help.

Kang also has ambitions for her career, but was faced with the prospect of giving up those ambitions – or giving up her job entirely – to care for a second child. In Beijing's soaring housing market, Kang and her husband couldn't afford a larger apartment, which they figured they would need if they had another baby. They were also worried that the capital's smoggy air could affect a new baby's health.

Source: www.theguardian.com/world/2015/feb/06/china-one-child-policy-problems-ageing-population

The difference between descriptive and reflective writing

Without developing reflection skills, many students tend to fall into the trap of describing rather than reflecting. It is important to know the difference between different types of writing as sometimes you will be asked to describe, and at other times you will need to reflect, which is the more difficult of the two skills.

Description

Descriptive writing is just what it says – a description of events. There is no discussion beyond description and there is no evidence of reflection.

Descriptive reflection

Descriptive reflection is somewhere in between description and critical reflection. Although largely descriptive, the description is not just about what happened but includes some discussion about why things happened.

Critical reflection

In this type of writing there is a 'stepping back' from the events, with an exploration of the role of the person in the events and actions. Critical reflection asks us to think about our practice and ideas and then to examine our thinking by asking probing questions.

ACTIVITY 3.13

Read the following extracts from blogs. Identify which of the three is description, which is descriptive reflection and which is critical reflection.

Blog 1

I had to deliver a presentation. I was scared about not saying the right things and not being able to answer questions properly. During the presentation I realise that I was trying to prove that I could present as well as my team mate. I wanted to impress everyone. Early on it went wrong and I began to panic. Trying to pretend I was confident made the situation worse. The more I spoke, the more my voice wobbled. It was only through talking over the presentation and the things that went wrong that I can now see several areas that I could get better.

Blog 2

I had to deliver the presentation. I was confident but I did spend quite a bit of time preparing. During the presentation I became nervous when I realised they were all waiting for me to speak and my nerves made my voice wobble. Afterwards I was disappointed that my presentation did not seem to have gone well.

Blog 3

I had to deliver the presentation. I spent quite a bit of time preparing it in the way that I have seen others make similar presentations. When it came to the presentation, I really wanted to do it well – as well as my team members had all done their presentations. Maybe I wanted too much to do well. I tried to be calm but failed and my voice went wobbly – that's how it felt to me anyway. My team member said afterwards that I looked quite calm despite what I was feeling.

Afterwards, I felt it was a disaster and it has left me feeling embarrassed in front of my team mates. However, the next day, I started to feel more positive and now need to think about why a simple presentation could have such an effect on me. I need to do some research on what makes a good presentation.

> **Reflection:** How did you do in Activity 3.13?
>
> Could you see the differences between the different types of writing?
>
> How confident do you feel about being able to reflect?

A third way to develop reflection skills

We have already explored two ways of reflecting: using the five key questions and the four prompts strategies. Here is a third, which will enhance your existing reflection skills.

This strategy identifies six stages for successful reflection.

ACTIVITY 3.14

For each of the six stages, record your own ideas based on an experience you have had. Use the examples given in the speech bubble as a guide only, and replace them with your own words according to the experience you are reflecting on.

1 Look back and describe what happened: the experience, idea or event. (Keep this part short, and use the past tense.)

> **Example:** We were asked to work in pairs; and instead of being able to choose our own, the teacher chose the pairs, which I thought was unfair as I ended up working with someone I wouldn't normally have chosen.

2 Think about how what you already know relates to the experience. (Here, use the present tense.)

> **Example:** I understand why the teacher grouped us this way, as previously we have chosen to work with our friends, and perhaps we needed to get a different perspective. Also, some of the less confident students don't participate much in class discussions, so this enables them to voice their opinions, without putting them on the spot.

3 Consider how it went. (Here you can include emotions/feelings.)

> **Example:** Initially, I was worried we wouldn't come up with any ideas; we sat in silence for a few seconds, then Marta got out her notebook and started to draw a mind map, as we discussed the issue. We found we could bounce ideas off each other really well, and I was surprised to learn how much easier it was to remember things when you made notes like that.

4   Identify the part(s), which you think you learnt the most from, why this was, and how you and others feel about it. (Part of reflection is discussing your feelings/thoughts with others and looking at things from different perspectives.)

> **Example:** I'd never considered making notes like that before, and I really enjoyed it and learnt from it, so it proved to be a useful strategy. For me, the most significant aspect was I felt as if I'd be able to remember the information better when we presented to the class next time. I always thought that I was more of a visual person and remembered by reading and looking, rather than by doing. Now I know better. Marta seems to think that if we look, hear and do, we'll improve our learning and memory. I think I agree with her now.

5   Explain how your analysis of the experience, idea or event might affect your future learning. (This is explaining what you might need to do/learn to impact on your future learning, so will mostly use the future tense, i.e. you are predicting.)

> **Example:** The knowledge I have gained from this experience is really useful as I can use this strategy in my future studies. My next step will be to have another look at other situations where I can apply this strategy, discuss it with others in my group, and start to reflect on my learning more regularly. I will also look at some other blogs.

6   Once you have discussed the experience and had further time to reflect on it, you can come back to your initial reflections, and add to them, creating further successful reflections.

Discussion point
With a partner, talk about whether you find it easier to reflect than you did before you started this section of the chapter.

Summary

- Reflection needs practice; the more you reflect, the better you will get at reflecting.
- Start to reflect by using the 'five key questions' strategy and develop to the 'six stages' strategy.
- Always keep in mind what you are being asked to reflect about.
- Keep a blog and add to it regularly – at least once per week.
- Explore the blogs of others to see what they are reflecting about and how they reflect.

3.04 Evaluation

SKILLS LINKS

- Chapter 1: Information skills, 1.02 Research
- Chapter 2: Critical thinking skills, 2.02 Evidence
- Chapter 2: Critical thinking skills, 2.05 Bias and vested interest
- Chapter 3: Independent learning skills, 3.03 Reflection

In Section 3.03, you saw that reflection allows us to analyse experiences and events so that we can continue doing what is working and change something that is not working or not going well. Reflection allows us to consider why things worked well or not. **Evaluation**, on the other hand, is the judgement about whether something worked well or not. When you evaluate something, you look at its strengths and **weaknesses**.

KEY TERMS

Evaluation: assessment of the strengths and weaknesses.
Weaknesses: the bad points or points that need improving.

138

▶▶

Reflection: Consider the following examples of evaluation and reflection.

The team worked well together.
This is an evaluation of how well the team worked together.

I think this was because we all knew each other beforehand, and we knew each other's strengths so could easily decide who was going to do what.
This is a reflection on why someone thought the team worked well.

Do you see the difference?

Discussion point
Discuss the following with a partner.

1 What might the reflection have looked like if the evaluation was: 'The team did not work well together'?

2 Give another example of evaluation and reflection.

The need for evaluation skills

Like the other skills in this book, evaluation skills need to be developed. Evaluation is a higher-level skill, so the ability to evaluate well will be useful not only for IGCSE and O Level Global Perspectives, but also for other subjects and for life in general.

For IGCSE and O Level Global Perspectives, you need to be able to evaluate source material when you are researching for information, both for your Individual Report and your Team Project. You could be asked to evaluate source material and the evidence used to support claims, arguments and perspectives within source material. As discussed in Section 3.03, for the Team Project you will have to write an individual reflective paper. Reflection and evaluation generally go hand in hand, so you need evaluation skills to be able to complete a reflective paper. The evaluation of sources, and the evidence and reasoning to support claims, arguments and perspectives, are largely covered in Chapter 2: Critical thinking skills. You should refer to this chapter to remind yourself of the key terms. There follows, however, a brief reminder of some of the key considerations and further activities to help you with the development of evaluation skills.

Evaluating sources

When evaluating sources, you should consider the strengths and weaknesses of the source in relation to the question you want an answer to or a specific argument: for example, whether nuclear power is a suitable replacement for fossil fuels, when looking at the global topic of **Fuel and energy**. As well as identifying each strength and weakness, you should try to develop your answers by justifying why you think the point you mention is a strength or weakness.

> **TIP**
> Always give a reason why you have chosen a particular strength or weakness of a source. Use the phrase: *this is a strength because . . .*

When evaluating sources, remember to consider:

- who wrote the information
- how likely the information is to be **biased**, inaccurate or one-sided
- whether the source quotes experts to support its **claim**, and if so, whether these have experience, **credibility**, expertise, **objectivity** and **consistency**
- whether other sources support the claims
- whether there are alternative views and sources that **counter** the information provided in the source.

KEY TERMS

Biased: showing an inclination or prejudice for or against one person or group, especially in a way considered to be unfair.

Claim: an assertion that something is true.

Credibility: being convincing or believable.

Objectivity: looking at something without bias, judgement or prejudice.

Consistency: logical coherence.

Counter: argue against something.

ACTIVITY 3.15

Read the following text. Decide whether you think the source is a good source to use to support arguments in favour of globalisation. Give three reasons for your decision.

> Globalisation has many benefits. It can bring wealth to some of the world's poor. For example, a lot of South-east Asia was really poor not so long ago, but thanks to international trade, many of these countries now experience growth. The United Nations provides many statistics on their website that support this. This means people are much better off now than their parents and grandparents were.
>
> Globalisation also helps protect the environment. Some people have suggested that in the past a country such as China could have produced as much pollution as it wanted to, but if these countries want to join the global marketplace, other countries can put pressure on them to clean up their act. I have seen how some countries are now thinking more about environmental protection in my work at the environmental protection agency.
>
> *Source*: Adapted from an international trade magazine

You probably noted that the argument on globalisation is one-sided as it comes from a trade magazine so just gives the benefits rather than any disadvantages of globalisation. Few sources of information are given, although the United Nations is cited and this might make the article more credible. No other sources of evidence are cited. The author works for an environmental protection agency, so the evidence given might be credible but there is little in the way of specific examples. For these reasons, you probably decided that this source is useful for supporting the argument for globalisation but that you would need to find other sources to add to the information here or to provide further evidence for the argument.

Evaluating evidence and reasoning

It is important to be able to evaluate the evidence and reasoning used to support claims, arguments and perspectives.

When evaluating evidence and reasoning, you should consider the strengths and weaknesses of both the evidence and the reasoning to support either a claim, an argument or a perspective.

TIP

When evaluating evidence and reasoning, always give explanations for your evaluation. Try starting with, 'the evidence for this claim is weak because . . .' or 'the reasoning is strong because . . .'.

Claims

When evaluating evidence and reasoning for a claim as a statement of something being true, remember to consider:

- what your criteria for evaluating the evidence are. You should decide before evaluating the evidence how you will determine its value. It is not good enough to say, 'This is bad' or 'This is good'. You need to be able to say why it is bad or good, for example, carbon emissions are bad for the environment because they cause air and water pollution.

- how good the evidence and the reasoning is. Rather than asking whether it is 'true', ask if it is 'dependable' and whether you are convinced.

ACTIVITY 3.16

Read the following text. Evaluate the evidence and reasoning presented for the claim that: 'Fast food is bad for kids' learning'. Do you think the evidence and reasoning for the claim is strong or weak, and why?

> **Fast food is bad for kids' learning**
>
> A new study published in the *Clinical Pediatrics Journal* (2014) suggests that children who eat regularly at McDonald's, KFC, Pizza Hut, and the like don't perform as well at school as their peers.
>
> 'Research has been focused on how children's food consumption contributes to the child obesity epidemic,' Kelly Purtell, who led the study at Ohio State University, told the *Telegraph*. 'Our findings provide evidence that eating fast food is linked to another problem: poorer academic outcomes.'
>
> The study used data from a sample of 8544 American schoolchildren, measuring their fast-food consumption at the age of 10 and then – after attempting to account for other factors – comparing that against academic results in reading, maths, and science at age 13.
>
> In science, for example, those kids that never ate fast food scored 83 points, compared to an average of 79 points for those who ate it every day. According to the *Telegraph*, theories as to why this is so are based on brain chemistry – such as a lack of iron, which leads to slower development, the effects of sugars in the diet, and so on.
>
> *Source: www.qz.com*

Discussion point

Compare your answer for Activity 3.16 with that of a partner. Did you agree that the evidence and reasoning for the claim was strong? What reasons did you give?

Arguments

When evaluating evidence and reasoning for an argument or a line of reasoning to support a claim, remember to consider whether:

- there is a clear statement of a **proposition** or a viewpoint and sufficient supporting evidence
- ideas are presented in a **logical** and connected way
- there are any weaknesses and **fallacies** in the evidence and reasoning, e.g. cause and effect.

KEY TERMS

Proposition: a statement putting forward an idea.

Logical: following on in a coherent way.

Fallacy: an error in reasoning or a mistaken idea.

ACTIVITY 3.17

Read the argument below and answer these questions:

1 Is a clear viewpoint expressed?
2 Is there evidence to support the claims made, and how strong is this evidence?
3 Are the claims to support the viewpoint presented in a logical and coherent way?
4 Are there any weaknesses in the evidence and/or reasoning?

Argument for cost-free primary Education for all

Education is vital for ending world poverty. With education, there are more employment opportunities, income levels are increased and there is an improvement in the health of children generally. In regions where access, attendance and the quality of education have seen improvements, there has also been a decline in the spread of HIV/AIDS and an increase in the health of the community in general. In fact, children of women who are educated are more likely to live past the age of five. Not only does education improve individual and family health, it also improves community health. In countries with good education systems, there is greater economic growth and a lower crime rate.

Reflection: Now consider that the origin of the source for the argument in Activity 3.17 was a site such as Wikipedia, or a source similar to Wikipedia. Do you think this would be a weakness, and why?

Perspectives

When evaluating evidence and reasoning for a perspective (global, national or local) or a viewpoint within a perspective (scientist, politician, teacher), remember to consider whether:

- evidence for the perspective is provided and, if so, whether it actually supports the perspective
- the reasoning is based on opinion, anecdotal evidence or value-judgements only
- hard data in support of the perspective is provided.

ACTIVITY 3.18

Which of these two perspectives do you think uses better evidence and has stronger reasoning?

Perspective 1	Perspective 2
According to the United Nations, a vegan diet is more sustainable and less demanding on the environment than a meat-and/or-dairy based diet, with a vegan diet taking about a 10th of the resources – land, water, fuel, etc. – to maintain. So from an ecological perspective, veganism is the best option for the future – our world resources can sustain a much larger population as vegans than omnivores. *Source: www.theguardian.com*	If God meant for mankind to eat a plant-based diet, why did He give Noah's family (and subsequent humans born) permission to eat meat? These humans and the animals with them had just survived a global deluge, one that covered the very mountaintops, during which all edible vegetation on the planet would have been destroyed. If God didn't intend for us to eat animals and we have access to healthy plant-based foods, should we consider a vegan diet? *Source: www.thisdishisvegetarian.com*

Evaluating the Team Project

For IGCSE and O Level Global Perspectives component 3, as well as presenting your key personal research findings in a clear and consistent way, making connections between the team and the personal elements, you will also need to evaluate the Team Project you complete as coursework. Once the Team Project has been completed, you write a Reflective Paper as the Personal Element of the Team Project. In this Reflective Paper, you evaluate:

- the strengths and limitations of the outcome your team produces in achieving the aims of the project
- the strengths and limitations of your own work processes.

This is independent work and forms part of the reflective paper, along with reflection on:

- the benefits and challenges of working as part of a team
- the strengths and weaknesses of your own performance as a team member
- your learning about different cultural perspectives
- your overall personal learning from taking part in the Team Project.

ACTIVITY 3.19

Imagine you have written the following two paragraphs for the Personal Element of the Team Project, to include in your Reflective Paper.

1   Identify the strengths and limitations of your team's outcome (a website to raise awareness about healthy living).

> **Project outcome**
> On the whole I think that we achieved our aim of making teenagers more aware about how they can lead a healthy lifestyle. Our website was not only seen by our peers in school, but also by contacts we have around the world. We gave people the link to our website and a survey to evaluate our website and were surprised at how many responses we got and how good the feedback was, highlighting strengths and weaknesses of the website. I agree with some of the comments. We focused mainly on food and we should have included something about exercise and sport. We might have included quotes from the different people we interviewed to make it more emotional rather than being just facts. Some of the facts were meant to shock, but I don't think they came from very reliable sources. We made the mistake of trusting what we read without looking for further sources of the same information. It is not text heavy and people found that good as the pictures and statistics made the viewers curious to know more about how to lead a healthy lifestyle.

  a   The strengths of the paragraph are . . .
  b   The limitations of the paragraph are . . .
  c   Suggested improvements include . . .

2   Identify the strengths and limitations of your own work processes.

> **Own work processes**
> As for my own contribution, I wasn't sure what I was supposed to be researching, so I suggested we made a plan. It then became clearer what we were all supposed to be doing. The short survey I put together that was sent to teenagers in other countries where we have a school link was a good way of finding out about how people keep healthy in those countries. I found out about walking backwards as a way of keeping fit – I didn't know it originated in China, but it is practised in Japan and in Europe now as well as in China. My time management was not efficient though and I did more research than trying to understand what I found out and this held the Team Project back.

  a   The strengths of the paragraph are . . .
  b   The limitations of the paragraph are . . .
  c   Suggested improvements include . . .

You should now feel more confident about what it means to evaluate something.

Summary

- Evaluation is a high-level skill worth developing.
- Focus on the strengths/successes and limitations/ weaknesses or failures when evaluating something.
- Always keep in mind where the evidence has come from when evaluating sources and evidence for claims, arguments and perspectives.
- Explore different sources of evidence about the same issue.
- Avoid Wikipedia or any other website that can be edited as you do not know who has written the information.
- Do not take things at face value. Always question whether the evidence and reasoning is strong or weak, and why.

Summary questions for Chapter 3

3.01 Memory

1 Explain why you think it is important to develop memory skills.

2 Explain how you think mind maps can help develop memory skills.

3.02 Note-taking

3 Explain why note-taking is a useful skill to develop.

4 Explain the benefits of a KWL chart for making notes.

3.03 Reflection

5 Identify which component in the IGCSE and O Level Global Perspectives syllabus requires you to write an individual Reflective Paper.

6 Explain the importance of being able to reflect on your experiences.

3.04 Evaluation

7 Which component in the IGCSE and O Level Global Perspectives syllabus requires you to evaluate sources and the evidence used to support claims, arguments and perspectives?

8 Explain the importance of being able to evaluate the outcome of the Team Project as required by the Reflective Paper for the Team Project.

Practising independent learning skills

So far in this chapter, you have been focusing on becoming a more independent learner by acquiring memory, note-taking, reflection and evaluation skills. The next section of the chapter is divided into three: developing independent learning skills, establishing independent learning skills and enhancing independent learning skills. Each section is designed to build on the section before. You can either work through each section in turn or choose the section that you feel is at the most appropriate level for you. You should see a progression in difficulty through the three sections.

Developing independent learning skills

This section uses the global topic of **Education for all**, which is one of the eight global topics listed in the IGCSE and O Level Global Perspectives syllabus for the Written Examination (Component 1). You will practise each of the skills using this topic as the vehicle for improving your independent learning skills.

SKILLS LINKS

- Chapter 3: Independent learning skills, 3.01 Memory
- Chapter 3: Independent learning skills, 3.02 Note-taking
- Chapter 3: Independent learning skills, 3.03 Reflection
- Chapter 3: Independent learning skills, 3.04 Evaluation

145

Reflection: What does this image make you think about?

Figure 3.12 Pupils in a classroom

ACTIVITY 3.20

Look again at Figure 3.12 and consider the following three questions:

1 Within the global topic of **Education for all**, what issue(s) does this picture make you think about?

2 Why has this picture been chosen?

3 If you see this picture in the future, will you remember the issue(s)? Why (not)?

ACTIVITY 3.21

Read the following text and answer these questions.

1 What is the main issue identified in the text?

2 What is the main purpose of the text?

Education Is For All

Very few girls from rural communities get the chance of continuing their education beyond primary school. High schools are far from where they live, and parents cannot afford to pay for accommodation in or near the schools. The charity 'Education Is For All' was founded to help provide the opportunity of a high school education for girls from rural communities. In September 2009, a boarding school was opened that allowed a number of girls to get a high school education who would otherwise not have been able to do so. However, as a charity, 'Education Is For All' relies on donations. Volunteers run the boarding house and the only paid staff are some of the teachers, who get a small salary. If you would like to make a donation, follow the link on the Education Is For All website.

To answer the questions, you might have had to chunk the information into two sections. As this was a relatively short text, you should have been able to do this and find the information to answer the questions fairly easily. With longer texts, you can still chunk information so that it is easier to find what you are looking for. Having an idea about what you want to find out is also useful when reading texts for information.

In examinations, you are given questions. Read the questions before looking at any source material so that you know what you need to find.

ACTIVITY 3.22

Identify the trend in the number of teenagers not in education in south and west Asia since the year 2000 from the text below.

Even though the number of teenagers out of education has fallen by nearly a third in south and west Asia since 2000, there are still 26 million out-of-school teenagers.

The next text extract is longer so you will need to make notes rather than relying on memory. As you discovered in Section 3.02, one way of making notes is to write down short pieces of information from the text.

ACTIVITY 3.23

Read the text and write down five short pieces of information from the text (in no more than five words each).

The millennium development goal of universal primary education by 2015 has not been achieved

An estimated 58 million children worldwide still do not go to school, meaning that there was 'no chance whatsoever' that the millennium development goal of universal primary education by 2015 could be achieved, the United Nations has admitted.

The United Nations released statistics that showed that not enough progress had been made in improving access to education since 2007. If current trends continue, it added, about 43% of those out of school – 15 million girls and 10 million boys – will probably never set foot in a classroom.

According to Unesco, the situation is particularly bad in sub-Saharan Africa, where population growth has left more than 30 million children out of school. Most of them will never start going to school, while those who do are unlikely to finish their studies. More than a third of children in the region who entered the education system in 2012 will leave before reaching the final year of primary school.

Despite the bleak forecast, Unesco points out that there are ways to solve the situation. Six government policies have helped countries such as Burundi, Nepal and Nicaragua to get more children into school.

For example, Burundi's decision to get rid of school fees in 2005 helped the number of children going to primary school rise from 54% to 94% in six years.

Source: Adapted from www.theguardian.com

Reflection: Look at the information you have written for Activity 3.23. Do you have mostly facts? Facts are important, as they can be used as evidence, but they will not help you remember what the text is about: the issues, perspectives, causes, consequences, solutions, etc. Go back to the text to see if you can write down five things (in more than five words) without including facts.

Discussion point

Share your information from Activity 3.23 with a partner. Consider both lists of information, discuss and choose the best five pieces to help you both remember the key points within the text.

ACTIVITY 3.24

Reflect on an experience you have had. Rather than describing this experience to someone, write a blog reflecting on the experience. The experience might have been something you tried for the first time, for example a long walk up a mountain, a camping experience or a field trip with school or friends. To reflect you need to include details to answer the following questions:

1 What happened?

2 What went well? Why?

3 What do I need to improve? Why?

4 What do I need to know?

5 What do I need to do now?

Compare your blog with the following blog entry:

Right near the end of the walk, I lost my balance and fell and sprained my ankle, as I wasn't looking where I was going. Until then, it had all been going well, especially as, when it rained, I had the right clothing with me so managed to keep dry. The climb to the top was hard and I was out of breath. I need to get fitter so that going up isn't so hard. I need to know how to make it easier to come down without putting too much strain on my knees. I will investigate long distance mountain-walking on the internet as there is bound to be some advice about what to do to make the way down easier.

Now try this strategy with a learning experience, either an individual piece of work you have done or a (mini) team project you took part in. You must answer all five questions when you write your blog, but as you can see from the example blog above, it does not have to be too long. Aim for between 100 and 150 words.

Reflection: Do you see the difference between what you have written and this blog in Activity 3.24? Does this blog answer the five questions asked? Does your blog?

ACTIVITY 3.25

Global perspective

How reliable do you think the following websites are in giving the 'global perspective' about education? You will need to explore the websites to answer this question for each of them and give reasons for your response. You can put these names into your search engine to find their websites.

'The United Nations'

'UNESCO'

ACTIVITY 3.26

Local perspective

1 How strong do you think the argument for this local perspective is?
2 What would make the argument stronger?

The number of children attending the village primary school fell and the local council felt that it would cost too much to keep it open so it was closed. School children had to go by bus to another school five miles away. The village school fell into decline. It was a pity because the school was at the heart of the community. Events used to take place there in the evenings and at weekends, and parents and teachers knew each other. Closing the school has meant that there is now more traffic on the roads as children are bussed to another school. They have to leave home earlier to get to school, and they get back home later, which affects their health. There is no time to play outside, and the laughter of children's voices is no longer heard in the village. As a result, houses are for sale for longer as families do not want to live in a village without a school.

The personal element of the Team Project

Once you have completed the Team Project, you write an individual Reflective Paper to reflect on:

1 the benefits and challenges of working as a team
2 the strengths and weaknesses of your own performance as a team member
3 your learning about different cultural perspectives
4 your overall personal learning from taking part in the Team Project.

You also evaluate:

5 the strengths and limitations of the outcome your team produces in achieving the aims of the project;
6 the strengths and limitations of your own work processes

Your Reflective Paper should also:

7 be well-structured, cohesive and comprehensive
8 present key personal research findings clearly
9 show connections between the team and personal elements
10 include citations and referencing as appropriate.

ACTIVITY 3.27

In this example of a completed section of a Reflective Paper, which of the above (**1–10**) have been included?

Reflective Paper

Our project aim was to raise awareness of the importance of education to reduce poverty in our local community. We wanted to make people within the community aware that the earnings a person gets increase by 10% for every year of schooling they get. This amounts to a 1% annual increase in Gross Domestic Product if good-quality education is offered to the entire population. So not only does education benefit the individual, it also benefits a nation. The outcome we made matched with the project aim in that we created a series of posters to illustrate the power of education in getting people out of poverty and the benefits they could get with an increased salary. We included the findings from our research, although because we only really interviewed people from international schools like ours, we couldn't show the range of cultural perspectives we had hoped for and should have done more secondary research so we could have shown different cultural perspectives better. The outcome that our group made was successful in achieving our aim as the people in the school noticed our posters and some adults commented on them at the open evening we had in school to showcase the work we had been doing for our Global Perspectives course. It was a pity we hadn't thought about asking for donations, which we could have then given to a local charity supporting education for all.

Establishing independent learning skills

This section uses the topic of **Poverty and Inequality** to develop independent learning skills further so that you feel that they are established. This topic is one of the eight global topics listed in the IGCSE and O Level Global Perspectives syllabus for the Team Project (Component 3). You will build on the skills you have acquired so far so that you start to feel more confident as an independent learner.

SKILLS LINKS

- Chapter 2: Critical thinking skills, 2.02 Evidence
- Chapter 2: Critical thinking skills, 2.03 Claims
- Chapter 3: Independent learning skills, 3.01 Memory
- Chapter 3: Independent learning skills, 3.02 Note-taking
- Chapter 3: Independent learning skills, 3.03 Reflection
- Chapter 3: Independent learning skills, 3.04 Evaluation
- Chapter 4: Collaboration skills, 4.01 Team work
- Chapter 5: Communication skills, 5.02 Writing

ACTIVITY 3.28

Find an image that makes you think about issues to do with poverty and inequality.

Create a mind map with 'poverty and inequality' in the centre and write down all the associations and connections you can think of. Use the image you have found to help.

Discussion point

Now you have associations and connections for the topic of **Poverty and Inequality** for Activity 3.28, discuss with a partner ideas for a Team Project. You have been given one idea. Try to suggest five further team project ideas.

1 Raising awareness about homelessness within a community

2 _____

3 _____

4 _____

5 _____

6 _____

ACTIVITY 3.29

Read the following text and write down three questions to help you understand and remember the key points. Make sure you are able to answer your questions, but, before revealing the answers, ask a partner to see if your questions elicit the answers you expect. If they do not elicit the answers you expected, amend them and ask your partner again.

Homelessness

People who are homeless are generally considered among the most vulnerable members of society – about 30% suffer from mental illness, about 20% are physically disabled, and a small number (approximately 3%) are HIV positive. However, rather than treating them as victims who need our support, many people are treating them as if they were criminals who need to be punished.

As well as a rise in the number of laws, the number of attacks on homeless people continues to increase. Treating homeless people like criminals is not going to resolve the problem of homelessness. It is expensive to arrest homeless people and put them in prison, and it can make the problem worse as homeless people go from the streets to prison and then back on the streets. Once someone has a criminal record, it is more difficult for them to get jobs or accommodation which could make them more independent.

If we are serious about ending homelessness, we need to look carefully at the causes of homelessness and the laws we already have, rather than spending money on creating new ones when budgets are already stretched. Punishing the homeless will do nothing to solve the causes of the problem.

Do some research about solutions to homelessness. Use the information you find and information from the text above to write a formal email to your local councillor about the issue of homelessness within your community and your suggestion for a course of action.

ACTIVITY 3.30

Causes and consequences of poverty

Copy and complete the example graphic organiser showing causes and consequences of poverty.

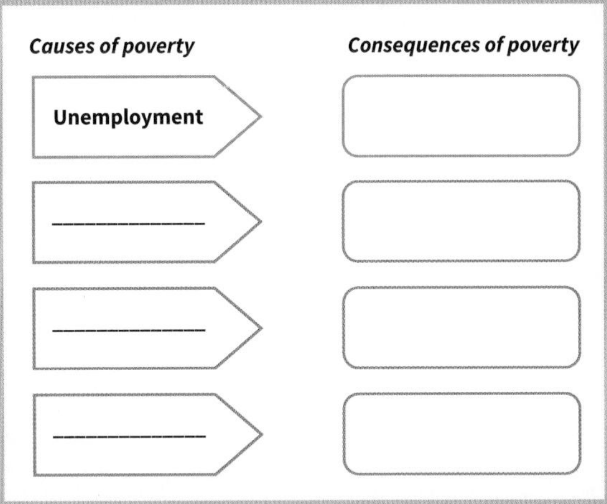

Figure 3.13 Causes and consequences of poverty

151

Discussion point

With a partner, see if you have the same consequences of poverty in your graphic organiser for Activity 3.30, and try to explain which one of these consequences you both think is the most significant and why.

ACTIVITY 3.31

Reflecting on global issues is an important part of IGCSE and O Level Global perspectives. Read the following text about poverty and answer the questions that follow.

Poverty and Inequality

Issues like illness, hunger and thirst are often both causes and consequences. The consequences of poverty are often related: one problem causes others. For example, lack of safe, clean water causes bad sanitation, which causes disease, and disease can result in inability to work, which leads to poverty, hunger, and so on.

Research has shown that people who have little money are more likely to commit property-related crimes. Social tensions exist when there is inequality in the amount of income people have. This is particularly the case when wealth is unequally distributed across a country and the rich get richer whilst the poor get poorer, and the rich are in the minority.

Poverty is an issue that can threaten the stability of a whole country. For example, in some countries there have been riots and uprisings in which people have protested about poverty. A lack of jobs and high levels of poverty amongst a significant number of people resulted in the demonstrations and unrest of the Arab Spring, for example, when the wealth of a nation had been retained by a few powerful people over many years. As a result, governments were overthrown as people turned to violence to voice their displeasure.

1 Reflect on what you have read by giving information in response to these four prompts:

   a Identify one important idea, piece of information or research finding that you learnt while doing this activity.

   b Ask yourself why you think this idea, piece of information or research finding is important.

   c Think about how what you have learnt connects with your own life.

   d Consider the questions you now want answers to and why these questions are important to you.

2 Record your thoughts in your blog.

3 Share your thoughts with a partner.

4 Add any further thoughts to your blog after discussion with your partner.

ACTIVITY 3.32

Claims

Choose <u>one</u> claim from the text about poverty and inequality in the previous activity.

Evaluate your chosen claim by answering the following questions:

1 What evidence is there to support your chosen claim?

2 Does the evidence convince you? Why/why not?

3 Do further research on the internet to find evidence to strengthen the claim and make a note of the relevant websites. Are these websites reliable? Why do you think this?

ACTIVITY 3.33

Here is a claim:

1 Do an internet search using your search engine to find the source of this claim.

2 Evaluate this claim as you did with your chosen claim in the previous activity.

3 Would you consider this a personal, local, national or global perspective? Why?

> In America we now have more income and wealth inequality than any other major country on Earth.

ACTIVITY 3.34

Read the short text below and answer the questions that follow.

From a . . . perspective

It is a fact that supermarkets are paying farmers in the area less money for their milk than it is costing them to produce. One supermarket has just agreed to pay a farmer near me about 25 euros per litre, but the milk costs 35 euros per litre to produce so it is not worth the effort. Those farmers that only have small dairy herds will be going out of business if the situation continues as it is. They are unlikely to find other work and so will soon fall into poverty. What they are being paid for their produce does not cover the cost of producing it. If they go out of business, everyone will suffer and what will happen to all the fields and the countryside?

1 Is the text written from a global, national or local perspective?

2 How strong do you think the evidence for this perspective is?

3 What do you think might make the perspective stronger?

ACTIVITY 3.35

Mini Team Project

Aim: To raise money for a local charity who give food and shelter to the homeless

Outcome: A poster campaign to persuade people of the importance of giving donations to charities who help provide food and shelter to homeless people

Read and compare examples A and B that follow, which might have come from two different Reflective Papers, and assess 'the strengths and weaknesses of own performance as a team member', according to the criteria in the table below. You should only tick one box for each example.

Level	Criteria	Example A	Example B
4	Clear and perceptive reflection on the strengths and weaknesses of own performance as a team member		
3	Clear reflection on the strengths and weaknesses of own performance as a team member		
2	Some reflection on the strengths and/or weaknesses of own performance as a team member		
1	Limited reflection on the strengths or weaknesses of own performance as a team member		

Example A – Reflection on own performance as a team member

I personally found this a very rewarding experience. My main contribution to the Team Project was creating the survey that we gave out to get responses to inform our poster outcome. I was also able to contribute in other ways like making the list of people who we wanted to view our poster campaign. I should have been able to work more quickly but I took my time. I felt that this might have been a weakness, but it didn't seem to have much effect on our progress.

Example B – Reflection on own performance as a team member

It is hard to write this part of the reflective paper, because of my personal experience. However, I will be realistic about the strength of my contribution. My contribution was the project itself. The other team members couldn't cope with the given tasks – one was silent and the other was absent. Therefore, I contributed by formulating and writing a plan with limited help from team members. I researched all the information needed for the production of the outcome, again with only a little help from one other team member. I contacted sources to show different cultural perspectives in the outcome and I wrote the Explanation. Finally, I produced most of the outcome. One of the posters was completed by another team member, but this wasn't very good and we didn't include it in our final submission. I feel that I have made far more contribution and effort to work in class and outside of class time to complete the project than anyone else in my team.

The weakness of my contribution was that I lacked the ability to lead and communicate with my team members. I feel that if I had tried harder to communicate with my team members about the problems they were facing completing the given tasks, I might not have had to do so much work myself at the end.

> **Reflection:** Just in case you need reassurance, example B might have been awarded a higher mark than example A in Activity 3.35. Can you see why? (It hasn't got anything to do with the length, although, if too short, work tends to be self-penalising in that you cannot include everything that is required.)

Discussion point

With a partner, discuss how you might strengthen example A in Activity 3.35.

Enhancing independent learning skills

This section uses the topic of **Trade and aid** to enhance your independent learning skills. This topic is one of the eight global topics listed in the IGCSE and O Level Global Perspectives syllabus for the Individual Report (Component 2). By working through the activities in this section, you will continue to build on the independent learning skills you have acquired so far.

SKILLS LINKS

- Chapter 1: Information skills, 1.02 Research
- Chapter 3: Independent learning skills, 3.01 Memory
- Chapter 3: Independent learning skills, 3.02 Note-taking
- Chapter 3: Independent learning skills, 3.03 Reflection skills
- Chapter 3: Independent learning skills, 3.04 Evaluation
- Chapter 5: Communication skills, 5.02 Writing

ACTIVITY 3.36

Look at the two images.

Figure 3.14 Money

Figure 3.15 Worker

Prepare answers to the following questions:

1 What do these two images have in common?
2 In what way(s) do you think they are contrasting?
3 What global issues do these images represent?
4 Put yourself in the images. Use your imagination. What can you see, hear, smell, taste and touch?

Using your answers to the questions, prepare one slide of a presentation to explain the issues to someone who is not doing IGCSE or O Level Global Perspectives. This could be a parent or a friend.

ACTIVITY 3.37

Here is an example of a text you might find whilst researching the term 'fairtrade' within the global topic of Trade and aid for your Individual Report.

1 Read the text and make notes of **five questions**, **five conclusions** and five pieces of supporting information in the suggested colours (red, blue and green).

Fairtrade

Fairtrade has been shown to increase standards of living and reduce risk and vulnerability for farmers and workers. The Fairtrade Minimum Price provides a safety net for farmers which can mean they are less vulnerable to price volatility. In turn, this can mean a better cash flow, greater access to credit and the ability to save more easily.

Food security is linked closely to economic growth, stable incomes and reduced risk and vulnerability. A better income means more money to buy food and the ability to invest in generating other food sources, such as growing new crops. This means farmers and workers can have more control over their lives when times are hard, worry less about how they will feed their families and be able to provide enough food for the people they care about, all year round. For example research in Colombia found an average 34 percent rise in income for Fairtrade banana farmers.

For workers, the Fairtrade Standards can improve job security through ensuring correct employment processes, contracts and leave entitlements. The combination of a more secure income and reduced vulnerability means farmers and workers are able to increase their assets and activities, such as paying school fees or boosting their savings, which raises their standards of living. While many still struggle with low incomes, the security that Fairtrade can offer means they are able to better plan and invest in their future. Fairtrade Premium investments can mean that farmers and workers benefit from services that they may otherwise have had to pay for, such as fertiliser and school fees. This frees up their finances for other things, and increases their security and resilience to unforeseen events. New research by the National Resources Institute at the University of Greenwich evaluated the impact of Fairtrade for coffee farmers and their organisations in Indonesia, Mexico, Peru and Tanzania. The study found that Fairtrade farmers often reported higher incomes than non-Fairtrade farmers. They were also becoming less vulnerable to shocks – for example price crashes – as a result of the Minimum Price and Premium.

Fairtrade believes the role of women in agriculture needs more visibility, recognition and value, and that gender equity is important to social sustainability. Currently, 350 000 women farmers and workers are part of Fairtrade, a quarter of the total.

Source: www.fairtrade.org.uk

---

2 Using the text and your own research, evaluate the issue of fairtrade from the perspective of one the following:

   a a farmer

   b a worker

   c a woman

   d a country/nation.

   When evaluating, remember to focus on the strengths, limitations and areas for improvement.

   You might need to do some further research. Why do you think this is?

3 How likely do you think it is that all trade will be fairtrade in the future? Don't forget to justify your response by giving reasons for your opinion.

Read the following advertisement.

Campaigners bake cakes to celebrate 20 years of the Fairtrade mark

Fairtrade campaigners from Wigtown organised a cake sale on September 18th 2014 to celebrate 20 years of the FAIRTRADE Mark in the UK.

In 1994, the FAIRTRADE Mark appeared on just three products: Green & Black's Maya Gold chocolate, Cafedirect medium roast coffee, and Clipper tea. Today, the FAIRTRADE Mark is the most widely-known ethical label in the world and UK shoppers can now choose from over 4500 Fairtrade products including tea, coffee, cocoa, chocolate, bananas, sugar, cotton, gold jewellery, cut flowers, wine and cosmetics.

Fairtrade benefits 1.4m farmers and workers in more than 70 developing countries, by ensuring they receive a fair, stable price for their produce, decent working conditions, and a Fairtrade Premium that can be invested in projects that will benefit their community, such as schools, hospitals, clean drinking water or climate adaptation programmes.

In 2013 alone, UK shoppers bought an estimated £1.78bn of Fairtrade products, which resulted in over £26m of Fairtrade Premiums being paid to producers. Throughout 2014, Fairtrade supporters around the UK including campaigners, schools, faith groups, universities and colleges, are celebrating 20 years of the FAIRTRADE Mark with a range of events and activities.

From small beginnings, the Fairtrade movement has gathered an enormous amount of support in the UK over the last 20 years as campaigners, businesses, the public and Fairtrade producers have worked together to spark a revolution and change the way that the nation shops. That should be celebrated, but it is only the beginning of the journey to make trade fair and sustainable for the farmers and workers in the developing world who grow our food. We all have the power to make trade fairer and we urge people to step up their support for Fairtrade, so that greater impact can be achieved over the next 20 years and beyond.

The Fairtrade Foundation will mark the 20th anniversary with a 'Fair Future' business conference in London in October. The event will bring together Fairtrade producers, businesses, NGOs, campaigners, academics and politicians to explore how the Fairtrade movement can build on the achievements of the last 20 years to create a fairer future and deliver lasting change for farmers, workers, their families and communities.

Find out more about the FAIRTRADE Mark and where to buy Fairtrade products at *www.fairtrade.org.uk*

Imagine you took part in this experience and reflect on it using the six steps.

1 Look back and describe what happened: the experience, idea or event.
(Keep this part short, and use the past tense.)

2 Think about how what you already know relates to the experience.
(Here, use the present tense.)

3 Consider how it went.
(Here you can include emotions/feelings.)

4 Identify the part(s) which you think you learnt the most from, why this was, and how you and others feel about it.
(Part of reflection is discussing your feelings/thoughts with others and looking at things from different perspectives.)

5 Explain how your analysis of the experience, idea or event might affect your future learning.
(This is explaining what you might need to do/learn to impact on your future learning, so will mostly use the future tense, i.e. you are predicting.)

6 Once you have discussed the experience and had further time to reflect on it, you can come back to your initial reflections, and add to them, creating further successful reflections.

Discussion point

Fairtrade is just one example of an issue within the global topic of **Trade and aid**. There are other issues. Discuss with a partner and give three more examples of issues to do with the global topic of Trade and aid.

ACTIVITY 3.39

Apply the Individual Report topic of **Trade and aid** to complete a KWL chart like the one below. Write down five pieces of information you already **Know** in answer to the following questions; list these in the **K** column.

Questions about trade and aid

1   How do countries trade with one another?
2   Why are some countries with plenty of natural resources poorer than some other countries?
3   Do richer countries have a responsibility to help poorer countries?
4   Which countries does my country trade with the most?
5   Why are some goods imported even though we produce similar goods at home?

Identify five pieces of information you **Want to know** about trade and aid and write them in the **W** column.

Save the KWL chart for use at the end of the activity.

KWL chart about trade and aid

	K	W	L
1			
2			
3			
4			
5			

Once you have completed the first two columns of your chart, you have an idea of what you need to find out, which is what you will record in the **Learnt** column.

Use the library and Internet resources to search for the information you need to add to the **Learnt** column. Once you have the necessary information, add this in note form to the **L** column.

Reflection: Think about the answers you might give to the following questions.

- What should I consider when I make decisions about whose products to buy?
- What effect does this have on the lives of others around the world?
- Are there some companies I should specially support, or boycott?

ACTIVITY 3.40

Use the information from this section to write down two questions that might be suitable for an Individual Report within the global topic of **Trade and aid**.

Chapter 4
Collaboration skills

Learning objectives

By the end of this chapter, you should be able to:

- understand the benefits of teamwork
- identify the roles and characteristics needed for effective teamwork according to different scenarios
- be able to work more effectively in a team
- be able to make decisions more easily
- be able to express yourself creatively.

Introduction

As you found in Chapter 3, IGCSE and O Level Global Perspectives develops your independent learning skills. It also enables you to work with others in collaboration. You can do this in class in pairs and in small groups and teams. The importance placed on teamwork is exemplified by the requirement to complete a Team Project as part of the course, as mentioned in the introduction to this book. Your teacher assesses this Team Project. You will be able to transfer the collaboration skills you develop to other subject areas. They will also be useful for future learning and when you are employed. In fact, many employers look for the ability to be able to work in teams as one of their recruitment criteria.

This chapter focuses on developing the following collaboration skills:

4.01 Teamwork   **4.02** Decision-making   **4.03** Creativity

4.01 Teamwork

SKILLS LINKS

- Chapter 1: Information skills, 1.02 Research
- Chapter 1: Information skills, 1.05 Planning
- Chapter 5: Communication skills, 5.03 Listening
- Chapter 5: Communication skills, 5.04 Speaking

Being able to work as a team member is important in sport, at school and in the workplace. Those who cannot work in teams often find it difficult to find and keep work.

Reflection: Think about something done as a team and why this works better done by a team than done by an individual.

You probably thought about a sport like football or rugby. The main reason why these are team sports is that each individual brings something to the team to enable the team as a whole to be successful in its aim – winning the game or match.

Figure 4.01 Individuals contribute to team success in sports like rugby

Discussion point

Discuss with a partner why you think teamwork is important. Does your partner share your viewpoint?

You might have discussed that teamwork teaches you to work together towards a common **aim** or **goal**. Others can often think of things you might have forgotten or missed. It is generally more motivating and interesting to work with others as they bring different perspectives and ideas to the task. You do not have to do everything on your own so you can achieve more, faster. Skills such as communication, **compromise** and **collective effort** are required for effective teamwork.

> **KEY TERMS**
>
> **Aim/goal:** something you want to achieve.
>
> **Compromise:** agreeing to a solution regardless of differing perspectives.
>
> **Collective effort:** activities by a group of people working together to achieve a common purpose.

Team roles

According to Dr Meredith Belbin, a well-known researcher in the field of teamwork, there are different **team roles** for effective teamwork.

> **KEY TERM**
>
> **Team role:** a tendency to behave, contribute and interrelate with others in a particular way (as defined by Dr Meredith Belbin).

These can be categorised under three headings as follows:

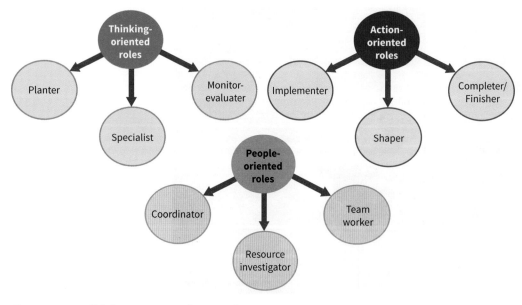

Figure 4.02 Belbin's categories of team roles

> **TIP**
>
> Find out more about team roles at: *http://www.belbin.com/*.
>
> Which of the team roles do you think you play in teamwork?

ACTIVITY 4.01

You are putting together a team of people for a difficult challenge that needs the best team possible.

Consider the following list of team member characteristics and choose a team of five from the list.

Team member characteristics

1   Likes to be in charge and can work with others.
2   Has some good ideas and likes to share them.
3   Likes to praise others but does not do much.
4   Likes to lead, but has difficulty following instructions.
5   Likes to talk.
6   Likes to do things and is creative.
7   Likes to listen but not good at sharing ideas.
8   Good at finishing a job; but not so good at starting one.
9   Gets things done but is quite argumentative.
10 Full of inspiring ideas, but not very realistic.
11 Very practical; good at hands on jobs.
12 Complains all the time about having to contribute.
13 Disappears when difficulties arise.
14 Is good at listening and likes to share ideas.
15 Follows instructions but does not like to be in charge.

Once you have five team members, consider the following scenario and decide whether you are going to leave your team as it is or change some of the members. You need to include yourself in the five (and decide which characteristics you bring to the team) so can choose another four members for your team.

Scenario

Imagine you are in charge of a search and rescue team which has arrived at a campsite in the mountains where a young child has gone missing. It is getting dark, and a search is being organised to find the child before nightfall. All the equipment is ready, but the track leading away from the campsite is narrow and the terrain is rough and uneven. Only a small group of five people will be able to set off in the initial search party. The rest will stay behind and join in the search in the morning if the child has not been found.

Who do you take with you?

Discussion point

Ask others in your class about the team members they have chosen in Activity 4.01 and why they have chosen them. See if you can come up with a rank order of the team member characteristics chosen by the class.

Reflection: Do you think that your choice of team member characteristics will probably change according to the task that needs doing? Why do you think this?

ACTIVITY 4.02

Read the following statements about effective **collaboration** and put them in order of importance (according to you), starting with the most important.

1 Effective collaboration relies on teamwork and the team must understand the goals and be equally committed to reaching them.

2 The team needs to be clear about the goals, accountability for their role and any outcomes.

3 Team members must trust each other and each team member should appreciate others' perspectives.

4 Each team member should feel able to express their thoughts, opinions, and potential solutions to problems and feel that they are being listened to.

5 Each team member should feel that they belong to the team. They are therefore committed to the team's decisions and actions.

6 Team members are always viewed as individuals with their own experiences, perspectives, knowledge, and opinions. After all, the purpose for forming a team is to take advantage of the differences.

7 The team is continuously trying to improve its processes, practices, and the interaction between team members.

8 The team agrees about how to resolve teamwork problems and all members of the teamwork towards mutual resolution of an issue or problem.

9 Members of the team make decisions together and have the support and commitment of the team to carry out the decisions made.

KEY TERM

Collaboration: working with someone to produce something.

Discussion point

Share your order of importance with a partner for Activity 4.02. Did they choose the same order as you? Discuss any differences and agree a final order that you are both happy with. You may need to compromise a little.

Team Project

As stated in the introduction to this book, in the Team Project for IGCSE and O Level Global Perspectives, you are required to work in a team to devise and develop a collaborative project into an aspect of one global topic from a choice of eight.

As a team, you produce one **Outcome** (e.g. a series of posters or a video-clip) and one **Explanation** (200–300 words) as a collaboration. You are assessed by your teacher on your ability to work in a team. You need to show that, in attempting to complete the project, you were an active and committed team member and there was evidence of effective teamwork throughout the process.

KEY TERMS

Outcome: the product of research aimed at achieving something.

Explanation: the project aim, a brief description of the project, and an explanation of how the team's exploration of different cultural perspectives has informed or supports the Outcome.

You might like to keep your own log of your contributions to the Team Project.

Team Project log

	Areas for comment/recording contributions	Comments
Week Date:	1 Support for team members 2 Completion of allocated tasks 3 Active contribution/participation 4 Commitment to Team Project	Helped produce a plan of action Helped to organise tasks for Weeks 1 and 2 Shared contacts for gathering different cultural perspectives
Week 1 Date:		
Week 2 Date:		
Week 3 Date:		
Week 4 Date:		
Week 5 Date:		
Week 6 Date:		

In the Personal Element of the Team Project; the Reflective Paper, you are also expected to reflect on the benefits and challenges of working as a team.

ACTIVITY 4.03

Read and compare Examples A and B below, from two different exemplar Reflective Papers, and assess 'the benefits and challenges of working as a team', according to the following criteria:

Level	Criteria	Example A	Example B
4	Clear and perceptive reflection on the challenges and benefits of working as a team		
3	Clear reflection on the challenges and benefits of working as a team		
2	Some reflection on the challenges or benefits of working as a team		
1	Limited reflection on the challenges or benefits of working as a team		

Example A – Reflection on benefits and challenges of working as a team

In my experience to date, it is generally true that more hands make lighter work and I can see that this was the case in this project as there were many benefits of working as a team, including being able to include different cultural perspectives on the issue, which we all contributed to. It benefited our work by listening to each other's perspectives, and sharing our ideas and research findings.

However, the fact that I managed to do more tasks than others in the team became a weakness. Instead of taking full control as a group leader, I trusted my group completely and therefore let them procrastinate for a long time before anything was done. In the end, these jobs were sadly left half complete or untouched. This was definitely a challenge of working in a team. I should have been very clear and strict as a leader, instead of being afraid to cause an argument.

Example B – Reflection on benefits and challenges of working as a team

Everyone in our group did a great job except for me. I was never available for visits because I was busy with something else outside of school or my parents took us on holiday. I wasn't able to give my own personal insight or help to my teammates when they asked because a lot of the time I didn't actually know what was going on. I have learnt that I need to manage my time better so I can understand what is happening and how to help.

If this whole thing was an individual piece, I certainly would have failed, but because we were a team, they were always there to help me and that is a definite advantage of working as a team. The time I have spent on this project and the information I have learnt has been very interesting and fun.

164

Even if you were unsure which level to award (1–4) for each example, you should have been able to spot the example that did a better job of reflecting on the challenges and benefits of working as a team according to the assessment criteria.

Reflection: Just in case you need reassurance, Example A in Activity 4.03 might have been awarded a higher mark than Example B. Can you see why?

Discussion point

Using what you now know about effective teamwork, with a partner, discuss what you could include to strengthen Example B in Activity 4.03.

Summary

- Collaboration enables teamwork as each team member works together towards a common aim/goal.

- Teams are made up of individuals who bring different characteristics and strengths to teamwork.

- Each team member should feel able to express their thoughts, opinions and potential solutions to problems and feel that they are being listened to.

- A Team Project log is a useful way of keeping track of contributions to teamwork.

- The Team Project for IGCSE and O Level Global Perspectives rewards active and committed team members and effective teamwork.

4.02 Decision-making

 **SKILLS LINKS**

- Chapter 1: Information skills, 1.01 Perspectives
- Chapter 1: Information skills, 1.05 Planning
- Chapter 3: Independent learning skills, 3.03 Reflection
- Chapter 3: Independent learning skills, 3.04 Evaluation
- Chapter 4: Collaboration skills, 4.01 Teamwork
- Chapter 5: Communication skills, 5.03 Listening
- Chapter 5: Communication skills, 5.04 Speaking

165

We all make decisions every day: what to wear, where to go, what to eat. Sometimes we make decisions that result in consequences we did not want or were not prepared for.

Reflection: Think about all the decisions you have made so far today. How many have you made? Were they easy or difficult decisions to make? Why/why not?

Decision-making guidance

Some decisions are easy to make without needing much thought. Others require more consideration. Some decisions we can and do make on our own and there are others that we make collaboratively. In this section, you will focus on the skill of decision-making and consider decision-making as part of collaboration. Figure 4.03 gives eight questions to consider in order to make a decision.

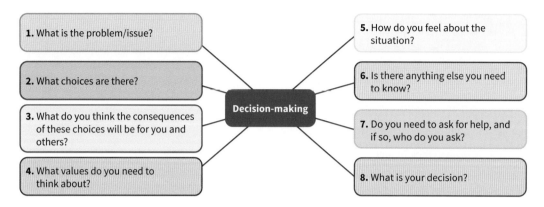

Figure 4.03 Decision-making questions

Once the decision has been made, you can then evaluate it by responding to the question:

- Do you think you made the right decision? Why/why not?

You might need to refer back to Section 3.04 on evaluation to remind yourself how to evaluate.

Discussion point

Imagine you are walking along the street and a homeless person asks you for money. Discuss with a partner your answers to the eight questions in Figure 4.03 for this situation. Can you reach a decision that you both agree on? Why/why not?

Figure 4.04 What would you do if a homeless person asked you for money?

Reflection: Think about a time when you think you might have made the wrong decision. Work through the eight decision-making questions in Figure 4.03 and reflect on why this decision might have been wrong.

Often there is no one right choice and you might think that very few decisions are totally wrong. Even if you feel you made the wrong decision at the time, you might be able to make up for it if a similar situation arises again. In the case of the homeless person in the scenario above, if you decided against giving money originally, you might have gone back and given them some money/food or you might give money/food to the next homeless person you see.

TIP

Decision-making is not a one-off event; we are always re-evaluating and making new decisions when we find out something new.

ACTIVITY 4.04

1 For each of the following issues, think about your decision, responding to the eight questions in Figure 4.03.

   a Whether to buy a Fairtrade bar of chocolate rather than what you normally buy even though the Fairtrade chocolate is a little more expensive.

   b Whether to travel abroad by plane on holiday when there are plenty of beautiful holiday locations in your own country.

2 For one of the following global topics, describe an issue on which you would be required to make a decision:

- **Water, food and agriculture**
- **Tradition, culture and identity**

Discussion point

Share your ideas from Activity 4.04 with a partner. Can you agree on the decisions you have made for issues **1a** and **1b** and for your own issue?

Reflection: Based on the discussion with your partner for Activity 4.04, did you think about changing your decisions or not? Give reasons for your answer.

Making decisions collaboratively

When working as a team, you discuss issues and make decisions collaboratively. This is teamwork.

Deciding on issues

One way of deciding which issue you might want to focus on for your Team Project is for each member of the team to choose one photo representing the topic. For example, for the global topic **Poverty and Inequality**, you could search on the internet using the key word 'poverty' and selecting 'images', or you could choose an image from a newspaper or magazine. You could do this at home and bring your image to the next lesson. In your team, you can place all your photos on the desk and answer the following questions about each photo.

1 What is the issue?

2 Who is it an issue for?

3   What is the message of the photo?

4   How many people might be affected by the issue and who are they? (Both in the photo and possibly not in the photo.)

5   What can be done to improve the issue?

Each member of the team chooses the photo/issue they find the most interesting and gives reasons for their choice. Others listen to the reasons and the team chooses one of the photos/issues for further investigation.

TIP

Don't forget that your Team Project should focus on an issue to do with one of the eight global topics for the Team Project and allow you to explore and communicate different cultural perspectives.

Team Projects

For the IGCSE and O Level Global Perspectives Team Project, which is assessed by your teacher, you have a choice of eight global topics to choose from. Issues for investigation can come from any of these global topics.

ACTIVITY 4.05

Individually, answer these questions for the photo in Figure 4.05:

1   What is the issue?

2   Who is it an issue for?

3   What is the message of the photo?

4   How many people might be affected by the issue and who are they? (Both in the photo and possibly not in the photo.)

5   What can be done to improve the issue?

Figure 4.05   Living in the Shebo village

Discussion point

Discuss your answers to Activity 4.05 with a partner.

Deciding on roles and responsibilities for Team Projects and group activities

When working as a team, you need to decide on the aim of your project, what information you need to know and therefore find out, which resources you are going to use (websites, books, actual people, etc.), what your outcome will be, and who is going to do what, when and why. Having a plan will help with this (see Chapter 1: Information skills, 1.05 Planning)

Having already been briefly introduced to Belbin's team roles in Section 4.01, you will now focus on other team roles and their responsibilities in order to form a team of four. You may decide to use Belbin's roles or you may decide to use the roles suggested below – the decision is up to you and your team mates.

Whichever role you take on will very much depend on your **work style.** According to industrial psychologist, David Merrill, work styles can be divided into four categories: **drivers**, **expressives**, **amiables** and **analyticals**. However, there is nothing to stop you adopting different roles for different Team Projects or group activities.

> **KEY TERMS**
>
> **Work style:** how someone chooses to approach a task.
>
> **Drivers:** people who take charge and lead.
>
> **Expressives:** people who are willing to share ideas, opinion and feelings.
>
> **Amiables:** people who are organised and like to perform work for the team.
>
> **Analyticals:** people who assess and evaluate work done to ensure deadlines are met and the project is completed well.

A. The leader

I am the leader. I facilitate the success of the team by assessing progress toward the team's aim and keeping the team on task and on track. I am responsible for getting all team members to participate and for making sure that all team members understand what needs to be done for the project. I also encourage new ideas and help the team work in new directions.

B. The recorder

I collect and share the information discussed during teamwork, and I create a written record of work being done, write out key ideas and keep copies of each member's work. I also prepare the materials for the final submission of the project.

C. The encourager

I encourage other team members by listening carefully, sharing ideas, making connections and expressing feelings. I also find the person who will help answer a question or resources that my team members need to complete work for the project.

D. The checker

I make sure that each team member understands what is being said, what work needs to be completed, and what the group has determined to be the project aim and outcome. I also make sure that the team is on track to meet deadlines and complete the project on time.

Figure 4.06 Team roles

ACTIVITY 4.06

Match the most suitable role (A–D) in Figure 4.06 with the appropriate work style. There are clues in the descriptions.

1 Amiable =   **3** Analytical =

2 Driver =   **4** Expressive =

Discussion point

Decide which role best suits your work style. Find three people in your class with the work styles suited to the other roles so that you can make up an effective team.

TIP

Remember that this course is not about learning and being able to regurgitate facts and information; it is about developing skills. So you don't need to be able to remember what the checker or the encourager do, but might find it interesting to read about certain roles and their typical responsibilities. Some team members might not fit easily into one category and might have more than one work style, which is fine. The main thing is to try to put together a team that has a range of different skills and work styles.

Deciding on a project aim

Project aims can vary from raising public awareness about an issue to doing or producing something to help resolve the issue.

ACTIVITY 4.07

With your team, consider a project aim for the issue of water shortages in a community.

Discussion point

Discuss your aim with a partner for Activity 4.07. Do they think it is a suitable aim for the issue? Can you think of a suitable Outcome together?

Deciding on an Outcome

The Outcome you choose should be suitable for the project aim. It should allow you to communicate your research into different cultural perspectives. Suggestions for your Outcome include:

- a poster, or series of posters
- an information leaflet or brochure
- a video-clip
- a series of photos, for example showing a fundraising event that you organised and took part in
- a song, which you perform live or produce as a video or audio-clip

- a poem, which you perform live or produce as a video or audio-clip
- a web page
- lessons you plan and teach, perhaps to a younger audience and in another school
- cartoons with captions
- a model or design for a solution.

The production of the Outcome is a chance for your team to show creativity (see Section 4.03).

Figure 4.07 There are many creative possibilities for your Outcome

> **!**
>
> **TIP**
> Writing an essay is not a suitable Outcome for a Team Project. The Outcome must be practical.

ACTIVITY 4.08

Decide on one suitable exemplar Outcome (either from the list above or an alternative) for each of these example project aims:

- To promote the importance of a healthy lifestyle, taking cultural norms into account (topic: **Disease and health**)
- To resolve the issue of a lack of water within a community (topic: **Water, food and agriculture**)
- To encourage the keeping of traditions within a local neighbourhood (topic: **Tradition, culture and identity**)
- To help support a charity providing food and shelter for the homeless within a community and taking cultural norms into account (topic: **Poverty and Inequality**).

171

How to collect information

Once you have decided on your team and have a plan of action, you need to decide where you are going to get the information you need to produce your Outcome and Explanation.

As discussed in Chapter 1 on Perspectives, you want to be able to include different cultural perspectives in your outcome and explanation, so either you can use contacts you have in other schools and collaborate via social media or you might be able to talk with people from different cultures in person depending on your location and your project aim. You might also use secondary research methods such as books about different cultures or websites giving views on the issue from different cultures.

Discussion point

Discuss with your team to decide where you are going to get information from different cultural perspectives from.

Summary

- Decision-making is an important life-long skill.
- Collaboration helps with decision-making.
- You will need to make decisions when embarking on group activities and Team Projects.
- Teams work better with a range of work styles and characteristics.
- It is always possible to change a decision.
- Planning is important for making decisions.

4.03 Creativity

SKILLS LINKS

- Chapter 1: Information skills, 1.05 Planning
- Chapter 2: Critical thinking skills, 2.02 Evidence
- Chapter 2: Critical thinking skills, 2.05 Bias and vested interest
- Chapter 2: Critical thinking skills, 2.06 Statements of argument
- Chapter 3: Independent learning skills, 3.03 Reflection
- Chapter 5: Communication skills, 5.03 Listening
- Chapter 5: Communication skills, 5.04 Speaking

Creativity is a natural human activity. We all have the ability to be creative. You might think that creativity comes more naturally to some people than to others. This might be true, but we all have the potential to be creative and can develop the skill of being more creative in how we think about and do things.

Edward de Bono is well known as an expert in the field of creativity. He was the first person to suggest that the human brain is a self-organising system. As a result of his study, he developed his thinking tools and creativity methods. These methods have helped many people and companies change how they think about things to come up with more creative solutions. He said:

'Creative thinking is not a talent, it is a skill that can be learnt. It empowers people by adding strength to their natural abilities which improves teamwork, productivity and where appropriate profits.'

Edward de Bono

TIP

Find out more about Edward de Bono by using your search engine and what you now know about how to do research.

KEY TERMS

Creativity: the ability to generate something new from already existing knowledge and ideas.
Concept: a difficult idea.

ACTIVITY 4.09

Try explaining a **concept** to someone who does not yet understand what it is.

Choose from these concepts: bias, value-judgement, vested interest or evaluation.

Observe how creative you are being in explaining your chosen concept so that someone else understands it.

Reflection: Consider the following questions:

What do you think being creative means?

What do you think being creative in IGCSE and O Level Global Perspectives means?

If you consider what you have to do for your Individual Report, you might have identified that proposing courses of action asks you to be creative. For the Team Project, your opportunity for being creative arises from your team's production of an Outcome that meets your project aim.

Thinking creatively

When Walt Disney created Disneyland, his friends and colleagues noticed that he went through different phases of thinking:

1   A *daydreaming or dreamer phase* to imagine his so-called 'grand vision'. A typical question that might have sprung to mind would be: 'What if I could build a magical city, like one out of a fairy tale, where people could come from all over the world to meet and talk to characters from films and have the best time of their life?'

2   The *realist phase* is the doing part, when the planning happens, keeping the overall goal in mind and considering how the project can be achieved.

3   Once the plan to achieve the goal has been created, the *critical review phase* looks over the plan to consider what changes are needed to make it the best method to achieve the goal.

This way of approaching problems and achieving goals by thinking, doing and reviewing has become known as the 'Disney Strategy' or the 'Disney Method'.

ACTIVITY 4.10

Do some research about Walt Disney and the Disney Strategy/Method.

Find one interesting fact to tell a partner that you think that they don't already know.

Don't forget to check your fact by using more than one reliable source of information.

Tell your partner your fact. Did they already know it?

ACTIVITY 4.11

Imagine you are planning a holiday. Use the Disney Strategy:

1   Envisage where you would like to go and what you would like to do.
2   Once you have this 'bigger picture', plan the holiday.

Next . . .

3   Review your plan. Aim to make it more cost-effective, time-effective and accessible for a group of your friends.

Discussion point

Share your thoughts with one or more of the friends that you have planned the holiday in Activity 4.11 for. Gain their feedback. Do they like your ideas? Why/why not? Do you need to go through the review stage again?

Reflection: Did using the Disney Strategy help you to think more creatively?

TIP

Goals are generally fixed. It is how we get there that might change. Consider what you might do if the hotel you wanted to stay in was fully booked at the time you wanted to go. It depends on the overall goal of the holiday. If the goal was to stay in that particular hotel, then you would change the time you went. If the goal was to go water-skiing, then you could stay in a different hotel.

ACTIVITY 4.12

Read the text below, then answer the following questions:

1 What do you consider to be the issue/problem that Allan is trying to help resolve?

2 What is Allan's overall goal?

3 Do you think Allan is achieving his goal?

4 Do you think Allan followed the steps outlined in the Disney Strategy to achieve his goal? Why/why not?

5 Do you think this course of action (handing out sandwiches) is an appropriate one to help solve the identified issue?

6 Could Allan's goal be achieved without collaboration? Explain your answer.

MINNEAPOLIS MAN HANDED OUT 520 000 SANDWICHES TO HOMELESS IN 1 YEAR. THAT'S MINNESOTA NICE

This man has dedicated his life to putting the needs of others before his own – regardless of what he's dealing with.

Allan Law, a former teacher in Minneapolis, spends his days in retirement helping those in need. For the past 14 years, Law has tirelessly delivered food and other supplies to people on the street during the late-night hours in which shelters and support centers are no longer open, according to NationSwell. Though he currently has arthritis and battled prostate cancer last year, the retired teacher has stayed committed to his work, and hasn't let his medical issues stop him.

It's this devotion that is the subject of a documentary, 'The Starfish Throwers,' which follows his journey, and the lives of two others whose missions are also to fight hunger.

'People say, "You're crazy," and I say, 'No. If I was homeless, or if I had a couple little kids that needed food or something, I would appreciate someone coming, giving a helping hand," he told Fox9.

During the day, Law collects sandwiches made by volunteers and donations from various groups through his organization, Minneapolis Recreation Development, Inc, according to the charity's website. Starting at 9 p.m., he begins his trek to deliver food in a van with the words, 'Love One Another' splashed on the side, traveling down the streets of inner city Minneapolis, ending his shift at 10 a.m.

Last year, Law says he delivered about 520 000 sandwiches, NationSwell reported. The retired teacher was unwilling to miss a day of work, even when he underwent prostate surgery, according to Edina Magazine. While in recovery, Law sneaked out, donning his nightgown, slippers and a turtleneck, determined to carry on helping the homeless.

The job is difficult and physically taxing for Law as he sleeps about two hours a day in his car, though he says what he does is a necessity. 'Am I glad I'm working 18 hours a day? No. But when you see a need you do it,' he told Edina Magazine.

He maintains that his work is more than making sure people don't go hungry.

'My commitment is not to feed people,' Law told the magazine. 'It's to change lives.'

Source: Huffington Post

TIP

See Allan Law in action by searching for 'Allan Law feeds the homeless'.

Discussion point

Discuss your answers to the questions about Allan Law's goal with a partner.

Courses of action

In Activity 4.12, clearly Allan needed the help of others in order to achieve his goal, but the original idea for the course of action he wanted to take, and took, was his own after researching the issue. The issue is a national as well as a global one, and Allan wanted to do something locally. Another course of action might have been to give food to a food bank and encourage friends to do so or to create a series of posters that highlight the need for people to donate food to food banks or soup kitchens. He might also have become a volunteer at the local food bank or with other community groups who help individuals and families living in poverty. Talking with grocery stores and restaurants in the area to encourage them to consider donating to food banks is another suitable course of action. All these are creative courses of action for the issue of feeding the homeless or poor within a community.

ACTIVITY 4.13

Consider the Individual Report topic **Digital world**. Some elderly people within your community find it a challenge to use a computer and have never used the internet, although it might help them in all sorts of ways. Propose one course of action to help encourage use of the internet amongst the elderly within your community. Collect ideas from the whole class and decide which is the most cost- and time-effective.

TIP

Courses of action can be short or long term. Courses of action for issues in an Individual Report should be global, national, local and personal.

For your Individual Report, you are not asked to solve world problems! Your global or national course of action might be an extension of an action that is already happening or that you would like to see happen as a result of what you have found out. Your personal course of action will stem from your research, as you will have discovered things that you had not previously known or considered. What you discover might also change your personal perspective, which ties in with any action you might take.

Some people find developing their creativity skills easier by using a creativity model such as the Osborne–Parnes model, which is often used in education and business. This model has six steps, which you could try to use both when completing your Individual Report and collaborating on your Team Project.

The Osborne–Parnes model

Step	Name	Action
1	Objective finding	Identify the objective, aim or goal
2	Fact finding	Gather relevant information
3	Problem finding	Clarify the issue or problem that needs resolving
4	Idea finding	Generate idea(s) for achieving the goal
5	Solution finding	Evaluate and improve idea(s)
6	Acceptance finding	Create a plan or course of action to implement idea(s) to achieve the aim or goal

Let us apply this model to a topic from your Global Perspectives course that you might consider for a Team Project: **Tradition, culture and identity**.

Imagine that you discover that a group of refugees have arrived in your community. Having been there a few days, they look unhappy. You think that they would be happier if they belonged more to the community.

You apply the Osborne–Parnes model to create a plan to enable them to belong more to the community. Here is how you might apply the six steps to this situation.

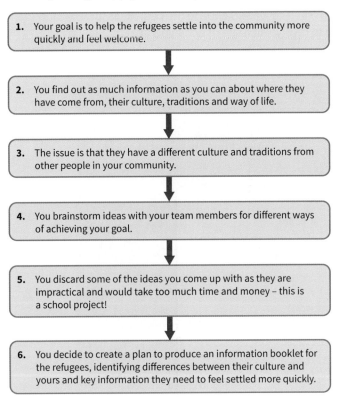

1. Your goal is to help the refugees settle into the community more quickly and feel welcome.

2. You find out as much information as you can about where they have come from, their culture, traditions and way of life.

3. The issue is that they have a different culture and traditions from other people in your community.

4. You brainstorm ideas with your team members for different ways of achieving your goal.

5. You discard some of the ideas you come up with as they are impractical and would take too much time and money – this is a school project!

6. You decide to create a plan to produce an information booklet for the refugees, identifying differences between their culture and yours and key information they need to feel settled more quickly.

Figure 4.08 Applying the six steps of the Osborne–Parnes model to a Team Project

Reflection: Is the Osborne–Parnes model a useful way of identifying a goal and creating a plan to achieve that goal?

ACTIVITY 4.14

Choose one of the eight topics for the Team Project and use the Osborne–Parnes model to identify a goal. You can do this individually to start with and then share your ideas with a partner who has perhaps chosen the same topic as you have.

TIP

Agree at the start of any teamwork or collaborative project not to discard any ideas and treat all ideas as worthwhile. You can start to look more closely at ideas, and discard some of them, later in the process of working together once you are clear about what you are trying to achieve.

Being creative collaboratively

When working in a team you can share ideas with each other and choose the best ideas for the goal, outcome, objective or course of action to resolve an issue or achieve a goal.

ACTIVITY 4.15

Read the following idea for a Team Project and answer the questions that follow.

Topic area: Poverty and Inequality

Aim: To encourage **empathy** for the difficulties of people suffering from poverty or inequality

Outcome: A poem

> Poverty and Inequality – a poem
> From Africa to India and within our own country
> Let us not allow people to go hungry
> Take action, however small
> To ensure equality for all
> Give generously to those in need
> Help rid the world of greed
> Equality for everyone is the ideal
> Daily for all to have at least one hot meal
> Trapped in poverty, poverty stricken
> Helping the poor must be our mission

1 Do you think the outcome of a poem suits the aim in this activity?
2 Do you think different cultural perspectives are communicated in the outcome?
3 How might you strengthen the outcome?

KEY TERM

Empathy: compassion and understanding for the situation of others who are perhaps less fortunate than you are.

Discussion point

Discuss your answers to Activity 4.15 with a partner. Does your partner agree with you?

Reflection: What other outcomes might suit the project aim in Activity 4.15?

Summary

- Everyone has the ability to be creative.
- Creativity can be developed.
- Collaboration helps with creativity.
- You will need to think creatively about courses of action for your Individual Report and an outcome for your Team Project.
- No idea should be thrown out at the start of a creative project.
- Ensure that your Team Project outcome is suitable for achieving your project aim.

Summary questions for Chapter 4

4.01 Teamwork

1 Identify one of Belbin's team roles.

2 Explain why you think teamwork is important.

4.02 Decision-making

3 Identify one work style that can benefit teamwork.

4 Explain the importance of collaboration when making decisions.

4.03 Creativity

5 Identify one suitable creative outcome for raising awareness of an issue.

6 Which of these outcomes is more realistic for achieving the project aim of finding out how different people keep fit and healthy and encouraging others to do so too?

   a To go on a field trip to see how people keep fit and healthy in a different country from your own.

or

   b To interview different people in the street about what they do to keep fit and healthy.

   Explain your answer.

Practising collaboration skills

So far in this chapter, you have focused on skills needed to make collaboration more effective. Teamwork, decision-making and creativity are all skills that benefit from collaboration. The next section of the chapter is divided into three: developing collaboration skills, establishing collaboration skills and enhancing collaboration skills. Each section is designed to build on the previous section. You can either work through each section in turn or choose the section that you feel is at the most appropriate level for you. You should see a progression in difficulty through the three sections. Each section uses one of the global topics for the Team Project to practise collaboration skills.

Developing collaboration skills

This section uses the global topic of **Water, food and agriculture**, which is one of the eight global topics listed in the IGCSE and O Level Global Perspectives syllabus for the Team Project (Component 3), to develop collaboration skills.

SKILLS LINKS

- Chapter 4: Collaboration skills, 4.01 Teamwork
- Chapter 4: Collaboration skills, 4.02 Decision-making
- Chapter 4: Collaboration skills, 4.03 Creativity

ACTIVITY 4.16

Look at the image in Figure 4.09 and answer the following questions:

1 What is the issue?

2 Who is it an issue for?

3 What is the message of the photo?

4 How many people might be affected by the issue and who are they? (Both in the photo and possibly not in the photo.)

5 What can be done to improve the issue?

Figure 4.09 Water

ACTIVITY 4.17

Look at the image in Figure 4.10 and answer the following questions:

1 What is the issue?
2 Who is it an issue for?
3 What is the message of the photo?
4 How many people might be affected by the issue and who are they? (Both in the photo and possibly not in the photo.)
5 What can be done to improve the issue?

Figure 4.10 Agriculture

ACTIVITY 4.18

1 Put the research terms 'water, food and agriculture' into your search engine and click on 'images' to choose an image that you think represents an interesting issue. Give the image to your partner to answer the five questions listed in Activity 4.17.
   Your partner will choose a different picture for you to answer the questions.
2 Choose one of the two images that you or your partner have found.
3 Identify an aim to try to 'improve the issue'.
4 Plan how you might achieve your aim.
5 Look at your plan and review it to make it the best plan you can to achieve your aim. Remember that, for the Team Project, you need to create an Outcome and write an Explanation to attempt to achieve your project aim.

ACTIVITY 4.19

1 Consider the following aim for a Team Project within the **Water, food and agriculture** topic:

   Project aim: To persuade young people of the importance of a varied diet by trying foods from different cultures.

2 Look at the Outcome and decide with a partner whether you think the Outcome meets the Project aim.

   Outcome: Poster about healthy eating

Figure 4.11 Healthy eating poster

Reflection: According to the descriptors in the table below (which has been written by the author), which level would you give the Outcome in Activity 4.19 at the moment?

How might you change the Outcome to reach the next level?

Level	Descriptors
	To meet the aim of the project:
4	Different cultural perspectives are clearly communicated in the Outcome and in the Explanation.
3	Different cultural perspectives are communicated in the Outcome and in the Explanation.
2	There is some evidence of different cultural perspectives in the Outcome or in the Explanation.
1	There is little evidence of different cultural perspectives in the Outcome or in the Explanation.
0	Does not meet the above criteria.

Reflection: Notice from the descriptors for the Outcome in Activity 4.19 that, in order to reach level 3 and above, you must present different cultural perspectives in both the Outcome and the Explanation.

1 Consider this sample Explanation for the same project aim.

2 What level would you give to this Explanation without seeing the Outcome?

3 Discuss with a partner the level you have given and the reasons for your decision.

Explanation

For our Team Project, we were interested in the celebrations we have throughout the year that are centred on food. We discovered by talking to students in lower grade classes that they eat a lot of fast food, which is very unhealthy as it is full of sugar and salt which makes us fat. We wanted to persuade Grade 7 students in our school of the benefits of trying different types of food and the enjoyment they could get from experiencing foods from other cultures. We allocated team roles to ensure that we could complete the project in the time frame we set ourselves. Each one of us was allocated a role by the self-appointed team leader. As well as this role, each one of us was responsible for researching at least one other culture or contacting a person from another country so that we could get together and share the information we found out before designing our series of posters. We contacted other schools that are doing IGCSE and O Level Global Perspectives in a few different countries: Indonesia, Australia and India. Then we produced a series of posters showing the healthy foods enjoyed by these cultures. Our Outcome shows that Indian food is generally healthy as there are a variety of vegetarian dishes that are eaten regularly. During Eid, anyone inviting guests will definitely have a Biriyani made with Basmati rice and mutton or chicken with chicken kebabs. Some prefer a turkey Biriyani every Eid. Indonesians prefer pork in soy sauce, pork rice, cakes and tarts. Usually, there are two buffet tables, one with pork dishes and one with halal food, like grilled fish, for Muslim guests. In Australia, prawns, crab and salads are very popular. Australians also eat a lot of meat but it is lean and often grilled.

299 words

ACTIVITY 4.20

Design the Outcome to go with the Explanation above. You should work in pairs or a small team.

Discussion point

Discuss with your partner whether you think your Outcome for Activity 4.20 and the Explanation in the Reflection point would now achieve level 4. If not, what changes do you need to make to ensure it achieves level 4?

Reflection: Consider how well you worked with your team/partner on the activities so far in this section. Where would you place yourself according to the criteria in the table below (which has been written by the author)?

Do you have any evidence to justify the mark you have given yourself (e.g. log or journal)?

Level	Descriptor	Marks
	When working on their Team Project:	
3	• Team members showed commitment to the Team Project at all times • The team collaborated well throughout the Team Project	5–6
2	• Team members showed commitment to the Team Project most of the time • The team collaborated well most of the time	3–4
1	• Team members showed commitment to the Team Project some of the time • The team collaborated well some of the time	1–2
0	• Does not meet the above criteria.	0

184

ACTIVITY 4.21

1 Which of these is the most suitable outcome for the project aim of:

'Raising awareness about the use and distribution of water from different cultural perspectives'?

a Drama sketch/skit

b Poster

c Video-clip

d Song

e Presentation

2 Give reasons for your answer.

Discussion point

Discuss your opinion and justification for your opinion for Activity 4.21 with a partner to see if you agree.

ACTIVITY 4.22

You read the text below on 'Water wasted through leakage' and want to take action.

Work with a partner or in a small team to:

1 Decide on an aim.

2 Decide on an Outcome.

3 Produce a plan of action.

4 Create the Outcome and the Explanation.

Don't forget to find out different cultural perspectives on the issue.

Water wasted through leakage

According to the World Health Organisation, approximately 1.2 billion people suffer ill health due to polluted water. The World Health Organisation also estimates that 15 million children die every year as a result of polluted water. This global crisis is getting worse. It is estimated that, by 2025, approximately 3 billion people in approximately 50 countries will face water problems, either from pollution or water shortages.

We all know that clean water is essential for human beings to survive. However, the rate at which we squander our most precious natural resource is disturbing. It is reported that over 32 billion cubic metres of clean water is lost every year due to leakage. In the developing world, the amount of water lost is sometimes as much as 60% of the total amount of water entering the distribution system. A reduction in this amount could give millions more people around the world access to clean water.

ACTIVITY 4.23

As well as using your creativity skills in the Team Project, you will use them for courses of action in the Individual Report.

1   Here are three courses of action for the issue of food waste:

   a   Individuals producing less food waste in the first place.

   b   Making good use of food that might still be fit for consumption.

   c   Better management of the food waste that is unavoidable, for example using food waste for biogas plants.

2   Which of these three courses of action encourages a personal response?

3   Which encourages a global response?

4   Which encourages a local/national response?

5   Choose one of these three courses of action.

   Write a short paragraph explaining how this course of action can help with the issue of food waste.

6   Suggest one further course of action to help deal with the issue of food waste.

7   Which of the eight topics for the Individual Report might the issue of food waste fall under?

Establishing collaboration skills

This section uses the topic of **Disease and health** to develop collaboration skills further so that you feel that they are established. This topic is one of the eight global topics listed in the IGCSE and O Level Global Perspectives syllabus for the Team Project (Component 3). You will build on the skills you have acquired so far so that you start to feel more confident as a collaborative learner.

SKILLS LINKS

- Chapter 4: Collaboration skills, 4.01 Teamwork
- Chapter 4: Collaboration skills, 4.02 Decision-making
- Chapter 4: Collaboration skills, 4.03 Creativity

ACTIVITY 4.24

1 Consider the following statement:

'Young people can and should be part of the solution to global and local health problems affecting themselves and the community at large.'
Source: www.un.org

2 Copy and paste this statement into a search engine (Google is suggested but you can use any).

3 Spend 20 minutes at most reading some of the health risks young people face.

If you are finding it a challenge to find information within this time frame, consult the World Health Organisation website and search for factsheets about the health risks young people face.

4 Join with a partner or small group and create a mind map of the health risks young people face around the world.

5 Add at least one detail/piece of evidence to each health risk.

6 Choose one of these health risks.

Decide on a suitable course of action for each of the following levels:

a Global

b National/local

c Personal.

Discussion point

Discuss the different types of action for part 6 in Activity 4.24 according to the level of response.

ACTIVITY 4.25

Focus on local action. Create an aim, and identify a suitable Outcome to achieve this aim at a local level (school, community).

Reflection: How effective do you think your Outcome for Activity 4.25 will be in achieving your aim? Explain why you think this.

ACTIVITY 4.26

Use the Osborne–Parnes model to identify an aim and an Outcome for a course of action for the following scenario:

Imagine that you discover that in your school many students miss classes because they are suffering from the symptoms of the common cold.

Use the start of the sentences for the six steps to help come up with your course of action.

1 Your goal/aim is . . .

2 You find out . . .

3 The issue is . . .

4 You brainstorm . . .

5 You discard . . .

6 You decide to create a plan to . . .

Discussion point

Discuss, with a partner or in a small team, the ideas you have for Activity 4.26.

ACTIVITY 4.27

1 Once you have a plan from Activity 4.26, decide on an Outcome to achieve your plan, keeping the aim in mind.

2 Create your Outcome and your Explanation to achieve at least level 3 of the assessment criteria below (which has been written by the author) (you will need to do some research into different cultures to achieve level 2 and above).

3 Ask another pair or small group to peer assess your Outcome and Explanation using the assessment criteria. Feedback (strengths and limitations) should be given.

4 Write a paragraph to evaluate the project Outcome (strengths and limitations) in view of the project aim. You should do this part on your own and then compare what you have written with a partner.

Level	Descriptors for Outcome and Explanation *To meet the aim of the team Project:*
4	Different cultural perspectives are clearly communicated in the Outcome and in the Explanation.
3	Different cultural perspectives are communicated in the Outcome and in the Explanation.
2	There is some evidence of different cultural perspectives in the Outcome or in the Explanation.
1	There is little evidence of different cultural perspectives in the Outcome or in the Explanation.
0	Does not meet the above criteria.

Reflection: For Activity 4.27, what might you do to improve:

1 your Outcome and Explanation?

2 your evaluation of your project outcome?

ACTIVITY 4.28

Imagine the following scenario: whilst researching diet and health, you discover that there is too much salt in the average diet. You come across the following text:

Reduce salt in your diet

Government policies should help people eat healthily, and this includes measuring the amount of salt that is within food and ensuring that there is not too much of it. Improving the eating habits of a population is not only an individual's responsibility. Below are some ways of making sure that a healthy amount of salt is eaten.

Global strategies for reducing salt intake include: creating policies to make sure food manufacturers produce healthier foods, raising awareness about the need to reduce salt intake through advertising and promoting healthy food in schools, workplaces, communities and cities.

Salt consumption at home can be reduced by not adding salt whilst preparing and cooking food, and by eating fewer salty snacks like crisps and peanuts.

National actions by the food industry should include reducing salt in products over time so that consumers get used to the taste and don't switch to alternative products, and promoting the benefits of eating reduced salt foods through consumer awareness.

Imagine you are proposing courses of action to try to reduce the salt intake of people, because if people continue to eat too much salt, they risk damaging their health. Eating too much salt can also put a burden on the health systems of countries. You can use the article to help you decide on courses of action, but you should write them in your own words and develop them further.

1 Use your own words to write down one global course of action. Add to the point so that it becomes more developed (an explanation or an example).

2 Use your own words to write down one national course of action and develop it further.

3 Use your own words to write down one personal course of action and develop it further.

4 Now propose one local course of action (the article does not tell you this but you should be able to suggest one).

ACTIVITY 4.29

Put the following steps into the most suitable order for completing a Team Project:

1 Choose team members
2 Give reasons for the choice of topic
3 Identify team roles
4 Choose the global topic
5 Identify tasks to be undertaken
6 Decide on the Outcome
7 Write the Explanation
8 Match tasks to team member roles
9 Carry out tasks (including secondary and primary research to gather different cultural perspectives)
10 Decide on the aim of the project
11 Identify the time frame for the completion of tasks.

You don't have to use a template to plan your Team Project, but it might help you. The form below shows an example plan for a Team Project. Evaluate it by identifying the following:

- Strengths
- Limitations
- Possible improvements.

Plan for completing a Team Project – Disease and health

Aim: To raise awareness about women's health issues		
Outcome: News article to be published on a facebook page		
Team members: Maha, Rula, Rita, Rosa		

Sources of information
Secondary:
World Health Organisation website
United Nations website
Women's health websites from different countries

Primary:
Interviews with medical staff at the local hospital – recorded interviews
Questionnaires completed by students from other countries – email, skype

Task	Who?	Time frame
Find information about women's health issues globally	Maha and Rita	1 week
Find information about women's health issues nationally	Rula and Rosa	1 week
Contact hospital to organise interviews with medical staff at the local hospital	All	1 week
Write up findings from recorded interviews from the hospital	Maha, Rula	1 week
Design questionnaire and email to group of students in another country (ask Miss D for contact details)	Rita and Rosa	1 week
Analyse and summarise findings from questionnaire	Rita	1 week
Start to organise research findings	Maha and Rula	1 week
Write news article (Outcome)	Maha and Rita	1 week
Write Explanation	Rula and Rosa	1 week

ACTIVITY 4.30

Use the example project plan template in the form below to create a plan for completing a Team Project within the topic of **Disease and health**.

Project aim: *To raise money to send to WaterAid, a charity that provides clean, safe drinking water around the world.*

Project plan template

Aim: To raise money to send to WaterAid, a charity that provides clean, safe drinking water around the world.		
Outcome:		
Team members:		
Sources of information:		
Task	**Who?**	**Time frame**

Enhancing collaboration skills

This section uses the topic of **Language and communication** to enhance your collaboration skills. This topic is one of the eight global topics listed in the IGCSE and O Level Global Perspectives syllabus for the Team Project (Component 3). By working through the activities in this section, you will continue to build on the skills you have acquired so far.

SKILLS LINKS

- Chapter 4: Collaboration skills, 4.01 Teamwork
- Chapter 4: Collaboration skills, 4.02 Decision-making
- Chapter 4: Collaboration skills, 4.03 Creativity

ACTIVITY 4.31

With a partner or in a small team, consider the following imaginary scenario:

All students in the international school you go to speak English. The support staff at your international school are from the local area and they have generally not had the opportunity to learn English. Therefore they are struggling to communicate with students. One of them has approached you to ask if you might teach them some basic English to help them to communicate with you and the other students.

1   Try to answer the following questions:

   a   What is the problem/issue?

   b   What choices are there?

   c   What do you think the consequences of these choices will be for you and others?

   d   What values do you need to think about?

   e   How do you feel about the situation?

   f   Is there anything else you need to know?

   g   Do you need to ask for help and, if so, who do you ask?

   h   What is your decision?

2   You have worked through the questions, and decided that you want to design a lesson/series of lessons to teach a small group of support staff some basic English.

   Answer the following questions:

   a   What is the aim of this Team Project?

   b   What is the Outcome?

   c   How might you show different cultural perspectives in the Outcome?

   d   How might you evaluate the strengths and limitations of the Outcome in achieving the project aim?

ACTIVITY 4.32

Read the following text about language.

Languages keep our brains active

According to a recent study, learning to speak a second language might help to keep our brains active, even in old age. The study showed that there was less mental decline in people who could speak a second language than in those who could not. Among the 800 participants who took part in the study, approximately 250 of them could communicate in at least one language other than English, and, of those, about 200 of them learnt their second language before they were 18 years old. Here are the benefits of speaking a second language:

Increased attention span
People who can speak more than one language are good at paying attention, especially when performing visual tasks like scanning a list for a specific name. They are also better at multi-tasking thanks to regularly moving between their native language and the foreign language while they are learning it.

Better at processing sounds
Another study in America was conducted with 50 student volunteers, of whom 25 were bilingual. They were exposed to different noises and sounds. The study found the bilingual group was far better at processing sounds compared to the monolingual group.

Indian schools

Indian schools are now introducing several new foreign languages apart from French and German to students from Class 3 onwards. Some schools are offering Mandarin to Class 6 students and it is proving to be very popular. Although Mandarin can be difficult to learn, children studying it commented on how useful it would be for their future. 'Mandarin is very different to English, but as I want to become an IT engineer, the language will help me in my career,' said a Class 7 student.

This activity requires you to work as a team.

Imagine you have been asked to make a video to show different cultural perspectives towards language learning in the hope of persuading people within your school of the importance of language learning.

Decide on the roles you think you are going to need to make your video. Here are some of the roles you might consider:

- Script writer
- Editor
- Camera operator
- Cue card holder
- Credits
- Reporter
- Props/equipment organiser

Team members can have more than one job and you might have more than one team member doing one job.

Consider the following questions:

- Are you interviewing people? If so, who, when and why are you interviewing them?
- What equipment, if any, do you need for your video shoot?
- Are you using a certain setting? How does the setting relate to your clip?

The table below shows an example script to stimulate ideas for your own project. The topic of the example is healthy eating.

Example script

Video	Audio
1. Students lining up in the school dining room.	We are here at Happy International School and the lunch hour has just started.
2. Close-up of one student being handed a burger and some fries	As students eagerly line up for their meal, we can see that burger and fries are a popular choice.
3. Close-up of the wrapping with the brand label 'Happy Fast Food' on it.	These are, however, not just any burger. They are not made by the school, but supplied by the fast food chain 'Happy Burgers'. At Happy International, it's 'Happy' fast food or nothing.
1. Wide shot of cafeteria showing Happy Fast food posters of burgers, milkshakes, ice cream, etc.	Last year, Happy Fast Food bought the rights to serve food at Happy International.
2. Zoom in to students eating at a table, with Happy fries, burgers, milkshakes, ice cream, etc.	Now, when students sit down to eat, they're surrounded by Happy Fast food branding and limited to their fast food and drinks.
3. Close-up of the first student as she speaks.	Student opinion is divided. Many students say that they like having 'Happy' food for lunch. Others think that there should be more choice and are worried that there don't seem to be many healthy options.
4. Wide shot of student's faces enjoying their food and listening.	
5. Close-up of second student speaking.	

Video	Audio
1. Wide shot of staff serving students and the Principal talking to some of the students. 2. Zoom in to Principal during interview. 3. Wide shot of parents outside the school gates. 4. Zoom into one parent as they are speaking.	'It wasn't an easy decision to make', says the Principal, 'but it's about money. The money we get from Happy Fast Foods enables us to spend money on other things likes trips out for students and other extra-curricular activities.' Parents have their concerns. They understand that money is needed for other things, but feel that the school has a responsibility to guide students into healthy eating habits and that they should provide more choice. In the words of one parent, 'I try to persuade my children at home of the importance of healthy eating, but if the school only provides what I consider unhealthy food, then this is undoing the work I am doing as a parent.'

Working in your small team, you are going to prepare a video to meet the aim of:

Showing different cultural perspectives towards language learning in the hope of persuading people within your school of the importance of language learning.

First, create a table like the one above and complete it to plan your script.

Once you have your script, create your video.

Show it to an audience to get their reaction to it. It might be your classmates or students from another class in your year or a younger audience.

Ask them the following questions:

1 Is it clear what the video is about?

2 Does it show different cultural perspectives about language learning?

3 What do you like about the video/what are its strengths?

4 What do you think might be improved (what are the limitations of the video)?

5 Do you think the video meets the project aim? Why/Why not?

Summarise the findings and write a paragraph using the headings:

- Strengths
- Limitations
- Improvements.

Reflection: If you were allocating marks for collaboration in this Team Project for Activity 4.32, what marks would you give yourself and why?

Would your team mates agree?

Use the criteria in the table on the next page (which has been written by the author).

Level	Descriptors	Marks
	When working on their Team Project:	
3	• Team members showed commitment to the Team Project at all times • The team collaborated well throughout the Team Project	5–6
2	• Team members showed commitment to the Team Project most of the time • The team collaborated well most of the time	3–4
1	• Team members showed commitment to the Team Project some of the time • The team collaborated well some of the time	1–2
0	• Does not meet the above criteria	0

Reflection: Now reflect on your work within your team. Write a paragraph including the following.

- Strengths of your own performance as a team member and the work you did in completing the video

- Weaknesses of your own performance as a team member and the work you did in completing the video

- Improvements you could make to your own performance as a team member and the work you did should you do this type of project again

- The benefits and challenges of working as a team

- What you have learned about different cultural perspectives

- What you have learned from completing the project

Chapter 5
Communication skills

Learning objectives

By the end of this chapter, you should be able to:

- understand the importance of developing communication skills
- identify the main points, gist and detail from written and spoken texts
- identify information from different types of written and spoken texts
- produce written summaries, paragraphs, and conclusions
- speak confidently for different purposes.

Introduction

Being able to communicate is a lifelong skill. We communicate on a daily basis using written and spoken words. However, good **communication** skills do not just happen, they need developing just like other skills. In this chapter, you will learn to develop your communication skills.

As well as demonstrating good communication skills whilst you are at school and for your examinations, you will need to show them when you apply for university and for jobs. The ability to speak appropriately with a wide variety of people whilst maintaining good eye contact, demonstrate a varied vocabulary and adapt your language to your audience and situation, listen effectively, present your ideas appropriately, write clearly and concisely and work well in a group all require good communication skills.

This chapter focuses on developing the following communication skills:

5.01 Reading   **5.02** Writing   **5.03** Listening   **5.04** Speaking

5.01 Reading

SKILLS LINKS

- Chapter 1: Information skills, 1.02 Research
- Chapter 1: Information skills, 1.03 Analysis
- Chapter 1: Information skills, 1.06 Questioning
- Chapter 3: Independent learning skills, 3.02 Note-taking
- Chapter 3: Independent learning skills, 3.04 Evaluation

KEY TERM

Communication: the means of transferring information from one place to another, either by using spoken and written texts or by non-verbal means.

In this section on reading, you will focus on responding to written texts. You can do this by speaking or writing. This section focuses on different strategies needed to be able to understand written texts.

Reflection: Why do you think it is important for you to be able to read and understand different types of text whilst following the Global Perspectives course?

Discussion point

Discuss with a partner and make a list of the different types of text you think you will meet and need to understand in IGCSE and O Level Global Perspectives.

TIP

During your Global Perspectives course you will be reading news articles to identify issues, perspectives and evidence and to draw conclusions. You will also come across other types of text such as poems, presentations, song lyrics, cartoon strips, diagrams, graphs and tables. In the examination you might be asked to study source material in order to answer questions so it is important that you are fully prepared to read these texts and to do as the questions require. For the Individual Report and Team Project you will need to research information and use it appropriately, as you discovered in Section 1.02 Research.

Reading strategies

Strategies you can use before, during and after reading a text are shown in the following table:

Before reading	During reading	After reading
Identify five words you expect to find in the text.	Summarise the first paragraph in one sentence.	Sum up the text in one paragraph.
Predict from the title what the text might be about.	Highlight ten key words to enable someone else to identify what the text is about.	Give your opinion about the text, giving reasons for your opinion.
Create possible sentences that might appear in the text from given word pairs.	Identify specific details, e.g. perspectives, issues, evidence.	The RAFT writing strategy – questions to enable you to understand texts by examining role, audience, format and topic.

TIP

The *RAFT writing strategy* focuses on the following:

The Role of the writer: Who are you as the writer? A tourist? A potential employee? A politician?

Audience: To whom are you writing? The government? A potential employer? Fellow students?

Format: In what format are you writing? A letter? An advertisement? A speech?

Topic: What are you writing about?

ACTIVITY 5.01

1 Predict what you think a text with the following title might be about:

Does globalisation bring more harm than good?

2 Now see if you can make sentences from these word pairs to identify some of the content of the text on **Globalisation**. For example, for the first pair you might have: 'Globalisation has failed to reduce poverty in the world'.

failed	poverty
force	development
riches	everyone
gap	widening
globalisation	worked

> **Reflection:** How did you do in Activity 5.01?
>
> Here is the whole section of the text about globalisation for you to check your sentences against.
>
> > It is clear that globalisation has failed to rid the world of poverty. Rather than being an unstoppable force for development, globalisation now seems more like an economic temptress, promising riches to everyone but only delivering to the few. Although global average per capita income rose strongly throughout the 20th century, the income gap between rich and poor countries has been widening for many decades. Globalisation has not worked.
> >
> > *Source: www.theguardian.com*
>
> The words shown in the word pairs are the key words you might have highlighted in the text when reading.
>
> To summarise this paragraph in one sentence, you could write:
>
> Globalisation has not worked because poverty still exists and the gap between rich and poor is getting wider.

Discussion point
Discuss the reasons for reading with a partner.

How to skim read

When skim reading, do not read the whole text word for word. Read the first and last sentence of each paragraph. Use any pictures, photos, title, sub-titles, key words and any other clues as to the content of the text. While skimming, try to understand what the text is about.

ACTIVITY 5.02

You have decided that you would like to do your Individual Report on the topic of **Family**. You are especially interested in how family life is affected by migration for economic reasons. You have found the following article and need to consider whether it is useful for your work or not. Skim read the article and come to a decision. Give reasons for your decision.

> **Migration crisis: 'Who can refuse these human beings? Who?' asks UN official**
>
> The Mediterranean migration crisis is a 'human atrocity' on a scale not seen since the second world war and can be tackled only with short-term generosity from European nations and a sustained global push to reduce extreme poverty over the coming decades, a senior United Nations official has warned.
>
> Philippe Douste-Blazy, a UN undersecretary-general and former French foreign minister, said the world had to understand that economic inequality was driving people from their home countries just as steadily as war.
>
> Douste-Blazy – who advises the UN secretary general on innovative financing for development and chairs Unitaid, which uses small levies on air fares to fund health programmes – also said migration to richer countries would increase unless more was done to improve life in the developing world.
>
> 'The wave was 10cm high two years ago,' he said. 'Now it's about 40cm high. But for your children, it will be 30 metres high. Why? Because 2 billion people in the world earn

Chapter 5 Communication skills

less than $1.25 a day. The difference between now and 20 years ago is that everybody looks at everybody now – it's the globalisation of the economy and the globalisation of communications: internet, TV, radio. It's very new.'

While he acknowledged that many refugees were fleeing violence and oppression in countries such as Syria, Eritrea, Somalia and Sudan, Douste-Blazy said 'we have 50% who are trying to escape from extreme poverty'.

Source: www.theguardian.com

Discussion point

Discuss with a partner whether the article in Activity 5.02 is suitable for the purpose you want it for.

Reflection: Might the article you have just read for Activity 5.02 be more suitable for the topic of poverty and inequality?

TIP

The difference between skimming and scanning.

Skimming helps you read a text quickly to decide whether you need to read it in more detail or whether you need to discard it. You skim read when you want to know the main ideas in a text. You skim to get an overall feel for a text, but you scan to find specific details in a text. Sometimes you will want to use both strategies. You skim to see if it is relevant and of interest and then you scan to find the exact details you need.

ACTIVITY 5.03

Now skim read the following text.

Does migration change life for the better for people from poor countries?

The report collated data collected by Gallup about the experiences of 25 000 migrants and 441 000 non-migrants in 150 countries. Respondents were asked what they have gained and lost through migration, how satisfied they are with their lives, whether they find it more difficult to find jobs or start a business, and whether they are likelier to report health problems.

The findings suggested the greatest gains in wellbeing come from migration to rich countries. Migrants moving from one rich country to another – the UK to Canada, for instance – reported the highest levels of life satisfaction, financial security, personal safety, and health.

In contrast, migrants who moved between developing countries – Indonesia to Malaysia, for example – seemed to fare similarly or worse, according to the report. They were also identified as the group least likely to feel optimistic about their lives.

According to Gallup data only 8% of adult migrants in developing countries, and 27% in rich countries, reported sending 'financial help' to family in another country.

Source: www.theguardian.com

Is this article more suitable for your purpose? If so, why?

How to scan

You do not need to read every word when scanning as you are looking for specific information, such as a date, an opinion, or a specific fact. It is a good idea to write down questions that you want answers to, so that you know what you are scanning for.

ACTIVITY 5.04

Scan the text in Activity 5.03 ('Does migration change life for the better for people from poor countries?') to find the following information.

1   How many countries did Gallup collect data from?
2   What percentage of adult migrants send financial help home to their families in developing countries?

TIP

Reasons for reading include:

- for gist (skim reading)
- for detail (scanning)
- to gain specific details (identify issues, perspectives, courses of action, etc.)
- to acquire new vocabulary
- tor developing ideas and add evidence
- out of interest.

The type of reading strategy you use will depend on the reason you are reading.

Summary

- When reading, you don't have to understand everything.
- Try to predict what a text is about by reading the title and looking at any visuals.
- Start by skimming a text to see whether it's useful to you or not.
- Ask questions so you know what information you are looking for.
- Scan texts to find specific information.

5.02 Writing

 SKILLS LINKS

- Chapter 1: Information skills, 1.04 Synthesis
- Chapter 1: Information skills, 1.05 Planning
- Chapter 2: Critical thinking skills, 2.01 Reasoning
- Chapter 3: Independent learning skills, 3.02 Note-taking

You will need to know how to write coherently and concisely for specific purposes throughout your time at school. You will be required to do some writing by hand in class and when completing your examinations, and will definitely use a computer to word process written texts.

Writing strategies

A lot of people don't know where to start when writing (sometimes referred to as suffering from 'writer's block'). Planning will help you to begin, as will writing summaries throughout the course, and writing first drafts.

Writing summaries

Writing summaries helps you build your skills in reading different texts. When you are doing research, writing a summary of what you read in your own words will avoid **plagiarism**. Also, if you write summaries during the course of study, then writing your Individual Report will not seem to be such a chore.

 KEY TERM

Plagiarism: presenting someone else's work as your own.

Summary writing guidelines

When writing summaries, keep the following in mind:

1 Do not copy the original piece.
2 Keep your summary short – aim for approximately 100 words, depending on the text you are summarising.
3 Use your own words.
4 Read the original piece with the questions who?, what?, when?, where?, why? and how? in mind and put the responses in your summary.
5 Describe the main ideas of the original piece.
6 Do not include your opinion of the issue or topic discussed in the original piece.

ACTIVITY 5.05

Read the summary and answer the questions.

Sustainable living **in Bradinton**

In 2014, Bradinton became a completely energy efficient community. Solar panels are installed on the roofs of all the houses. These panels capture energy from the sun, which is converted and used to power home appliances like computers, televisions and fridges. This natural use of solar power reduces the people of Bradinton's reliance on energy sources such as oil and gas, which are harmful to the environment. Bradinton has become a completely environmentally aware community that can be used as an example for other communities.

1   How many words does the summary contain?
2   Does the summary give you information to answer the questions: who?, what?, when?, where?, why? and how?
3   Does the summary contain any opinion?
4   Do you think summary writing is a useful skill to enable you to summarise information from any research you do and to build up your Individual Report?

Discussion point
Discuss your answers to the questions in Activity 5.05 with a partner.

First drafts

For a **first draft**, don't worry about the quality of what you write, just get started. Try not to worry too much about the accuracy of what you write or the fluency of your sentences. The ideas are what matter for first drafts.

KEY TERM

First draft: a version of a piece of work, such as the Individual Report or the Explanation for the Team Project that you write before working on the final version.

Reflection: Have you written first drafts before?

Do you find them useful? Why/Why not?

You should be building up your written work to create your first drafts. You don't need to write an Individual Report in one session. You can even start in the middle. Rather than staring at a blank page, skip the introduction and jump in at **paragraph** two. You can come back and write the introductory paragraph at the top when you have finished.

KEY TERMS

Paragraph: a group of related sentences that develop one main idea or new aspect of an argument in a clear and logical way. Typically, a paragraph will be a minimum of four or five sentences but not usually longer than half a page. Each paragraph should include a topic sentence, a supporting sentence and a piece of evidence.

Topic sentence: this sentence gives the topic and the main idea and is usually the first sentence in the paragraph.

Supporting sentence: develops the point you are making using information, explanation and examples, and provides a smooth flow from one sentence to the next.

Evidence: you should support all the points you make with evidence from source material.

ACTIVITY 5.06

Read the following paragraph from an Individual Report within the topic of Humans and other species about the consequences of mass tourism.

Answer the following questions:

1 What is the **topic sentence**?

2 Give an example of a **supporting sentence**.

3 What **evidence** is presented?

Notwithstanding governments' considerable attempts to deal with the negative consequences of mass tourism across the globe, often by passing laws, the effects of mass tourism continue to cause problems, one of which is the amount of destruction to the local environment. According to the World Wildlife Fund (2015), the hunting and poaching of endangered species for ivory, and in particular at the moment rhino horn for medicine, is on the increase and poaching gangs are becoming more organised and using increasingly more complex methods of trafficking because of the potential profits they can obtain from trading these items. Strict laws do not seem to be working to stop these gangs from carrying out this illegal and highly destructive practice. Furthermore, according to ECPAT International (2015), even though world leaders are committed to ending the sexual exploitation of children, it is still a global consequence of mass tourism with hundreds of thousands of tourists reported to practise sex tourism and to abuse poverty. In addition, there is a noticeable worsening in the behaviour of young people associated with tourism, such as alcohol-related issues, violence and general disregard for the local environment, which some governments find difficult to stop despite their best efforts.

Sources:

World Wildlife Fund (2015), www.worldwildlife.org/threats/illegal-wildlife-trade

ECPAT(2015), www.ecpat.net/

203

Discussion point

Discuss your answer to the questions in Activity 5.06 with a partner.

Applying your learning to the Individual Report

For your Individual Report, the main idea for each paragraph (topic sentence) will be about an issue identified from the question you have set yourself. Your supporting sentences will then focus on the perspectives and the viewpoints within these perspectives about the issue, the causes and consequences of the issue and the course(s) of action you propose to help resolve the issue. For each area, you will want to use evidence to back up the points you make and evaluate the sources of information you use.

If you find it difficult to write, you might want to try speaking and recording your work and then transcribing what you have said. In this way, you can achieve your first draft and work from this.

> **TIP**
>
> Explore some speech to text transcription apps to see how you can turn your spoken work into written work. Use any search engine to search for 'speech to text apps'.

For the Individual Report, you need to write a research report that meets the assessment criteria (a maximum of 2000 words). Marks are awarded for communication; your ability to structure your report and to present arguments, evidence and perspectives clearly and effectively.

When planning to write your Individual Report, you will need to pace yourself and give yourself enough time. You should have been building up notes, summaries and paragraphs whilst working and exploring issues within lessons. You can refer to these once you have your Individual Report question. Don't forget that when you have your question, you will need time for:

- planning
- questioning
- writing your first draft
- **revising**
- writing your final draft
- ensuring your report is within the limit of 2000 words
- adding your reference list
- **proofreading**.

KEY TERMS

Revising: the process of re-reading a text and making changes (in content, organisation, sentence structures, and word choice) to improve it. During revision, you may want to add, remove, move and substitute text (the ARMS treatment).

Proofreading: the last thing you do before declaring a piece of written work is 'finished'. Pay attention to your grammar: make sure every sentence has a subject and a verb, and that they agree with each other. Correct all the spelling errors, especially the ones that spell-checking misses (such as 'there'/'their', and 'to'/'too').

Time frame for an Individual Report

You might want two weeks for research, two weeks for writing, two weeks to let your draft 'sit' while you think about any changes that need making, and a few days to revise and proofread. During your writing time, set aside time to write something each day. Try to write no more than 500 words in any one sitting. This is much more manageable than writing 2000 words at once, and should be straightforward if you have been keeping notes and writing summaries during class time. It is also a good idea to get to the end of a section each time: it is easier to begin writing again on the next 500 words.

Checking your work

Every sentence should direct your reader towards your conclusion. Questions to ask yourself include:

1 Is the topic of each paragraph clear?
2 Does each sentence in the paragraph contribute to a deeper understanding of the paragraph's topic?
3 Does this sentence add to my argument, or does it just take up space?

4 Does this sentence follow on from the sentence before, and lead into the following sentence?

5 Have I included evidence to support the argument I am making?

6 Have I evaluated the sources of information I have used?

7 Have I used citations and referenced them all in a reference list at the end of the report?

> **Reflection:** How often have you used these questions for checking your work?
>
> Do you think these questions will be useful for when writing your Individual Report?

Writing the conclusion

The purpose of your conclusion is to summarise and make final comments on the ideas you have presented in your Individual Report. It should not contain new evidence. The conclusion should be a strong answer to the question posed at the start of your report and the last paragraph or two should be a justification of your personal perspective using the evidence you have presented throughout your report.

Conclusions checklist

You can use this checklist for writing conclusions:

When writing a conclusion, create a new paragraph.

Remember to:

1 Signpost to the reader that you are about to conclude by using words such as: in conclusion, to summarise, finally, to conclude.

2 Sum up your findings in answer to your research question.

3 Give your personal perspective and justify it based on the evidence presented in your report.

4 Only include evidence that you have given in the main part of your report.

5 Check that your conclusion is a coherent answer to the question you set in the title of your report.

ACTIVITY 5.07

Read the following conclusion to the Individual Report about the consequences of mass tourism for the global topic of **Sustainable living**.

> Mass tourism is on the increase and we cannot prevent this, because quicker and cheaper transportation means that people are able to travel all over the world. What we can do is persuade governments and individuals about their collective responsibility to protect the environment in areas where mass tourism is happening and ensure that tourists abide by local rules and regulations. It is not acceptable that endangered species are threatened by poaching and hunting, so stronger action needs to be taken to stop this practice. Furthermore, without the demand for products obtained as a result of hunting and poaching, this practice would soon disappear as it would not be profitable enough to warrant the risk of imprisonment and hefty fines.

It is clear that things are starting to change and this will mean that tourism can be beneficial to an environment rather than harm it. More and more people are becoming aware of the need to protect endangered species so access to certain areas is heavily restricted. The protection of children is at the forefront of the international political agenda; and restrictions on groups of young people are in place in some areas that have previously suffered from violence and general disregard for the environment on the part of alcohol-fuelled gangs.

Do you think this is a strong conclusion to the Individual Report about the impact of mass tourism? Give reasons for your answer.

Discussion point

Discuss your thoughts about the conclusion in Activity 5.07 with a partner.

You probably felt that this is a strong conclusion as it summarises and makes final evaluative comments on the ideas presented. Although you do not have access to the rest of the report, you can see that the conclusion does not present new evidence. There is justification of a personal perspective using the evidence presented in this section of the report. You might also have been able to work out what the question was (What are the consequences of mass tourism and what can be done to protect affected environments?).

Writing answers under time pressure

You need to be able to pace yourself and ensure that what you have written is legible, whilst dealing with the added pressures of time and stress that inevitably come with taking any examination. This takes practice.

TIP

It is a good idea to practise the type of questions you need to answer, and to time yourself so you know roughly how long you have to spend on each question. Questions that carry more marks will take longer for you to answer, so be prepared.

ACTIVITY 5.08

Read the text from the **Fuel and energy** topic about 'No more fossil fuels' and answer the question. Note how long it takes you to write your answer.

> No more fossil fuels
> Lack of transport, broken down cars
> Less computer, less television
> Increased costs, goods unavailable
> Fewer jobs, less working hours
> No more fossil fuels

Question: Which one of the consequences of fossil fuels running out do you think is the most serious? Explain your answer (4 marks).

Reflection: How long do you think it would have taken you to write this?

> *Lack of transport is the most serious as without transport people will not be able to get to work very easily. This will mean that they will only be able to work near to where they live. This is not such a problem if they live and work in a city, but if they live in a rural area they might not be able to work to earn money to feed their families. Having less TV is not very serious because there are other forms of entertainment that don't need fossil fuels.*

Summary

- The hardest thing about writing is getting started.
- Try a speech to text app if this helps with writing.
- Get the ideas down first, you can check structure and grammatical accuracy later.
- Summaries help you to use your own words and show understanding of the material read or listened to.
- Write paragraphs throughout your course of study so it comes more naturally when you come to write at length.
- Ensure each paragraph has a topic sentence, supporting sentences and evidence.
- Write by hand in class as you will need to in examinations.

5.03 Listening

 SKILLS LINKS

- Chapter 1: Information skills, 1.02 Research
- Chapter 1: Information skills, 1.03 Analysis
- Chapter 3: Independent learning skills, 3.02 Note-taking
- Chapter 3: Independent learning skills, 3.04 Evaluation

In this section on listening, you will focus on responding to spoken texts. We can respond to spoken texts in a variety of ways, in speech and writing. This section focuses on different strategies needed to be able to understand spoken texts.

Reflection: Why do you think listening skills are important for IGCSE and O Level Global Perspectives?

Discussion point

Discuss with a partner and make a list of the different types of listening text you think you will meet and can use during the IGCSE or O Level Global Perspectives course.

TIP

Listening material includes listening to texts such as speeches, presentations, songs, advertisements, films, documentaries, etc. For the Individual Report and Team Project you will need to research information and use it appropriately. This information can come from texts that you listen to as well as from those that require you to read.

Listening strategies

Strategies you can use before, during and after listening to a text are shown in the following table:

Before listening	During listening	After listening
Predict from the title of the text what the text might be about and how many people might be speaking.	Use any visuals and make notes to recall what the text is about.	Write down the main issue and at least two supporting details.
Write down six words or phrases that you expect to hear.	Write questions prompted by what you are listening to.	Reproduce the message of the text orally.
Identify what you want to know before listening and produce a table to collect information (who, what, where, when, how, why, cause, effect, impact, etc.)	Write down specific details for further research, e.g. perspectives, issues, evidence.	Give your opinion about the text, giving reasons for your opinion.

ACTIVITY 5.09

1 Below is the summary of a video clip. Write down what you think the clip will be about and six words you think you might hear during the clip.

> **Education is a right for all** not a privilege for a few. In October 2012, Pakistani schoolgirl Malala Yousafzai was shot in the head by the Taliban for publicly stating her belief that girls, as well as boys, are entitled to an education. Malala survived and received treatment in the UK for her injuries. This film was produced while she was still recovering in hospital to highlight the campaign for Global Education.

2 The video clip is approximately four minutes long. Watch and listen to video clip: *www.truetube.co.uk/film/education-all*
3 Make notes to help you recall the key information presented in the video clip.
4 Use the notes you have to identify what the main issue is and at least two supporting details.

5   Tell a partner what the video clip is about.

6   Write down your opinion of the video clip, giving at least one reason for your opinion.

7   Identify areas for further research.

Reflection: How did you do in Activity 5.09?

You will probably have identified what the clip was about from the short description and might have been able to predict some key words that appeared in the clip. You should have been able to use the visuals to help you make notes. You might have noticed the change in the **tone** of the clip (music and presenter's voice) once it moved from the issue to the courses of action towards the end (the tone becoming more optimistic and upbeat). The pictures and statistics given will have helped you identify supporting details for the main issue (of children not being in school).

KEY TERM

Tone: a quality in the voice of the speaker that expresses the speaker's feelings or thoughts, often towards the person being spoken to or the topic being spoken about.

Using a variety of texts

Spoken texts can be just as useful as written texts for finding out information and make a change from reading all the time, as can texts without any language at all. When you first think about the topic for your Individual Report, have an initial look to see whether you are going to be able to find suitable, accessible texts, both to read and to watch and listen to.

TIP

Always copy and paste web addresses and add the date that you found particular sources of information. You can keep a Word document for this. If you get into the habit of writing down how long video clips are, this will make it easier later when you need to gather relevant information in order to answer the question you have set for your Individual Report or to use for your Team Project.

ACTIVITY 5.10

Investigate the topic of **Humans and other species**.

1   Do an initial search to see whether there are any suitable video clips that you might gain information from. Try to find short (no more than five minutes) video clips.

2   Once you find a suitable video clip, copy and paste the web address onto the Word document where you have been gathering information for the topic, and add the date.

3   Watch the video clip and make notes. It might be useful to remind yourself about what you are looking for (e.g. perspectives and viewpoints, causes and consequences of issues, possible course(s) of action).

4   Once you have watched the clip, create a written summary using your notes to help.

ACTIVITY 5.11

Imagine you are interested in this sentence from the text you read about the consequences of mass tourism whilst working through section 5.01:

'According to the World Wildlife Fund (2015), the hunting and poaching of endangered species for ivory, and in particular at the moment rhino horn for medicine, is on the increase and poaching gangs are becoming more organised and using increasingly more complex methods of trafficking because of the potential profits they can obtain from trading these items.'

Do a search for a video clip by putting 'truetube' and 'rhino horn' into your search engine.

The video clip is at: *www.truetube.co.uk/film/tiger-fur-and-rhino-horn*

Discussion point

Discuss with a partner whether you think the video clip mentioned in Activity 5.11 is suitable for the purpose you want it for.

TIP

Try using this website for short, suitable video clips about global issues:

https://www.truetube.co.uk

Listening in class and when working in teams

As well as access to information from multimedia (audio and visual), listening skills are important for activities done in class and when working in teams. Team members feel that their ideas are worthwhile if you listen to them, which increases their confidence, and you get different perspectives about issues and information that you may not previously have considered.

ACTIVITY 5.12

Are you an **effective, active** listener?

Complete the quiz below to see how good an effective and active listener you are. Try to be as honest as you can.

	Statement	Yes	No
1	I listen more than I talk.		
2	I maintain good eye contact.		
3	I try not to give much advice.		
4	I look interested when someone else is speaking.		
5	I wait for someone to finish before I start speaking.		
6	I give positive comments as feedback.		
7	I use appropriate body language (nod, shake head).		
8	I ask questions that show I'm listening.		
9	I avoid other distractions like answering my phone or texting whilst listening.		
10	I don't assume I know what the other person is talking about.		

The more you answered 'yes', the more developed your listening skills are.

KEY TERMS

Effective listening: listening to the words of the speaker and the meaning of the words.
Active listening: the process in which the listener takes active responsibility to understand the content and feeling of what is being said and then checks with the speaker to see if he/she heard what the speaker intended to communicate.

Reflection: For any statement that you answered 'no' to in Activity 5.12, consider its importance and how you are going to develop your listening skills further.

ACTIVITY 5.13

Pair up with a partner. Interview your partner for three minutes to find out what global issues are important to them and why. You should encourage your partner to share their opinions and justifications for these opinions, by listening actively.

Swap roles and allow your partner to ask you questions about the global issues that are important to you and why.

Reflection: Evaluate your listening skills during the pair Activity 5.13 using the following questions:

1 How did you feel in each role (as the interviewer and the interviewee)?

2 Were you distracted while listening?

3 Do you feel like you know more about the global issues your partner feels are important and why after this activity?

4 How could you improve your listening skills?

Now evaluate your partner's listening skills during the pair activity using the following questions:

1 Did you feel your partner listened to you?

2 Was there anything you noticed during this activity that made you feel your partner was or wasn't listening to you?

3 How do you think your partner could improve their listening skills?

Discussion point

Discuss with your partner how you think you could improve your listening skills to see if they agree with you and you agree with them.

Summary

- When listening, use any visuals and make notes to help you understand the text.

- After listening, try to tell someone else what the text was about.

- An effective listener listens to words and the meaning of the words of the speaker.

- An active listener takes active responsibility to understand the content and feeling of what is being said.

- An active listener checks with the speaker to see if he/she heard what the speaker intended to communicate.

5.04 Speaking

SKILLS LINKS

- Chapter 1: Information skills, 1.04 Synthesis
- Chapter 1: Information skills, 1.05 Planning
- Chapter 1: Information skills, 1.06 Questioning
- Chapter 2: Critical thinking skills, 2.01 Reasoning

Speaking is a skill that many of us take for granted. Effective speaking involves being able to speak in a public context clearly and with confidence, but at the same time showing your own personality. Skills in speaking clearly, confidently and in a reasoned way can be developed, like the other communication skills in this chapter.

TIP

Communication skills are rated as essential to an employer when interviewing candidates for a job.

Starting out

It is important to get used to the sound of your own voice. When you are at home or with friends, you can generally speak in the way that you want to. However, when speaking in class and in public, there are certain **conventions** to follow.

KEY TERM

Convention: a custom, or a way of acting or doing something that is widely accepted and followed.

The best way of getting used to how you sound when speaking is to make a recording. You can do this at home – perhaps using a mobile phone or a computer.

KEY TERM

Sustainable living: a lifestyle that attempts to reduce an individual's or society's use of the Earth's natural resources and personal resources.

ACTIVITY 5.14

1 Find a short article to read aloud, for example the following about Sustainable living.

> **Climate pledges by 140 countries will limit global warming – but not enough**
>
> Plans submitted by 140 nations to limit their greenhouse gases would go some way towards tackling climate change, but not enough to prevent the planet from warming by well over 2°C compared to pre-industrial times, experts say.
>
> The plans by countries from Albania to Zimbabwe, led by top emitters China and the United States, were submitted by an informal United Nations deadline on Thursday as building blocks towards a climate accord that negotiators will try to clinch at a summit in Paris in December.
>
> A Climate Action Tracker (CAT) by four European research groups projected the plans, if implemented, would limit average temperature rises to 2.7°C above pre-industrial times by 2100, down from 3.1°C estimated last December.
>
> That is still clearly above the 2°C level that governments have accepted as the threshold beyond which the Earth would face dangerous changes including more droughts, extinctions, floods and rising seas, which could swamp coastal regions and entire island nations.
>
> *Source: www.theguardian.com*

2 Read the article through silently to yourself first.
3 Read the article aloud in your normal speaking voice. Don't worry if you make mistakes, just continue to read to the end.
4 Read your article a third time, and this time record yourself as you are reading. Then listen to yourself to see if you can identify any aspects that make what you say less effective.
5 Try to practise as often as you can, with different lengths of text. This will give you confidence when it comes to speaking up in class or presenting to an audience.

TIP

When reading aloud, don't rush. You may feel you want to speed up and get it over with quickly, but this will cause you to mumble, making it difficult for people to understand what you are trying to say.

Use varied intonation rather than the same tone of voice, which can give the impression that the speaker is bored.

Try to hold the text at eye level, rather than lowering your head to read it, and project your voice as if you were talking to someone at the back of the room.

Try to pause for a couple of seconds at the end of a sentence or paragraph. Pausing also allows you to emphasise key points and gives your audience time to take in what you have said.

213

Reflection: These activities all involve speaking: debates, discussions and presentations. Can you think of any others?

Discussing global issues

ACTIVITY 5.15

Look at the image.

Figure 5.01 Building project

Discuss the photo with a partner or in a small group using the question words: what (is happening)?, when?, where?, how? and why?

You might have discussed the topics of **Changing communities**, **Migration** or **Sustainable living**. The photo is a new build being built in a forest area. The issue is probably that there needs to be more places for people to live, hence the building going on.

Reflection: Did you have an equal discussion or did one person dominate?

TIP

Use these prompts to help with a discussion or conversation.

1 Take turns and make sure that each person contributes to the discussion.

2 Ask each other, 'Would you like to add to my idea?' or 'What do you think about this?'

3 Ask questions to check what the other person is saying and show that you understand, for example, 'Do you mean … ?' 'Can you tell me more about that?' or 'Can you say that in another way?

214

ACTIVITY 5.16

Using your search engine, find an image to do with any of the global topics to discuss with a partner or small group. Use question words to guide the discussion. You might also discuss the issues, perspectives, causes, consequences and courses of action to do with the topic. Use the guidelines in the Tip to have a more effective discussion.

Reflection: Was this discussion for Activity 5.16 better than the last? Why/why not?

Debating global issues

You will probably have had some **debates** in class. Your teacher will have presented a **proposal** and asked you to take on a particular **standpoint** for the debate or you will have been given free choice on the standpoint you take. Whatever the situation, you will always need to prepare your arguments for a particular standpoint you take.

KEY TERMS

Debate: a formal discussion on a particular issue in a public meeting, in which opposing arguments are put forward and which usually ends with a vote.

Standpoint: a point of view, attitude, position, way of thinking or perspective.

Proposal: putting something forward for consideration.

215

ACTIVITY 5.17

Choose one of the following three proposals. Decide whether you are for or against the proposal and give reasons for your standpoint. You may need to do some further research so that you can justify your standpoint.

1 All students should be allowed to use cell phones and other electronic devices during lessons.

2 Renewable forms of energy should be subsidised by the government.

3 Animal testing should be banned.

Discussion point

Try out your arguments for Activity 5.17 with a partner to see if they are in agreement with you or have a different perspective.

Presentations

Presentations have become a common way of getting a message across to an audience in school (perhaps given by your teacher or fellow classmates) and in the workplace. Indeed, you may have decided to create a presentation as the Outcome for your Team Project. In preparation for this, you will have wanted to practise with a couple of mini-presentations – perhaps with a partner or within your class.

Mini-presentation

ACTIVITY 5.18

In this activity, you will prepare a mini-presentation to practise your presentation skills.

1   Choose a picture (from the internet) that relates to one of the global topics. Here is one you could use that falls within the topic of **Humans and other species**.

Figure 5.02 Monkey about town

Create a short presentation (no more than two minutes long) about the picture. Make notes but not a script. Notes should take the form of bullet points to act as prompts.

2   Be prepared to answer questions about the picture and the wider topic for a further two minutes.

3   In pairs, present the picture for two minutes without interruption.

4   Ask your partner questions about their picture and about the wider topic for two minutes (not repeating what you have already heard).

5   Swap over and repeat the activity with another picture your partner has chosen.

Reflection: Is this a good way of developing your speaking skills?

ACTIVITY 5.19

Have a look at the following slide from a presentation aimed at raising awareness about litter and the need to keep the **Environment** clean so that disease does not spread.

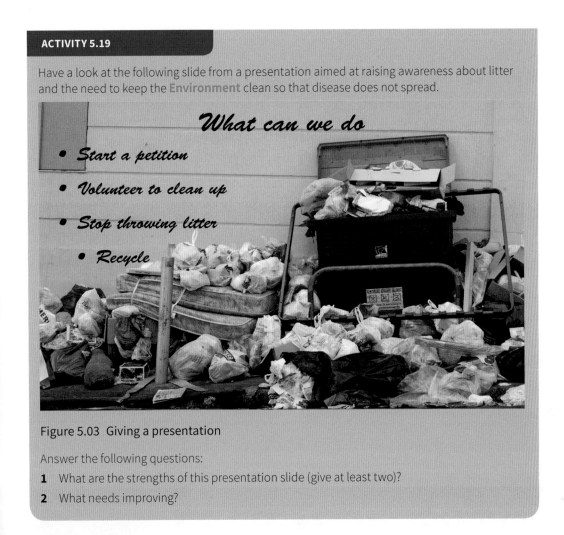

Figure 5.03 Giving a presentation

Answer the following questions:

1   What are the strengths of this presentation slide (give at least two)?
2   What needs improving?

Discussion point

Discuss your evaluation of the presentation slide in Activity 5.19 with a partner to share your ideas.

TIP
Evaluation involves identifying strengths and areas that need improving.

Guidelines for presentations

When creating presentations, keep the following in mind:

- Who is the intended audience (younger children, teenagers, parents, etc.)?
- What is the purpose (persuasion, raising awareness, advice, etc.) and how does the purpose affect the language (if it is to persuade then persuasive language should be used) and tone you should use? Remember to keep the message and the language simple and straightforward and to vary your tone when speaking.
- Is it a suitable length? It must not be too long – remember the attention span of most people is quite short – psychologists suggest about three minutes! Therefore break the presentation down into different sections of about three minutes with something to stimulate the audience between each one – perhaps some humour or an interesting graphic or a cartoon to reinforce a point.

- How are you making it engaging? An effective presentation needs to be engaging and 'grab the attention' of the intended audience, especially if you are trying to get something from the audience and/or persuade them to do something.

- Don't stand behind a table or lectern, try to connect with your audience. Use notes rather than a script.

- What illustrations and examples are you using and why are you using them? It is important to use illustrations to help people understand key points and perspectives, especially if you want them to take action.

Summary

- Speaking skills need developing like any other communication skill.
- When discussing global issues, it's important to take turns and involve everyone in the discussion.
- Arguments for and against proposals for debates need prior preparation.
- Speaking in front of an audience needs practising.
- Presentations should be created and given for a purpose, not be too long, and be informative and engaging.

Summary questions for Chapter 5

5.01 Reading

1   Identify one reading strategy.
2   Explain the difference between skimming and scanning when reading a text.

5.02 Writing

3   Explain the importance of first drafts when writing.
4   Identify **two** of the steps you should take when writing an Individual Report.

5.03 Listening

5   Explain why listening skills are worth developing.
6   Identify **one** characteristic of an effective, active speaker.

5.04 Speaking

7   Identify one type of speaking you will need to be able to do during the Global Perspectives course of study.
8   Explain the importance of being able to speak clearly and with confidence.

Practising communication skills

The focus of this chapter is communication skills and so far you have been looking at ways of developing your ability to read, write, listen and speak. This section of the chapter is divided into three; developing communication skills, establishing communication skills and enhancing communication skills. Each section is designed to build on the section before. You can either work through each section in turn or choose the section that you feel is at the most appropriate level for you. You should see a progression in difficulty through the three sections.

Developing communication skills

This section uses the topic of **Family**, which is one of the eight global topics listed in the IGCSE and O Level Global Perspectives syllabus for the Individual Report (Component 2). You will practise each of the skills using this topic as the vehicle for improving your communication skills.

 **SKILLS LINKS**

- Chapter 5: Communication skills, 5.01 Reading
- Chapter 5: Communication skills, 5.02 Writing
- Chapter 5: Communication skills, 5.03 Listening
- Chapter 5: Communication skills, 5.04 Speaking

ACTIVITY 5.20

Reading practice

1 Look at the <u>title only</u> of the text below, and predict what you think the text is about.
2 Before reading the whole text, predict five words that you think might be in the text.
3 Read the text to see if those five words are in the text. If they are, ask yourself whether these five words gave you a clue about the content of the text or whether a different five words would have helped more.
4 Answer the following two questions:
   a Why does the older boy live away from home?
   b What is Andrea's perspective about living apart as a family?
5 Sum up the text in one paragraph of not more than 100 words.

> **Does living apart make for a happy family life?**
>
> An increasing number of families live apart, but class themselves very much as being together as a happy family unit. It depends how you define family life. For the Alimercia family, mum, Andrea; dad, Alejandro; and their four children all live, work and go to school in four different places.
>
> They are not the only ones with an unusual family life. As the economy changes and a job for life is a thing of the past, many families find themselves living together at weekends and holidays only. For the Alimercia family, this involves the older boy at university in one part of Australia, living with grandparents whilst he is studying. The two younger boys attend a residential school in the next state from where Andrea lives with the baby. Meanwhile,

Alejandro works away during the week as when he was made redundant from his job as an engineer in his home town, he needed to move further afield to find work. Life seems to work that way for the time being, although Andrea finds that she is looking forward to going back to work once the baby is old enough to go to preschool. 'I really miss working, and unlike Alejandro, my job as a teacher is fairly secure and they have already told me that when I'm ready, I can go back. I'd be really happy if Alejandro could get a job back here in the future, but for now, I'm happy with the situation. Besides, developments in technology mean that we can talk to and see each other whenever we want to.'

Alejandro is aware that his current job is not safe and that he might have to move again, but does not seem to be over-concerned. 'There will always be work for engineers and I'm not worried about working away from home as long as I get to see my family at weekends and for holidays.' In fact, both Andrea and Alejandro agree that living apart means that they do not take each other for granted and enjoy every moment they spend together as a whole family.

6 Now do a self-assessment of your summary.

How many of the following apply to your summary:

	Self-assessment criteria	Yes	No
1	Not copied from the original		
2	Less than 100 words		
3	In my own words		
4	Answers questions: who, why, what, where, when, how and why (as many as applicable)		
5	Gives the main ideas of the original piece		
6	Does not contain my opinion		

Reflection: Did you skim the text first and then scan it to find out why the older boy did not live at home and what Andrea's perspective is?

Which form of reading helped most with writing your one-paragraph summary?

Discussion point

Discuss with a partner whether the text for Activity 5.20 above might be suitable for your Individual Report about how family life is affected by migration for economic reasons.

ACTIVITY 5.21

Writing a paragraph

Imagine you have decided on the following title for your Individual Report.

Is family life being affected by technology?

1 Which of these two topic sentences do you think is best for the start of your Individual Report and why?

    a *In this report, I am going to talk about technology.*

    b *The last twenty years have seen immense changes in the way our lives have been and continue to be affected by technology.*

2 Now you have your topic sentence, what else do you need in your paragraph?

3 Which of the following is the supporting sentence and which is the evidence for the first paragraph of your Individual Report about whether family life is being affected by technology'?

a In fact, according to a recent study, 8–18-year-olds spend over seven hours a day using some form of media for entertainment, totalling over fifty hours per week.

b We are spending more time on our own than with the rest of the family, inside on the computer and watching television than we are outside in the fresh air.

4 Read paragraph two of the text in activity 5.20 again. Identify the following:

a the topic sentence

b a supporting sentence

c a piece of evidence.

Discussion point

Compare your answers to the questions in Activity 5.21 to those of a partner to see if you have the same.

ACTIVITY 5.22

Put this paragraph in the correct order of topic sentence, supporting sentence and evidence.

a Research shows that there is a link between the amount of time spent in front of screens and being overweight.

b Globally, there has been an increase in the amount of overweight children.

c One of the main reasons that parents support the government's proposal to restrict the amount of time children spend in front of screens such as computer screens and televisions is that they are concerned about their children's health.

ACTIVITY 5.23

Writing a conclusion

Consider these three conclusions to an Individual Report entitled 'Is family life being affected by technology?' How effective are they?

a In conclusion, technology has brought many benefits to society in general. However, from the research I have done, I think that developments relating to new technology are affecting family life in a more negative than positive way.

b To conclude, family life has changed tremendously over the last few decades and not least because of the impact of technology. Homes have got bigger, meaning that family members can avoid seeing each other from one day to the next. As everyone is busy with work, school, and after school activities, there is simply less time for families to spend time together. Adding technology to this means that parents and children are emailing and texting each other more than they are talking, thereby affecting family relationships.

c In summary, technology affects family life in a lot of ways, some positive ways – the time that we can save to invest in family relationships; and some negative – new technologies are preventing people from interacting and spending time with their family.

Look back at the Conclusions Checklist in section 5.02 of this Chapter. Answer the following questions.

1 Do you think each of these conclusions is suitable for the question posed for the Individual Report?

2 Give one strength of each conclusion.

3 How might each conclusion be improved?

Discussion point
Discuss your thoughts for Activity 5.23 with a partner.

ACTIVITY 5.24

Writing for a written examination

This is an example of an exam-style question, together with its allocated marks and mark scheme (which has been written by the author).

1   Answer the following question:

Do you think migration is affecting family life in a mainly positive or negative way? Explain your answer. (3 marks)

You may use any of the texts in this section to write an answer to the question, keeping in mind the mark scheme. Don't forget to time yourself to see how long it takes you to answer the question.

2   Once you have written your answer, share your answer with a partner for peer assessment against the marking criteria.

Marks	Marking criteria
3	**Clearly reasoned**, structured argument; usually at least two developed points clearly linked to the issue.
2	**Some reasoned** argument; usually at least one developed point with some link to the issue.
1	**Limited argument**; usually one undeveloped point.

222

Reflection: How did you do in Activity 5.24?

What improvements do you need to make to be able to answer this type of question?

ACTIVITY 5.25

Listening practice

Use a search engine to find a short (no more than 5 minutes) listening text/video clip related to how family life is affected by technology. For the listening text/video clip you find:

1   Copy and paste the website address and the date you find the text into your record of information about the sources you use as you work through the course. It would also be a good idea to note the topic and the issue, in this case how family life is being affected by technology.

2   Make notes to help you recall the key information presented in the text/video clip.

3   Use the notes you have to identify what the main issue is and at least two supporting details.

4   Once you have your notes and have finished listening, explain to a partner what the video clip is about.

5   Write down your opinion of the text/video clip, giving at least one reason for your opinion.

6   Identify at least one area/issue for further research.

ACTIVITY 5.26

Speaking practice

One way of gaining further information about an issue is to take part in discussions and debates. Not only do you get to express your own standpoint, but you can listen to others' perspectives and review your own standpoint or strengthen it further.

Imagine that you are taking part in a debate. The proposal is:

'Technology is destroying family life.'

1 For the purpose of this activity, you should choose one standpoint only:

Yes – technology is destroying family life.

No – technology is not destroying family life.

2 You should prepare an argument for the standpoint you have chosen. You may need to do some research.

3 Once you have your argument, find someone in your class who has chosen the other standpoint to you and have the debate with them.

4 Answer the following questions:

a Do you still agree with your original standpoint? Why/Why not?

b Did your partner convince you about their standpoint? Why/Why not?

c Does your partner agree with your standpoint? Why/Why not?

d Do you feel that your argument was strong enough to convince others of your standpoint?

Establishing communication skills

This section uses the topic of **Biodiversity and ecosystem loss** to establish your communication skills. This topic is one of the eight global topics listed in the IGCSE and O Level Global Perspectives syllabus for the Individual Report (Component 2). You will build on the skills you have acquired so far so that you start to feel more confident when communicating with others.

SKILLS LINKS

- Chapter 5: Communication skills, 5.01 Reading
- Chapter 5: Communication skills, 5.02 Writing
- Chapter 5: Communication skills, 5.03 Listening
- Chapter 5: Communication skills, 5.04 Speaking

ACTIVITY 5.27

Reading practice

What do you know about how species loss happens?

Did you know, for example, that the main causes of species loss are:

1 Pollution

2 Climate change

3 Habitat loss

4 Invasive species

5 Unsustainable trade

Did you also know that human activity is responsible for each of these?

We are responsible because of the resources we use and the waste we throw away.

The greatest threat to species from these five causes of species loss is habitat loss, which according to the World Wildlife Fund affects more than 2,000 mammal species globally.

1 Use a search engine to search for a written text about 'habitat loss'. Once you have your search results, discard any articles from Wikipedia.

2 Have a look at the web addresses to see if there are any websites that you know and recognise as being credible.

3 Choose an article from one of these websites.

4 Skim the text to see if you are able to answer the following questions:

  a What is the issue?

  b What are the causes of the issue?

  c What is the perspective/viewpoint?

5 If you are unable to answer these three questions, find another text that gives answers to them. Once you have found your text, bookmark it and/or copy and paste the web address and add the date you find it.

6 Now scan the text to answer the questions and the following two, which might be in the article or you might need to think about.

  a What are the consequences if the issue continues?

  b What can be done (course(s) of action) and at what level (global, national, local, personal)?

7 Find someone in your class who has done the same activity and answer the same questions about the text they have found. If you bookmark their text, you can add this to your reference list as a source of information about this topic.

224

ACTIVITY 5.28

Writing a summary

Using the answers to the questions from Activity 5.27, for either your text or your partner's text, write a summary of the text, keeping to the guidelines for summary writing. Ask your partner to peer assess your summary using the checklist below:

	Criteria	Yes	No
1	Not copied from the original		
2	Less than 100 words		
3	Uses own words		
4	Answers questions: who, why, what, where, when, how and why (as many as applicable)		
5	Gives the main ideas of the original piece		
6	Does not contain opinion		

Discussion point

Gain some feedback from your partner about how you might improve your summary for Activity 5.28.

Give advice to your partner about how they might improve their summary.

ACTIVITY 5.29

Writing a paragraph

Here is a topic sentence for the question, *'Is climate change the main threat to biodiversity?'*

Climate change is a serious threat to biodiversity.

1   Do some research to find two suitable texts to skim and scan.

2   Add a supporting sentence to this topic sentence (in your own words).

3   Add a piece of evidence to back up your supporting sentence (don't forget to copy and paste the website address and date where you get your evidence from as you will need to reference it later).

Discussion point

Share your work in Activity 5.29 with a partner to see if they used the same article and evidence.

Reflection: Did you find Activity 5.29 easy to do?

Don't worry if you didn't: you can build up your summaries and paragraphs throughout the course and the more you practise writing them, the easier it will become.

ACTIVITY 5.30

Writing a conclusion

Here is a possible conclusion to an Individual Report entitled:

'Is climate change the main threat to biodiversity?'

Read it and answer this question.

Without having seen the rest of the report, do you think this is a strong conclusion? Give reasons for your opinion.

In conclusion, from the research I have done, my perspective has changed, as I did originally think that climate change was the main reason for ecosystem loss and species extinction. It is clear that climate change is one of the main threats to the loss of the variety of species in the world, and particularly in my own country because of the extreme weather conditions we have experienced in recent years. However, it also appears to be the case that climate change is only one of the threats to biodiversity globally. Others include the over-hunting and over-fishing of species, the invasion of non-native species in an area and pollution.

In fact, habitat loss seems to be the biggest threat to biodiversity globally as it is the key reason species become extinct. As noted, however, there are ways of preventing habitat loss, and therefore species extinction, so that a variety of species can continue to thrive.

Discussion point

Discuss your opinion on the conclusion in Activity 5.30 with a partner to see if they agree with you.

ACTIVITY 5.31

Writing for a written examination

When writing for a written examination you need to consider the type of response needed.

What is this question asking you to do?

How might you go about persuading people in your community not to destroy an area of forest to build a new road?

1 Write a letter persuading people in your community not to destroy an area of forest.

Or

2 Write about the methods you are going to use, who you need to involve and what you need to do to persuade people not to destroy an area of forest.

Did you choose option 2? If so, you are correct. Remember to always read the question before starting to write your response.

Now write a suitable response to the task.

Discussion point

Discuss what you have written for Activity 5.31 with a partner or your teacher.

Your answer might have included the following:

The people you might need to persuade are the local council, businesses, families.

All these people might be able to do something to prevent the forest being destroyed and a new road being built.

You might also have written about taking action like putting up posters, talking to people individually or at a meeting.

You would tell them the reasons for not destroying the forest, which might be that there is already a perfectly good transport system/road, and taking away the forest could mean that some species lose their habitat, adding to the local and global threat of loss of biodiversity and ecosystem loss.

Listening

As well as helping with perspectives, issues, causes and consequences, listening texts can be useful for thinking about and proposing your own courses of action for an Individual Report. You don't need to attempt to solve world problems. If you think that something that is working already could work in your local area, then you can propose it as a course of action. You might think it could work, but needs a few changes for it to work in your area. Try to avoid proposing a course of action that is already happening. Be realistic but creative!

ACTIVITY 5.32

1 Use a search engine to find a short video clip about the reintroduction of wolves into Yellowstone National Park in the United States in 1995.

2 Use a note-taking strategy to note down the key information from the clip.

3 Answer the following questions:

a What did you learn from this clip?

b Do you think that what was learnt from this clip could be a course of action elsewhere to help with biodiversity and ecosystem loss?

Discussion point

Share your answers to the questions in Activity 5.32 with a partner.

ACTIVITY 5.33

Here are some proposals for a debate.

1   Should we stop deforestation?

2   Is globalisation responsible for the loss of biodiversity?

3   Is economic prosperity more important than environmental protection?

Choose one of these three proposals. You should prepare an argument for both the yes and no standpoints for the proposal you have selected. You may need to do some research.

Once you have your arguments, find people in your class to have your debate with.

Answer the following questions:

a   Which of the standpoints (yes or no) do you agree with and why?

b   Was this your original preferred standpoint or did someone in your group persuade you with their argument?

c   Do you think that with a little preparation, you would be able to argue for a standpoint that you didn't necessarily agree with at the outset?

ACTIVITY 5.34

Discussing perspectives

Figure 5.04 Stone quarried from a mountain   Figure 5.05 Enjoying mountain life

1   Look at the two photos. Make some notes independently about what the issues and perspectives in the photos are and to answer the questions: what (is happening), when, where, how and why?

2   Discuss the photos with a partner or in a small group using the question words: what (is happening), when, where, how and why? Identify the issues and the perspectives.

Enhancing communication skills

This section uses the topic of **Fuel and energy** to enhance your communication skills. This topic is one of the eight global topics listed in the IGCSE and O Level Global Perspectives syllabus for the Written Examination (Component 1). By working through the activities in this section, you will continue to build on the communication skills you have acquired so far.

SKILLS LINKS

- Chapter 5: Communication skills, 5.01 Reading
- Chapter 5: Communication skills, 5.02 Writing
- Chapter 5: Communication skills, 5.03 Listening
- Chapter 5: Communication skills, 5.04 Speaking

Global topics

As you will have noticed, the global topics within the three groups for the IGCSE O Level Global Perspectives course are quite broad. As you are researching information for one topic area, you might come across information for a topic within another component list. This is fine as there will be overlap when looking at global issues. For example, even though the topic of fuel and energy is in the list for component 1 (Written Examination), some of the issues might also be relevant to the topic of sustainable living which is one of the topics for component 2 (Individual Report).

ACTIVITY 5.35

1   Using a search engine of your choice, type in one of the following three questions:

   a Can renewable energy replace fossil fuels?

   b Whose responsibility is it to ensure we don't run out of fossil fuels?

   c Why are we still using fossil fuels?

2   Choose one of the reading texts in the list that looks like it might give information about: perspective(s), issue(s) – cause(s), consequence(s) and course(s) of action.

3   Skim read this text and if it meets the criteria you are looking for, copy and paste the website address into your list of references and add the date.

4   Make notes under the headings: perspective(s), issue(s) – cause(s), consequence(s) and course(s) of action.

5   Now choose option **a** (Can renewable energy replace fossil fuels?) even if you chose it at the start of this activity. Add one of the following countries to the question to get a different perspective (India, China, Albania, Costa Rica or Afghanistan). Copy and paste the website address where you find a suitable article to give you a different perspective on the issue(s) – cause(s), consequence(s) and course(s) of action you found previously. Make notes to go with the ones you already have from the other article you read.

6   Now, use the same question, but add the country where you live to get a different list of reading texts. Follow the same procedure to gain the national perspective about the issue(s) – cause(s), consequence(s) and course(s) of action.

Reflection: Which of the three questions at the start of Activity 5.35 do you think is the best option for an Individual Report for the topic of 'sustainable living' and why?

Discussion point

Discuss your viewpoint about the the most suitable question for an Individual Report from Activity 5.35 with a partner to see if they agree with you.

Reflection: What other issues are relevant to the topic of 'sustainable living'?

ACTIVITY 5.36

Writing paragraphs about issues from different perspectives

1 Using the notes you have from the reading activity (Activity 5.35), write two paragraphs for an Individual Report entitled, 'Can renewable energy replace fossil fuels?'

   The first paragraph should focus on the global perspective. The second paragraph should focus on the national perspective (the perspective of the country where you are living).

   Don't forget to refer to the material about writing summaries and paragraphs earlier in this chapter.

2 Once you have your two paragraphs, ask a partner to look at them. You can also look at your partner's work. When reviewing work, you are looking to see whether each paragraph contains at least one:

   - issue
   - cause of the issue
   - consequence of the issue (should it continue)
   - course of action.

   The two paragraphs will be different as they will be looking at the issue from two different perspectives: global and national.

Discussion point

You and your partner should give each other verbal feedback for the work done for Activity 5.36. Identify two strengths of the work and one area you think needs improvement.

Reflection: Do you agree with your partner's feedback?

ACTIVITY 5.37

Writing a conclusion

1 Use the paragraphs you wrote for Activity 5.36 to write a conclusion to the question:

   'Can renewable energy replace fossil fuels?'

2 Once you have written your conclusion, ask your teacher to review it to see if it sums up what you have written in your two paragraphs.

3 Act on the guidance given by your teacher to amend your conclusion as necessary.

You should now have a global perspective, your national perspective and a conclusion which includes your personal perspective in answer to the question: 'Can renewable energy replace fossils fuels?' You can now go back and write the introduction.

Reflection: Has the completion of the activities in this section been a useful way of building up an Individual Report?

What else do you now need to add to meet the assessment criteria?

Remember that your Individual Report assesses the following skills:

- Research, analysis and evaluation
- Reflection
- Communication

Writing practice

Even though there are no specific marks for communication for the Written Examination, as the marks are for research, analysis and evaluation, it is still important that you are able to communicate your ideas in writing. In question 4 in particular, you are asked to develop a line of reasoning and what you write needs to be clear, coherent and well-structured.

ACTIVITY 5.38

Consider the following question?

'If the use of fossil fuels were limited, which do you think should be given higher priority; the use of fossil fuels for transportation or for private households?'

Look at the two responses A and B.

Which of these two responses do you think is better and why?

Response A

I think that fuel for transportation should be given priority over fuel for household use, as households, particularly in the developed world, generally use too much fuel and limiting its use might actually get people to think more about how much they are using. For example, we don't need to have the heating on in the house when we are out at school and work all day long. This is a waste of fuel, which could be used for other purposes. We should also make sure that we don't leave televisions and computers on standby as this uses up fuel.

Using fuel for transportation is much more important as without transportation, services would suffer because people would not be able to get to their work places which might be some distance away. For example, nurses and doctors might not be able to get to hospitals and people might die as a result. People might also die if ambulances and fire engines cannot get to the scenes of accidents because they don't have any fuel.

Without transportation, we would not be able to get food in the shops as a lot of what we eat is transported from one place to another. Developing countries also rely on charities to deliver food and medicines. It is unlikely that these will get to the people that need them without fuel for transportation.

Response B

Using fuel at home has to be the priority because without fuel we wouldn't be able to do anything such as read or watch television. We might get cold if we don't have any heating.

It is more important to keep warm than have fuel for transportation as it doesn't really matter if we don't go anywhere. There are too many cars on the road so if we limited fuel we wouldn't have so many cars on the road and this would help the environment.

So overall I think we should make households a priority for the use of fuel.

Discussion point
Share your viewpoint about Activity 5.38 with a partner.

Reflection: How can the weakest response be made stronger? Give two pieces of feedback to help improve this response.

ACTIVITY 5.39

Listening practice

Imagine that someone in your class is finding it difficult to find information about alternative energy sources to fossil fuels. They would prefer something to watch and listen to rather than read. Using a search engine, input 'alternative energy' to find video clips.

Find a suitable clip from a credible source.

Watch the clip and write some appropriate questions to help them identify perspective(s) and issue(s).

You might like to work with them to discuss and answer the questions.

Reflection: How did you benefit from working with someone else during Activity 5.39?

How do you think your partner for this activity benefitted from working with you?

ACTIVITY 5.40

Speaking

Discussions and debates do not always need to happen in class. They are part of daily life and can be prompted by something you have read, heard, seen or watched.

Look at Figure 5.06:

Figure 5.06 A topic for discussion

Make notes about the following:

- What words and phrases come into mind?
- What questions might you ask in connection with this image and the topic in general?
- What responses do you think you will get?

Show the image to a partner and ask them the questions you have prepared.

Reflection: Did they respond as you expected to the questions you asked in Activity 5.40?

ACTIVITY 5.41

1 Formulate three proposals for a debate on the topic of fuel and energy or sustainable living. You can use the Internet to gain ideas but should always use your own words.

2 For each of your proposals, prepare one argument for and one argument against the proposal.

3 Choose one of your proposals to debate with a partner, decide on your standpoint and give them time to prepare the other standpoint.

4 Ask a third member of your class to act as the chair person for the debate.

5 Once the debate is over, agree on who had the most convincing argument (the chair person gets the final say).

Reflection: Do you agree with the final decision about whose argument was stronger in Activity 5.41?

Have you changed your standpoint?

Glossary

Active listening: the process in which the listener takes active responsibility to understand the content and feeling of what is being said and then checks with the speaker to see if he/she heard what the speaker intended to communicate.

Aim/goal: something you want to achieve.

Alleviate: ease, lessen, reduce.

Amiables: people who are organised and like to perform work for the team.

Analyse (command word): break something down.

Analyse: break down a global topic into issues and explore the causes and consequences of these issues.

Analyticals: people who assess and evaluate work done to ensure deadlines are met and the project is completed well.

Anecdote: short story, usually to make the listeners laugh or think about a topic.

Argument: a line of reasoning to support a given perspective, idea, action or issue.

Assertion: another word for a statement or claim.

Association: linking groups of ideas to each other.

Assumption: something that is accepted as true or as certain to happen, without proof.

Benefits: advantages of doing something.

Biased: showing an inclination or prejudice for or against one person or group, especially in a way considered to be unfair.

Biodiversity: the variety of plant and animal life in the world or in a particular habitat.

Cause: is responsible for making something happen/is the reason behind something happening.

Challenges: difficulties that arise that need to be overcome.

Chunking: breaking down information into smaller, more manageable pieces.

Citing: quoting from or referencing a particular author or publication, usually in the main body of the work.

Claim: an assertion that something is true.

Collaborate: work together with others.

Collective effort: activities by a group of people working together to achieve a common purpose.

Command word: a command word in a question indicates the type of answer required.

Communication: the means of transferring information from one place to another, either by using spoken and written texts or by non-verbal means.

Compare (command word): look for and state the differences / similarities.

Comparison: a consideration of the similarities and differences between two things or people.

Compromise: agreeing to a solution regardless of differing perspectives.

Concept: a difficult idea.

Conclusion: a judgement or decision reached.

Consequence: happens because of something else/ is a result or effect of something.

Consider (command word): think about the different choices given.

Consistency: logical coherence.

Context: background or circumstances that form the setting for an event, statement, or idea.

Convention: a custom, or a way of acting or doing something that is widely accepted and followed.

Counter: argue against something.

Course of action: A plan or method used for achieving a specific aim or goal.

Creativity: the ability to generate something new from already existing knowledge and ideas.

Credibility: being convincing or believable.

Credible: how convincing or believable something is.

Critical thinking: actively applying, analysing, synthesising, and/or evaluating information gathered from observation, experience, reflection, reasoning, or communication.

Cross-reference: reference to another source that gives the same or similar information, or elaborates on the original.

Cultural perspectives: the way that individuals are shaped by their environment as well as social and cultural factors, such as nationality, race and gender, which affect their viewpoint.

Culture: the ideas, customs, and social behaviour of a particular people or society, or a particular group of people within a society.

Debate: a formal discussion on a particular issue in a public meeting, in which opposing arguments are put forward and which usually ends with a vote.

Deduction: the process of reaching a decision or answer by thinking about the known evidence.

Disguised: hidden, camouflaged or covered up.

Documentary films: factual films/programmes about real-life issues.

Drivers: people who take charge and lead.

Economic: to do with money.

Ecosystem: the living things, from plants and animals to microscopic organisms that share an environment.

Effective listening: listening to the words of the speaker and the meaning of the words.

Elicit: to draw out (information; a reaction, answer, or fact) from someone.

Emotive words: moving language, used by the writer or speaker to try make us feel something.

Empathy: compassion and understanding for the situation of others who are perhaps less fortunate than you are.

Encode: translate into understanding.

Ethics: principles of what is right and wrong that govern a person's behaviour in a particular context, for example when conducting an activity like research.

Evaluate (command word): identify strengths and weaknesses.

Evaluation: assessment of the strengths and weaknesses.

Evidence: the available facts or information to support an argument, indicating whether something is true.

Exaggeration: too much emphasis on something.

Explain (command word): a detailed response that gives reasons for how and/or why.

Explanation: details about how the outcome meets the project aim and shows different cultural perspectives.

Expressives: people who are willing to share ideas, opinion and feelings.

Face value: to take something someone is saying at face value is to believe that it is the truth, rather than looking for evidence, any hidden meaning or the bigger picture.

Fact: Something that is known or can be proved to be true.

Fallacy: an error in reasoning or a mistaken idea.

Family: a basic social unit consisting of parents or guardians and their children, considered as a group, whether living together or not.

First draft: a version of a piece of work, such as the Individual Report or the Explanation for the Team Project that you write before working on the final version.

Generalisation: an overview, lacking specific evidence or details.

Gist: the general meaning of a piece of text.

Global: relating to the whole world.

Globalisation: process by which national and regional economies, societies, and cultures have become integrated through the global network of trade, communication, immigration and transportation.

Goals: aims or the end product to show achievement of something.

Graphic organiser: also known as a concept map is a communication tool that enables you to express knowledge, concepts, thoughts, or ideas, and the relationships between them.

Implied: suggested or pointed towards something.

Identify/Give/State (command words): answer briefly by picking out an answer.

Indicates: shows/demonstrates something.

Indigenous people: groups of people who are native to a particular country and have specific rights as a result their historical ties to a particular area.

Inequality: the unfair situation in society when some people have more opportunities, money, etc. than others.

Infer meaning: to suggest or point towards something, similar to imply.

Inference: an idea or conclusion reached based on evidence and reasoning.

Information: Facts gathered about something or someone that helps our understanding.

Issue: an important topic or problem for discussion or debate.

Jump to conclusions: to assume something without using any evidence that might suggest otherwise.

Justify (command word): explain why / give reasons for something.

KWL chart: a graphic organiser that helps people organise information in three columns.

Limitations: what is not done well and could be improved upon.

Local: related to a particular community or area.

Logical: following on in a coherent way.

Long-term goal: an aim that might take a few weeks, months or years to achieve.

Manageable: to deal with easily.

Memory: the ability of the mind to store and remember learning.

Narrative data (qualitative): descriptive data, usually used to find out what people think about a situation or issue.

National: related to a particular country/common to a whole country.

NGO: non-governmental organisation.

Notes: a short record of key points or ideas written down to aid memory.

Numerical data (quantitative): information about quantities that can be measured and written down with numbers. Examples are your height and your shoe size.

Objectivity: looking at something without bias, judgement or prejudice.

Opinion: A belief or judgement formed about something, not based on fact or knowledge and which cannot be checked.

Outcome: the final product following a period of collaboration to achieve the project aim that shows different cultural perspectives.

Paragraph: a group of related sentences that develop one main idea or new aspect of an argument in a clear and logical way. Typically, a paragraph will be a minimum of four or five sentences but not usually longer than half a page. Each paragraph should include a topic sentence, a supporting sentence and a piece of evidence.

Personal: related to yourself.

Perspective: a particular way of regarding something/ a certain world view.

Plagiarism: intentionally or unintentionally copying the words and phrases of someone else and passing these off as your own work.

Planning: the process of setting goals, developing strategies, and outlining tasks and schedules to accomplish these goals.

Prediction: what someone thinks might happen in the future.

Prejudice: opinion that is not based on reason or actual experience.

Primary data: information originally obtained through the direct efforts of the researcher through surveys and interviews.

Problem: a difficult issue needing a course of action or solution to improve or resolve it.

Proposal: putting something forward for consideration.

Proposition: a statement putting forward an idea.

Reasoning: thinking about something in a clear and sensible way.

Referencing: listing sources of information referred to in a piece of work, usually at the end of the work.

Reflection: serious thought or consideration about something you have done or something that has happened.

Reliable: able to be trusted/ believed.

Reputable: well thought of.

Reschedule: to do the tasks/what needs doing another time.

Research: the investigation into and study of materials and sources in order to establish facts and reach new conclusions.

Research methods: the methods used to gather data and information that will be used in your work to support the points you make.

Review: a critical appraisal of a book, play, film, hotel or other service or product, published in a newspaper, magazine or on a website.

Secondary data: information obtained from published sources on the internet or in books.

Selective: carefully choosing information as the best or most suitable for your purpose.

Self-aware: aware of your own character, feelings, motives and desires.

Short-term goal: something you want to achieve soon, in the near future. The near future can mean today, this week or this month.

SMART plan: a plan that is specific, measurable, achievable, results-focused, and time- bound.

Social: to do with people.

Solution: A means of solving a problem or dealing with a difficult situation.

Sources of information: a publication or type of media where specific information can be obtained, for example reliable websites of government agencies, charities and voluntary organisations, newspapers, books and documentaries.

Specific detail: the detail required to answer a question.

Standpoint: a point of view, attitude, position, way of thinking or perspective.

Statistics: the collection and analysis of numerical data for the purpose of evidence in support of claims for arguments.

Strengths: the benefits or good points about something.

Summary: a brief statement or account of the main points of something.

Supporting sentence: develops the point you are making using information, explanation and examples, and provides a smooth flow from one sentence to the next.

Surfing the internet: to spend time visiting a lot of websites on the computer.

Sustainable living: a lifestyle that attempts to reduce an individual's or society's use of the Earth's natural resources and personal resources.

Synthesise: the combination of two or more sources of information to form something new and original that might support an argument.

Team role: a tendency to behave, contribute and interrelate with others in a particular way (as defined by Dr Meredith Belbin).

Tone: a quality in the voice of the speaker that expresses the speaker's feelings or thoughts, often towards the person being spoken to or the topic being spoken about.

Topic sentence: this sentence gives the topic and the main idea and is usually the first sentence in the paragraph.

Understatement: too little emphasis on something.

Value judgment: a judgement about whether something is good or bad, right or wrong, depending on their standards or priorities.

Verifying: making sure that something is true, accurate, or justified.

Vested interest: a personal reason for involvement or interest, especially an expectation of a financial or other gain.

Viewpoint: a particular attitude, perspective or way of looking at an issue.

Weaknesses: the bad points or points that need improving.

Wikipedia: a free, open-content online encyclopaedia created through the collaborative effort of a community of users known as 'Wikipedians'.

Work style: how someone chooses to approach a task.

Index